STRATEGIES FOR
SOFTWARE ENGINEERING

WILEY SERIES IN SOFTWARE ENGINEERING PRACTICE

Series Editors:

Patrick A.V. Hall, *Brunel University, UK*
Martyn A. Ould, *Praxis Systems plc, UK*
William E. Riddle, *Software Design & Analysis, Inc., USA*

Fletcher J. Buckley • Implementing Software Engineering Practices

John J. Marciniak and Donald J. Reifer • Software Acquisition Management

John S. Hares • SSADM for the Advanced Practitioner

Martyn A. Ould • Strategies for Software Engineering
The Management of Risk and Quality

David P. Youll • Making Software Development Visible
Effective Project Control

Charles P. Hollocker • Software Reviews and Audits Handbook

STRATEGIES FOR SOFTWARE ENGINEERING

THE MANAGEMENT OF RISK AND QUALITY

Martyn A. Ould

Quality and Technical Director, Praxis plc

JOHN WILEY & SONS

Chichester • New York • Brisbane • Toronto • Singapore

Copyright © 1990 by Martin A. Ould
Published by John Wiley & Sons Ltd
        Baffins Lane, Chichester,
        West Sussex PO19 1UD, England

Reprinted July 1994

Chapter 5 is reproduced in revised for from *Software Engineer's Reference Book* by kind permission from the publishers, Butterworths Scientific Ltd.

Figures 6-1 to 6-6 are reproduced, with permission, from *Testing in Software Development*, published by Cambridge University Press, 1987.

Other Wiley Editorial Offices

John Wiley & Sons, Inc., 605 Third Avenue,
New York, NY 10158-0012, USA

Jacaranda Wiley Ltd, G.P.O. Box 859, Brisbane,
Queensland 4001, Australia

John Wiley & Sons (Canada) Ltd, 22 Worcester Road,
Rexdale, Ontario M9W 1L1, Canada

John Wiley & Sons (SEA) Pte Ltd, 37 Jalan Pemimpin 05-04,
Block B, Union Industrial Building, Singapore 2057

British Library Cataloguing in Publication Data available.

Printed and bound in Great Britain
by Bookcraft [Bath] Ltd.

CONTENTS

PREFACE   ix

1   GRASPING THE SNAKE   1

1.1   Early brain damage   1
1.2   Down with risk   1
1.3   Up with quality   3
1.4   Silver bullets   4
1.5   Sharp instruments   5

2   PLANNING STRATEGICALLY   8

2.1   Technical Plans   8
2.2   Technical planning at bid time   13
2.3   Technical planning at project inception   15
2.4   Preparing a Technical Plan   16
2.5   Writing the Technical Plan   22
2.6   The life and times of a Technical Plan   26
2.7   Reviewing a Technical Plan   27
2.8   Chapter recap   28
2.9   How to read the rest of this book   29

3   PLANNING FOR RISK REDUCTION   30

3.1   What is a process model?   30
3.2   Why have process models?   31

3.3   Which process model?   *35*

3.4   The V process model   *38*

3.5   The V process model with prototyping   *44*

3.6   The evolutionary development process model   *54*

3.7   The incremental delivery process model   *58*

3.8   The exploratory process model   *64*

3.9   Blending process models   *67*

3.10   Detailed risk reduction manoeuvres   *68*

3.11   Preparing the input to your plan   *69*

3.12   Chapter recap   *70*

4   PLANNING FOR QUALITY ACHIEVEMENT   71

4.1   Introduction   *71*

4.2   Modelling a system   *72*

4.3   The system models defined   *81*

4.4   The system models in practice   *86*

4.5   Technical planning and system models   *89*

4.6   Preparing the Technical Plan   *91*

4.7   Chapter recap   *96*

5   ESTABLISHING A QUALITY CULTURE   98

5.1   A definition of quality   *98*

5.2   Quality assurance   *103*

5.3   Quality control   *108*

5.4   Quality planning   *116*

5.5   Chapter recap   *119*

6   PLANNING FOR QUALITY CONTROL   122

6.1   What is quality control?   *122*

6.2   Over-the-wall testing   *129*

6.3   V&V potential of methods   *130*

6.4   Quality factoring and the verification chain   *140*

6.5   Developing a verification strategy   *144*

6.6   Developing your Quality Plan   *148*

6.7   Chapter recap   *149*

7   PLANNING RESOURCES   153

  7.1   The culmination of a journey   *153*
  7.2   Preparing the Resource Plan   *155*
  7.3   Preparing the monthly report   *173*
  7.4   Factors affecting productivity   *176*
  7.5   Metrics and indicators   *179*
  7.6   Chapter recap   *184*

8   THE 14 DILEMMAS OF SOFTWARE ENGINEERING   186

  8.1   Changing is hard   *186*
  8.2   Breaking the blocks   *188*
  8.3   Handling the risks of innovation   *189*
  8.4   Getting the basic experience   *190*

9   RÉSUMÉ   192

  9.1   Clouds to concrete   *192*
  9.2   Getting there   *193*

10   A WORKED EXAMPLE   199

  10.1   Introduction   *199*
  10.2   The Invitation to Tender   *200*
  10.3   The Technical Plan   *204*
  10.4   The Quality Plan   *210*
  10.5   The Resource Plan   *217*

11   EXERCISES   224

    BIBLIOGRAPHY   232

    ABBREVIATIONS   238

    INDEX   240

PREFACE

If you are a technician at heart than you will no doubt think that the problem of successful software engineering is a technical problem to be solved by technical means. If you are a manager you will no doubt think that it is a managerial problem to be solved with managerial techniques.

As both technician and manager over the years, I have tried to understand just what makes for a successful software development project: one that produces what the client wanted at the agreed price and date. My conclusion is that, aside from universal management skills such as the ability to motivate, someone managing a software development project must be able to make a technical assessment of the problem to be solved, and to go from that assessment to the plans and standards that are the manager's tools. In this book I describe a process that I call *technical planning*. It is a process designed to lead the manager through that assessment and on to the formulation of the traditional resource plan. En route, the manager will

* assess the risks and uncertainties in the project and find ways of handling them

* assess the special features of the system to be built and choose appropriate methods for dealing with them.

The important point to note is that, in each of the above, a technical assessment leads to a managerial decision – hence the combination of terms in the phrase *technical planning*. This is the first major strategic tool this book presents the manager.

In recent years, there has been a move within the software industry to smarten up its act, in particular to worry more about the quality of its product than it has traditionally done. There has been some confusion over precisely what *quality* means for software, and for a software development manager there must be a concern about how they will manage quality into the software that their team finally delivers to the client. So *quality planning* is another concern for the manager. Too often this topic is approached from general notions and purely managerial actions get suggested.   But here again I believe the matter is principally a technical one, and it is only by a technical assessment of the quality requirements on the system that appropriate and effective measures can be chosen by the manager in constructing a quality plan for their project. The second major strategic tool that this book presents the manager is therefore to do with quality planning.

The subtitle of this book – *The Management of Risk and Quality* – summarises these two themes.

To round off the picture I show how the decision making processes I offer the manager lead to the starting point of the traditional resource plan. Lest anyone believe I think this is a simple matter, I have added a chapter devoted to a discussion of precisely why introducing new software engineering practices is difficult. And, of course, I offer some possible solutions from my own experience that might help you in your own situation.

So as not to raise expectations in unwarranted ways, I should stress that this book is very much about strategies and planning, and hence, with the exception of a little on the topic of checking project progress, the execution of a project is not covered. There are many aspects to project management that deserve books of their own – people management, client management, change control, contractual aspects and so on – but I leave these aspects to those other books. For the view from the other side of the fence – ie the view of the *buyer* of software systems – I recommend *Software Acquisition Management* by Marciniak and Reifer [Marciniak 1990].

I would like to thank Praxis plc for giving permission to publish the book. Many of the ideas that have gone into the book come from work that I have done as Quality & Technical Director, and derive from the technical and quality culture that the company has developed over the years, not to mention from discussions with colleagues. My thoughts on process models were very much helped along originally by discussions with Keith Southwell (now of Logica Cambridge) when he and I set up the *Sesame* project in Logica between 1983 and 1985; subsequently with Dr Gerry Wolff (now at the University of Wales, Bangor), particularly with regard to the importance of Barry Boehm's *Spiral Model*; and with Clive Roberts in the area of formal process modelling during the work we did on the *IPSE 2.5* project in 1986.

My thanks also go to Fletcher Buckley for pointing out the UK-isms and my free-wheeling use of terms in the drafts. Any remaining re-definitions of well known terms are all my own work! In particular, I have chosen to use the phrase *quality feature* to describe an aspect of quality, whether it be functional or non-functional. The word I would have preferred was *attribute* but this is used (eg in [IEEE 830] to mean a *non-functional* aspect in contrast to *function*, although the IEEE standard glossary [IEEE 729] also defines *software quality* as *the degree to which software possesses a desired combination of attributes*! Neither the ISO nor IEEE vocabularies has a word for both sorts of aspect so I have chosen the shorter of the two words (*feature* and *characteristic*) from the ISO definition of *quality*. Ah well.

On a further point of pedantry, I have used *they, them,* and *their* in their (genderless) singular usage in order to avoid the offensive *he, him, his* and the ugly *he/she, s/he,* etc combinations. It is an old usage known to Fowler [Fowler 1931] whose view, though he admits it to be "disputable", is that it "should never be resorted to". It is common in speech and I dispute with Fowler on this point. Rushers to dictionaries will find the Oxford English Dictionary recognises the usage – "often used in reference to a singular noun ... applicable to one of either sex" – and gives a quotation from a 1526 publication by Wynkyn de Worde (who took over Caxton's press) that reads "Yf ... a psalme scape ony persone, or a lesson, or else yet they omyt one verse or twayne". Such fun.

Chapter 5 *Establishing a Quality Culture* is a revised form of a chapter that I wrote for *Software Engineer's Reference Book* [McDermid 1990] edited by Professor John McDermid, published by Butterworths Scientific Press. My thanks go to Butterworths for permission to include that chapter here.

Finally, my thanks go to Apple for inventing the Macintosh.

Martyn Ould, Hinton Charterhouse, July 1990

A Short Biography

Martyn Ould read Mathematics at Cambridge University before joining ICL in 1970 to work on operating systems. After this and a spell at the King's College Hospital Computer Centre investigating the computerisation of medical records, he joined Logica in 1974 where he worked for eleven years mainly on real-time system development in the fields of radar, sonar, digital television and communications, subsequently helping to found the *Sesame* project, a corporate initiative on software engineering.

He joined Praxis in 1985 where he is now Quality and Technical Director of Praxis plc with responsibility for defining and promoting the company's quality and technical policy. He has served as a member of a number of national committees and working parties in the areas of methods, software standards, education and safety-related software. He lectures frequently to industrial, government and academic audiences.

He is a co-author of *A Practical Handbook for Software Development* (Cambridge University Press, 1988) with Nick Birrell, and co-editor with Charles Unwin of *Testing in Software Development* (Cambridge University Press, 1986) written by the British Computer Society Working Group on Testing and published in the BCS's *Monographs in Informatics* Series. He is a corporate member of the BCS and a Chartered Engineer.

1

GRASPING THE SNAKE

1.1 EARLY BRAIN DAMAGE

I've started many projects up in my twenty-odd years in software engineering and I can't remember not enjoying the early heady days of each, not least because there is so much to do and so much to be organised and all at once. The client is waiting to get started, you have staff arriving, office space needs to be acquired, the computers and software are arriving soon, your management are demanding plans and forecasts – and you haven't the faintest idea what you're up to. Everyone is looking to you to get this ship out to sea – the right way up. Where do you start?

For the first month or so – let's assume this is a development that is expected to run for a reasonable time, say a year or two – the pressure is immense and you need something to hang onto, something to build on, not least so that you don't forget things. And because there is so much managerial work to be done there is little time to get to grips with the problem to be solved and to understand it sufficiently that you know what you have let yourself in for. Brain damage seems to creep over you and it gets harder and harder to get hold of this snake that is already wriggling out of your grasp.

Managing a software development project – like managing anything – is about understanding what you have to do and retaining that understanding, grabbing the snake and then keeping a firm hold on it. It's my contention that, if you don't understand the problem you've been set to solve, you're more or less doomed unless very clever or very lucky. And that means taking enough time out to get that understanding. Which is what this book is about.

1.2 DOWN WITH RISK

Life's a pretty unpredictable venture altogether, with software development one of the black spots. No manager needs to be reminded just how risky a venture writing 100,000 lines of code can be.

About half way into a project I once discovered that (thanks to a good technical authority and a good team of software engineers as it happened) I had time in the day to think through a number of scenarios for the rest of the project: what happens if release 3b of the custom hardware doesn't arrive on time? how much testing could we get done with release 3a? suppose the new discs don't have the performance we've been promised – do I have any escape routes? And so on. Like other project managers I have spoken to since, I found this is a pretty unnerving feeling to get during a project. It's one that experienced managers get to be suspicious of in themselves (and in others if they claim to be feeling it): if you've time to think, you're either doing a brilliant job or something terrible is going wrong and you haven't spotted it!

As it turned out, things were indeed steaming along nicely, and the time I had to work over possible disaster scenarios was well spent because it helped me really understand the *dynamics* of my project. In particular, I started to get to know all the downstream risks and I could plan to handle them *today*. Now, a moment's thought will tell you that the greatest number of risks are present at the start of the project. And that's just the moment when you don't have the time to think your way through them.

This book won't tell you how to make time at the start of the project. For that you must either work longer hours or become an expert in one of the many "how to manage your time" techniques (though I'll recommend a favourite of mine to you: [Oncken 1984]). I'm going to assume that you have made yourself enough time to carry through the techniques I'm going to describe. If you haven't, I can only wish you bon voyage.

A major part of the technique is about analysing the problem you have been set in a systematic way so that you can spot the major areas of uncertainty and the major areas of risk, and can plan to minimise them or even circumvent them downstream. Forewarned is forearmed.

This analysis I call *technical planning*. It is something people do all the time if they have the snake under control. What I shall do in this book is to present it to you in an orderly fashion, so that you can do it in a step-wise and orderly fashion too. When you do technical planning, you will make a technical assessment of the risks and uncertainties inherent in the system you are going to build, and from that assessment deduce what you are going to do about them in your project. In other words you will be planning about all the things that you *don't* know about.

It is always easier to write down what you know than what you don't know. It's a bit to do with the embarrassment of saying "I don't know" that makes this so. We've always been taught to say what we know – exams are an obvious part of our up-bringing which reinforces this. But the most important thing about planning is writing down what you *don't* know, because what you don't know is what you must find out. And a good plan is one that recognises risks and uncertainties and contains activities downstream that will handle them. You don't have to answer all the problems at the planning stage – you simply have to know they exist and to plan for tackling them at some later date.

I have often noted that people who are late producing their plans at the start of their project are late because they feel they cannot issue the plan until they have solved all the problems the project faces. "Well, I can't say what training we'll need, until we've decided on the language we're going to use, and I can't decide that until we've done our preliminary analysis of the system." And as long as the plan doesn't get issued, the project rolls along in no particular direction at all.

So, technical planning is designed to make you find out what you don't know and to plan to handle it in the future. That way you get a project plan out early and you have the snake under control before it slips out of your grip. As the time to tackle those risks and uncertainties comes along, your plan will have the activities there to do it. You have given yourself room to move.

1.3 UP WITH QUALITY

That's half the story. The other half is about making sure – from the outset – that the system you deliver is one that you will be proud of: one that has all the quality features your client expects of it. Once again we start thinking about this issue right at the start of the project. The problem here is one of pitching the quality at the right level. No client is going to thank you for gold-plating or for delivering a grisly user interface or a flaky application.

When the system is first specified, we describe it in terms of what it should do (its *functional* quality features) and how it should be (its *non-functional* features). Taken together these features form the specification, and they are our target. Being sure we hit that target with what we deliver is not simply a matter of crossing our fingers and hoping all will be well when the system is put together. It is about making sure that we translate those requirements in the final system into requirements on each of the intermediate things that we produce: the designs at various levels, the code, subsystems and so on. This process of *quality factoring* is generally badly handled in my experience. Crossing fingers is easier but generally less reliable.

I once managed a project that was building a transaction processing system. In the specification we had performance figures to do with the maximum transit times for transactions under certain loadings. One of the key activities we undertook was a crude analysis of the paths that would be taken by those transactions and some estimates of the path lengths in number of instructions and number of operating system calls. By doing some experimentation with operating system calls to see how long they took, we were able to come up with some estimates of the time that a transaction would take to traverse the code, and hence to emerge from the system. We could not be absolutely certain that things would be OK on the night, but we knew we were not completely out of court with the design we had.

Achieving the required quality is therefore first about factoring quality requirements into quality requirements on intermediate deliverables. It is then about understanding the sorts of verification and validation that make checking for those requirements possible. And this is something that comes from an understanding of what our methods can do for us – what I call the *V&V potential* of a method.

But how do we choose the right methods in the first place? Again, this an area where we can ask some quite straightforward questions to find the answer, questions that form another part of the technical planning process. These questions are designed to make us decide what are the essential characteristics of the system we are building and then choose the methods that concentrate on those characteristics. The key feature of a screw is that it has a slot in the top for inserting something with which to turn it. A hammer doesn't fit at all, a coin fits reasonably well, but a screwdriver gives us leverage too. We need to make the same assessment of a system to choose the method that fits and gives us the best leverage.

1.4   SILVER BULLETS

In his paper *No Silver Bullet* [Brooks 1987], Fred Brooks says "... we see no silver bullet. There is no single development, in either technology or in management technique, that by itself promises even one order-of-magnitude improvement in productivity, in reliability, in simplicity.... [but] a disciplined, consistent effort to develop, propagate, and exploit [many encouraging] innovations should yield an order-of-magnitude improvement. There is no royal road, but there is a road." He then distinguishes between *essential* difficulties that are inherent in a problem such as software engineering, and *accidental* difficulties that attend the solution of the problem but aren't inherent. For software, essential difficulties stem from the conceptual aspects of the software; whilst we create accidental difficulties such as awkward languages and poor tools. If conceptual problems are to be efficiently tackled we must look at how we formulate complex conceptual structures, and Brooks addresses a number of "promising attacks":

*   buying a product rather than building bespoke – otherwise known as avoiding the conceptual problem altogether

*   refining requirements perhaps through rapid prototyping – that is, concentrating on the most difficult part of the conceptual task

*   developing software incrementally rather than all at once – the conceptual leaps involved in growing a system are smaller and easier than those required when building one

*   breeding good designers, the people who know the meaning of the phrase *conceptual integrity*.

Other proffered bullets to slay the werewolf of software development such as Ada, object-oriented programming, artificial intelligence, expert systems, "automatic" programming, and graphical programming will, says Brooks, only give us improvements at the margin as they attack only the accidental difficulties of development.

In his list of promising attacks, I think Brooks highlights two crucial features of a successful development project: a successful strategy and successful methods. The strategy is designed to minimise the risks inherent in software development;

the methods are designed to solve the conceptual problem that is left. Risk management and appropriate methods are the main topic of this book.

1.5   SHARP INSTRUMENTS

So, though there are unlikely to be many silver bullets with which software development managers can load their pistols for guaranteed success, for the manager prepared to treat the topic with the same measure of science that the designer approaches the problems of design, there are a number of sharp instruments that can be wielded to good effect, and it is these that this book describes. Briefly put, the methods I describe are designed so that you can

- reliably choose the correct strategy for your software development in a way that minimises exposure to technical risk
- reliably choose the development methods and tools that are most appropriate for the system your team will build, and choose them in a way that gives your client the required degree of quality in the system
- reliably plan your project on the basis of your chosen strategy and methods
- reliably carry through the development in line with those plans, keeping risk to a minimum and quality to the required level.

In an earlier book *A Practical Handbook for Software Development* [Birrell 1988] Nick Birrell and I presented the software engineering manager with the available options to be made when choosing development methods. This book takes the next step and shows how the choice between those options can be made using a rigorous decision making mechanism, and it goes on to show how those choices can be implemented through the project.

By reading this book you will learn three techniques. The first – *technical planning* – is a technique designed to lead you, the manager, through the decision making process that should start every software development project. Technical planning provides you with the information required to choose strategy, methods, and tools, and has as its twin goals the reduction of downstream risk and the increase of delivered quality.   The second technique covered is that of *quality planning* which is designed to lead you to define a verification strategy for your development.

The third technique – *resource planning* – takes the outputs of technical and resource planning and helps you produce a costed Resource Plan for the development, a plan that now takes into account all the risks, uncertainties, the characteristics of the system, the verification requirements and so on. The overall aim is of course is to get to a plan that gives you the greatest chance of success. The three techniques and how they fit are illustrated in figure 1-1, and one of the main purposes of the rest of this book is to elaborate this simple picture to the degree that you can get on with such a venture yourself.

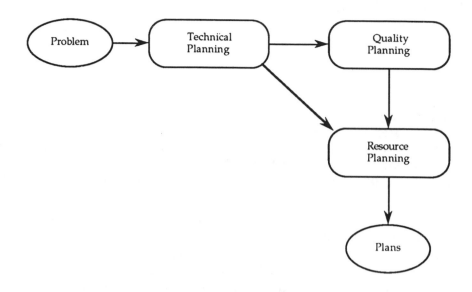

Figure 1-1. The strategy summarised

Chapter 2 will provide you with an overview of the technical planning process, in particular its two main steps:

- getting the project's shape (the *process model*) right by looking at the risks and uncertainties

- choosing the methods you will need by looking at the nature of the system you are about to build.

The results of these choices you will record in your Technical Plan.

Chapter 3 expands on the notion of the process model and gives you clear guidance on how to analyse the system you are building and how to get the right shape for your project: one that minimises your exposure to risk and uncertainties.

Chapter 4 expands on the second question, giving you a procedure for analysing the system you are building and choosing methods that will give you the most leverage.

Chapter 5 introduces the notion of *quality*, defining such terms as *quality assurance*, and *quality control*, and describes how a Quality Management System works.

Chapter 6 looks in detail at the question of how to set the right quality levels for each deliverable your project is to produce (including the technique of quality factoring), and how to define verification and validation activities to check that they have been achieved.

Chapter 7 is the culmination of the processes you will have learnt in earlier chapters: it shows how all the decisions you have now made yield most of the input you require to draw up a full and realistic resourced project plan. It also suggests a straightforward and reliable way of regularly checking progress and reforecasting outcome.

In chapter 8 I tackle a number of blocks that are frequently met by those introducing new software engineering approaches to the work of their teams or their organisations: my Fourteen Dilemmas of Software Engineering. I suggest practical ways in which you can remove these blocks – for they are real and you should know them.

Chapter 9 gives you a resumé of all that has gone before – a "cut out and keep" of the ideas in the book – while chapter 10 illustrates all those principles with a worked example. In fact, as you read chapters 2 through 7 you might like to glance at the worked example in chapter 10 on the fly so that you can see the principles at work.

Chapter 11 contains a number of exercises on the ideas in the book. They're not obligatory for the industrial reader (!) but might help to prompt some self-questioning about the ideas.

I hope that, with an understanding of the strategic planning process I describe, you will be able to grasp that snake at the start of the project and have it firmly under control right through to successful delivery of your system to your client!

2

PLANNING STRATEGICALLY

2.1   TECHNICAL PLANS

Software engineers are nice people

I have occasionally sat in sessions when a project is being started and the project manager is discussing the plans with the line manager, or when a bid is to be made to a client and the person doing the estimating is discussing the estimates with the salesperson. Software engineers are generally kindly folk, wanting to please (after all, they are in the business of providing bespoke systems to their clients – not unlike tailors), and so often I have heard them let their estimates be talked down to meet the client's or the department's budget. "Surely we understand how to build this sort of thing well enough that you don't need so long in the design phase?". "Our software engineers haven't used Ada before but moving from FORTRAN shouldn't be hard – we pay them enough – knock that training out". "Surely you can achieve higher productivity figures than those – increase them by 20% and see what the figures look like". And so on.

Don't misunderstand me – I'm not making a point about salespeople or line managers here. I'm simply reminding us that when push comes to shove compromises have to be made in any commercial venture. The question is: do we know *what* compromises have been made? I believe the only way of ensuring that we do is to start with a plan that has been systematically constructed from the best information, a plan that says "this is the ideal project shape, duration and cost". That's the right starting point for compromise.

Now I'm not suggesting my ideal project is one where I can take as long as I like with as many staff as I like. Barry Boehm has pointed out [Boehm 1981] that there is an ideal duration and staffing for any project and pushing the various factors to either side of that ideal – and this includes lengthening the project – actually makes it less ideal. Obvious really, but when we start to chip away at the budget or the timescale do we keep a note of the risks that we are introducing by moving away from the ideal? I contend that if we start from a plan that has recognised all the uncertainties and all the risks then we shall be clearer in our minds what compromises we are making and hence what extra risks we are – for sound commercial reasons – taking on, and what extra burdens we are therefore asking the project manager and team to shoulder.

In [Jackson 1975] Michael Jackson gives the programmer the advice "don't optimise; but, if you must, do it last". He is saying in effect that we should get the design right first, and then introduce risks by trying to make it run faster. The same advice holds for project managers: "don't compromise on the ideal plan; but, if you must, do it last" – get the plan right first, then introduce risks to get the 'right' answer.

Technical planning is about getting the plan right first.

Software engineers are optimists

What sort of risks and uncertainties are there in the average software development project? Here are a few that might ring a bell:

- what sort of screen layouts will the terminal users want?
- what sort of performance will the database give us?
- will the development machine provide us with sufficient power to do stress testing of the system?
- will we be able to use the facilities in the new language we have adopted?
- how will the first functions we deliver to the users affect their view of what the subsequent facilities should look like?
- will our design deliver the real-time performance required?
- how does this configuration management tool that we have just bought work?

Some sample answers to these might be

- the first ones we give them
- enough
- probably
- no doubt
- not enough to worry about
- and so on.

Yes, we've all done it. And worse, we might have done it unknowingly. We *assumed* the users would be happy – grateful even – for what they got; that the database would run terrifically fast; that we could start using that new tool tomorrow... We never even thought that there might be some uncertainties here. And as a result we ignored the accompanying risks.

As well as being kindly, software engineers are known for their remarkable optimism (speaking charitably – some would call it short-sightedness). Things go wrong and it's a surprise. For an industry well versed in the corollaries of Murphy's Law, we are notable for our ability to pretend that it has been temporarily suspended on our projects.   My advice to project managers is always "plan for the worst, hope and work for the best". That way you have some chance of being pleasantly surprised. Of course, it might be simply that we don't like to admit that there could be problems in the development ahead which, right now, we're not sure how we're going to solve. So our plans take no special heed of them.

Technical planning is about taking heed of potential problems.

Horses for courses

Since around 1975 there has been a growth industry in software engineering methods.   In the early 1980s Nick Birrell and I felt that there was such a plethora that the software engineer needed to be able to get some overall view of the methods arena, and we wrote *A Practical Handbook for Software Development* in which we described most of the major runners, described the strengths and weaknesses of each, and showed how they fitted into the overall development process: methods for systems definition, methods for design, methods for programming, and so on. A point we were at pains to make was that the choice of the most appropriate methods was one of the most important activities for the software engineer, and that that choice would depend on what the major features of the system being built were. Some systems are principally about data, its structure, flow and transformations. Other systems are about control, its structure flow and change. The more the method chosen for the problem in hand concentrated on the central issues, the more leverage it would give to the software engineer.

This is a theme that I shall continue in this book. In particular, I shall give some techniques for analysing the system you have to build and thence for choosing the methods most appropriate to build it. There is nothing magical about it. It is simply a matter of matching technology to problem, and to do that we first have to be able to characterise systems and then know what methods treat which characteristics the best.

I was once system designer on a project building a sonar system. The project involved the development of a great deal of special electronics and the software we were to develop was to carry out the major real-time tracking functions in one of the computers attached to all this equipment. The software had to run in several different modes: live, simulation, and replay. There were many options that controlled its operation and it had to be resilient to loss of data from the various sensors to which it was ultimately attached. I remember struggling for weeks trying to come up with an architecture that would support all this variety, as well as running on the machine we had to use, together with its operating system. Finally – and not without help from the excellent team I had – we came up with a scheme by which we effectively partitioned the system into a number of discrete components and then modelled the different ways in which they could be combined and the different interactions that would exist between them – which would trigger which and so on. The scheme worked very well and we built a resilient and very flexible system. Moreover, because we had a model of the dynamics of the system we were going to build before we had actually written the code, we were able to exercise it and see if it would behave in the way we wanted it to.

It was some two years later that I read about Petri Nets and realised that we had invented a Petri Net-based system, even to the point of inventing special coloured tokens with special properties. Petri Nets – if you haven't come across them – are simply a way of modelling concurrent cooperating processes. The basic principles are very simple but very powerful. If only I had known about the method before we had started the project! I would then have been able to have determined what was most important about the system we had to build, namely the need to organise around forty loosely coupled processes in a way that was changeable dynamically – and we could then have got on and done it that way. I would also have known of the analysis that you can do on a Petri Net to determine its properties, such as whether or not it can deadlock or reach a state from which it cannot "move".

That experience proved to me that a technical appreciation of the nature of the problem being solved was vital to effective planning of the system, and it is one of the reasons that the analysis necessary to get that appreciation forms part of the project planning process.

Technical planning is about planning for the problem to be solved.

Bringing realism to our plans

By now it should be clear that I am concerned with discovering at the outset of the project what is hard about it and what is uncertain about it, and then planning it in a way that tackles those hard bits head-on and explicitly deals with those uncertainties. This process of analysis of the problem and the synthesis· of the plan is what I call *technical planning*. It is *technical* planning because it looks at the technical attributes of the problem. In particular it asks two major questions:

1   what are the uncertainties of the problem we have to solve, and what do we need to do during the project to resolve them?

2   what are the properties of the system we have to build and what does that tell us about the way we must build it?

The answers to these two technical questions give us all the basic information we need to write our Resource Plan. The process of asking them and answering them is what technical planning is all about. You will be surprised at how much important information answering these questions yields.

In particular, the answers to question 1 will lead to decisions about the overall shape of your project, what you will commit to and when, what major decision points there will be and when, what iterations you will allow for and when, and so on. They will lead to your choosing what is called a *process model*, or what was once called a *lifecycle*. The term *lifecycle* really isn't very helpful since it presupposes that there is indeed a cycle and this is not always so. The term *process model* is much more precise: it says that we have a model of the process, in our case the software development process. We must start our project planning with a process model of the development that we are going to undertake, in just the same way that we start the planning of an aircraft, say, with a model of its overall shape: a fuselage, main wings for lift, canard wings perhaps for manoeuvrability, landing gear, a single jet engine. These major parameters will be determined from consideration of the principal properties we want from the aircraft. In the same way, the process model of our project will reflect the main parameters of the project: in particular its risks and uncertainties. The model will differ from project to project since the uncertainties and risks differ from project to project.

In chapter 4 we look in detail at the sorts of process model that we might choose for our project. Suffice it to say here that the sorts of things that might constitute such a model will include

- a division of the project into phases with decision points between them, so that we have commitment to a new phase as it becomes understood during the previous phase

- the inclusion of a prototyping activity to remove uncertainty in some aspect of the problem

- a small number of iterations around an activity that, we believe, we cannot guarantee to get right first time

- the development of the core of the system followed by new functions as the need for them becomes apparent, rather than trying to define them all up front.

You can see from each of these examples that something that worries us about the project at its outset is causing us to elaborate the model in a way that reduces our risks downstream. Always a wise move!

The answers to the second of the questions above lead us to a choice of the methods we will use to build the system: methods for requirements capture and analysis, system definition, system design, program construction, verification and validation, configuration management, and all the other activities we need to go through. This is covered in detail in chapter 5.

The result of our technical planning will be a document: a *Technical Plan*. This is the starting point for the construction of the traditional Resource Plan that we will go on to produce and that describes what activities will be done, and in what order, by whom and how long they will take.

When to write a Technical Plan

Technical planning is important at three points in the life of your project: when the work is initially contracted for, when the project is started to develop the software, and during the project whilst development is taking place. The context I will assume is that you are in a competitive bidding situation and therefore have to prepare a proposal to your would-be client in order to win the contract. You need to produce a competitive price and timescale without taking unacceptable risks. If you are doing software development as an internal service the situation will be slightly different but the need is the same: to prepare an estimate of effort and timescale that you are confident with and your (internal) customer is happy with.

When you draw up your Resource Plan, you will make estimates of the timescales and the costs of the planned development. To a large extent, these will depend on how the project is tackled at a technical level, and on the requirements for training, familiarisation, equipment purchase and tool purchase. The Technical Plan therefore provides input to the Resource Plan.

In chapter 5 I describe the process of *quality planning* during which you define the *quality features* or levels needed for the various deliverables your project will produce, and during which you define the procedures your team will use to check that these features have been achieved at the required levels. Quality planning results in a *Quality Plan* in which you record these decisions about the features, the levels you require, and how you will check for them. Your Technical Plan complements your Quality Plan by describing the technical strategy that you will adopt to develop the deliverables in a way that they achieve the quality features described in the Quality Plan.

Once a project is running, the Technical Plan can act as a work instruction for the entire project, describing how the system is to be developed – the approach, the methods, the tools – and giving a common framework to the technical side of the project. In general, therefore, it is not disposable and generally needs to be maintained.

In summary, the Technical Plan is an essential component of the trinity of plans prepared at the start of a project and used during a project to guide work: the Technical Plan, the Quality Plan and the Resource Plan.

Finally, a Technical Plan is written by a project for the project.

2.2   TECHNICAL PLANNING AT BID TIME

At bid time you have two main concerns: producing a good (ie credible) estimate of the costs, and convincing the client to buy from you. Let's take them in turn.

Estimating development costs

The costs of a development are determined by a number of factors. Boehm's COCOMO cost estimating model uses (inter alia) the following [Boehm 1981]:

- "computer turnaround time"
- "analyst capability"
- "programmer capability"
- "programming language experience"
- "use of modern programming practices"
- "use of software tools".

It is clear from Boehm's analysis that the technical approach to be taken, the skill levels of the staff, and the availability of a good development environment are major factors to be considered in costing projects. Put another way this says that getting a reliable estimate is going to be very difficult unless some level of technical planning is carried out. A Technical Plan provides a framework that is designed to reduce the chance of overlooking costs and cost factors. In particular, it makes us look carefully at the following:

- choice of overall approach
- choice of (alternative) methods
- training in methods
- familiarisation with methods
- choice of tools
- training in tools
- familiarisation with tools, packages, etc
- development hardware
- development software licences
- maintenance hardware
- maintenance software licences.

Requirements for development hardware and software are of particular importance. These differ from project to project: in some cases you might buy or acquire the necessary facilities (eg via rental or loan from the client) especially for the project; in other cases you might use in-house facilities.

Presenting a good technical case

It may be that you are bidding for work in a competitive situation and hence need to convince your prospective client that you have a sound technical approach in mind. You will want to get that message across in the proposal you submit. Your Technical Plan can provide useful input to that case. Clearly you should use caution in proposing too detailed a technical solution, as this may subsequently constrain an implementation. The aim is to offer enough evidence that you have understood the problem and are proposing an effective method of reaching a detailed solution, but not enough that you cannot implement a different solution should you win the job and find that you need to make certain changes.

You might on the other hand be planning work for an internal organisation. Again there is a strong likelihood that your proposed costs and timescales will need to be soundly justified, and again your Technical Plan can help make your case for you.

The Technical Plan can be used to record the technical issues considered and the decisions made during the bidding process. In one sense it is the technical areas of risk and uncertainty that are the most important as these define work that is still to be done for the proposal and some of the *commercial* risks and uncertainties. Early drafts of the Technical Plan might therefore contain more questions than answers. Additionally, I recommend that you record any alternatives you considered, together with the reasons that they were discarded.

Finally, it is worth bearing in mind that a high quality Technical Plan produced at bid time can itself be used as a sales aid and given to the client. It can help to demonstrate the (presumably high) level of thought that you have devoted to the client's problem, and your concern with having the right approach for their problem. An external audience for a Technical Plan would of course view it with different eyes from an internal audience, so you need to take care to ensure that both the form and contents of a Technical Plan are appropriate if it is to be given to your client.

2.3   TECHNICAL PLANNING AT PROJECT INCEPTION

When you win a development contract and the project is set up to undertake it, you have to draw up plans:

- from the technical point of view – the Technical Plan

- from the quality point of view – the Quality Plan

- from a resources point of view (people and money) – the Resource Plan.

If you prepared a Technical Plan at bid time, your new plan can be a refinement of the earlier one:

- What were originally statements of intent ("we will train everyone with the Whizzo™ theorem prover") are now turned into statements of action ("an in-house course on the Whizzo™ theorem prover will be arranged with Pode Systems plc for week 8").

- Outline requirements for development facilities ("we will need two Suns for the theorem prover") must be turned into actions for acquisition ("the Computing Facilities team has been requested to make available two Sun 3/260's with ... for week 18").

- Above all, the project inception Technical Plan is more specific about the activities to be undertaken and the deliverables to be produced.

  For instance, a statement at bid time that a System Specification would be written using VDM might now be expanded into a detailed description of the form the System Specification will take and how VDM will be used to produce it. Or, if object-oriented design was proposed in the bid, then this might be refined to describe the principles of design that will be used – in other words what precisely is meant by "object-oriented design" in this project – and to describe the precise form the design will take.

The relevant sections of the Technical Plan (see below) can thereby act as a statement of *technical strategy* for your project team. There are significant dangers, especially with large projects, that junior staff do not have clear understanding of how the development is to be done, and hence how their contribution is to fit in. They end up looking over the shoulders of the technical authority trying to figure out what is going on. The Technical Plan can be a major way of ensuring your staff know what is going on and what part they will play.

But one of the principal reasons for reworking the Technical Plan now is that since the original work was done during the bidding stage it is quite possible that new risks and uncertainties have emerged and old ones have gone away. So a reappraisal will be needed to check on this.

2.4   PREPARING A TECHNICAL PLAN

In this section we take an overview of the process of drawing up a Technical Plan as a preamble to subsequent chapters.

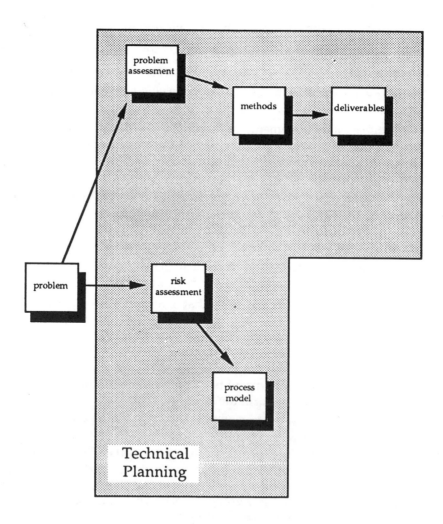

Figure 2-1. The main steps of Technical Planning

That process has three steps:

1   analysing the problem to be solved and choosing the technologies to be used

2   making plans based on those choices

3   determining the implications of those plans and choices.

These are dealt with in the next section. We then look at how to draw up the Technical Plan as efficiently as possible, and give guidance on the likely life history of a Technical Plan. Figure 2-1 summarises the main steps; we shall see two more diagrams like this for Quality Planning and Resource Planning, and all three will come together over the coming chapters.

Choosing the technologies

There are three parts to this step:

1.1 By looking at the risks and uncertainties in the development of the system and your level of understanding of it, you can choose an overall approach to development that minimises the risks and tackles the uncertainties.

1.2 By looking at the type of the system to be built, you are led to a choice of appropriate technologies for such a system, which in turn will define the training required, the acquisitions that have to be made, and how the system will be maintained after delivery.

1.3 Finally, you need to take into account any expectations the *user* has of how the system is to be developed and to reconcile these if necessary with your technical assessment.

We now look at the three substeps briefly – they are dealt with in detail in chapters 3 and 4.

Step 1.1 – Characterising the required development

In order to choose the overall approach to development you need to answer one question about the system to be built, viz *what are the risks and uncertainties that face me in this development?* Answers to this question – and there can be several answers – will help you to decide which basic process model should be used to structure the development approach. Five sample models are described in detail in chapter 3:

•   the V process model

•   the V process model with prototyping

•   the evolutionary development process model

•   the incremental delivery process model

•   the exploratory process model.

Warning: these models should be considered as examples and starting points only; every project must make its own variation – perhaps a mixture of these – to match the risks and uncertainties peculiar to its situation.

Part of the more general question is *how well is the system requirement understood and finalised?* If for instance there is already in existence a good System Specification (ie one that is complete, unambiguous, ...) then development can proceed in the traditional fashion using the *V process model* - in other words, the choice of process model or development approach is easily made.

However, if there is only some (informal) expression of requirements, or if the System Specification is not good, the choice of approach is not so obvious. The traditional V process model can still be used, but only the initial system specification stage can be estimated and planned with any reliability. We might, therefore, undertake to produce a System Specification within a certain time and for a certain price. Once that System Specification has been agreed the remaining stages of the process model can be estimated and embarked upon.

Things might not be so simple, as, for example, in situations where the client does not appear to have even a clear *mental* model of what they want, so that the direct path to a System Specification and thence to a system is not appropriate. Some degree of prototyping might be necessary to elucidate the requirements of the client on the ikiwisi (I'll know it when I see it) principle. This prototyping might be of the throw-away variety intended solely to establish the required functionality of the system so that it can be written up in a System Specification, agreed and then developed – the *V process model with prototyping*. It might be of the more radical variety: viz a series of increasingly extensive partial systems the last of which is the one that is delivered and put into service – the *evolutionary development process model*. If each of the partial systems is actually put into use by the client then the model is the somewhat different *incremental delivery process model*.

The topic of prototyping as an approach to the development of ill-defined systems is covered in detail in chapter 4.

In some situations there might not be a definitive system for which it would make sense to write a detailed specification of what is required. This situation is typical of AI applications and some research-oriented projects. Only by exploring a number of different implementations, often working entirely bottom-up, building on the better understood areas and so on, can progress be made. This style of working is defined as the *exploratory process model*.

The key point is that a judgement must be made about how well the requirements and functionality of the system are already understood. This judgement then leads to a choice of development approach designed to reduce the risk that the wrong system is produced or that the right system is never produced.

Step 1.2 – Characterising the required system

Your choice of development methods for the project depends on certain characteristics of the system to be built. You can determine those characteristics by answering the following questions:

* is the system principally a data-oriented system or principally a control-oriented system?

* is the system a concurrent system?

- to what extent are we concerned with critical software?
- is the target environment (on which the delivered system will run) also a suitable development environment?

These questions are most relevant where a new development is being undertaken. Enhancement and porting of existing software are generally constrained by the way the existing software was originally constructed and the available documentation.

In this book I concentrate on new developments. I shall treat each of the above questions in turn, looking briefly at how the answers lead to particular technologies, or classes of technology, appropriate to the development.

Is the system principally a data-oriented system or a control-oriented system?

A system can be viewed from a number of viewpoints. The relative or absolute timing of its actions might be the most important problem to be faced during design; ie the system could be considered to be principally a control-oriented system and the design method should take account of this. Software controlling machinery or reacting to sensors in real-time is typically control-oriented.

On the other hand, a system principally concerned with the processing of particular data structures can generally be considered a data-oriented system and is best approached using data-oriented methods. Software involving a database is typically data-oriented: transaction processing systems or batch data processing systems, for instance.

Many systems are a combination of these two extremes, of course, and account will need to be taken of this. In many cases data-oriented subsystems feature in a control-oriented system and a combination of methods is appropriate.

Is the system a concurrent system?

What is important here is whether the system must handle the problems of concurrent processing or each program can be treated as a free standing serial process. We can ask such questions as "does the designer want the system to retain control of the sequencing of processes?", and "must the system have close control over the relative or absolute timing of processes and state changes?".

A transaction processing system often requires the ability to handle a large number of simultaneous transactions. However, in some cases a transaction processing environment can be bought that handles the necessary simultaneity. In such a situation each transaction becomes a serial process and the designer need pay no heed to interactions between processes.

In situations where no stock solution exists (for example, by using some form of application generator), handling concurrency becomes a problem for the developer and a different approach is required. In particular, the design of the system needs to address the dynamic control structure of the system, the control relationships between the separate processes, the concurrency model, and so on.

For more details specifically on the development of concurrent systems and the techniques available to handle them, see chapter 4.

To what extent are we concerned with critical software?

The required reliability of the software is a determinant of the approach taken to development, the methods used, and the tools applied. Critical software with a high reliability requirement, such as software controlling a nuclear reactor, demands the use of formal methods of specification, design, implementation and testing. This demand must be turned into strategic requirements on the project and recorded in the Technical Plan.

Is the target environment also a suitable development environment?

The run-time target environment – hardware, software and operating system – to be used by the system is not necessarily an appropriate environment for the *development* of the system. In such cases, some or all of the components of the target environment need to be replaced by components more appropriate to development. For instance, the development of embedded microprocessor software might be best undertaken under UNIX on a mini, perhaps augmented by a cross-development facility purchased specially for the project.

Step 1.3 – Recording the client's requirements

It is not unusual for clients to lay down their own requirements on the process (how development is to be done – methods and tools) and on the product (its expected lifetime, change frequency, etc). Such expectations are normally spelt out in the Invitation to Tender (ITT) but, at project inception, it is worthwhile digging to find out if there are unspoken requirements or perhaps prejudices in favour of certain approaches. These might need to be followed or even overcome.

A typical example is that a requirement that development should be done using a particular method, for instance SSADM [NCC 1990, Downs 1988] which is a technique preferred by UK Government and by many public bodies in the UK for administrative computer systems, or MASCOT [JIMCOM 1987] which is preferred by the UK Ministry of Defence for real-time systems. Clients might also demand the use of particular tools (eg for configuration management and change control) to allow them to absorb the new system into their own development and maintenance environments. Indirect influence might stem from the fact that the client is employing a consultant who favours a particular approach.

Should an approach, method or tool look appropriate that conflicts with your client's requirements or expectations, you will need to resolve this conflict before making a commitment either way.

The questions addressed in the three steps described above are designed to give you information on what technologies you need to apply to solve the problem and to achieve the quality requirements on the system. You want to choose technologies that give good coverage of the problems to be solved, that are appropriate (ie do not stop you doing things you want to do) and that are cost-effective (ie can be taken on board at a reasonable cost).

Once you have chosen your process model, your methods, your tool support and the development environment you have all the information you need for your Technical Plan. In addition to recording the actual choices made, technical planners should aim to record briefly any alternative choices considered and why they were rejected in favour of the final choice. This will assist subsequent analysis of the project, help new project staff understand better why the project is being undertaken the way it is, and assist the technical planner in making clear and rational decisions.

Making plans

Once you have chosen the technology necessary you need to make plans to ensure that your choices are put into action. These plans cover training and the acquisition of development and maintenance environments in particular.

Step 2.1 – planning the training

Planning training of your staff is of course an iterative business: your choice of software engineering techniques is, to some extent, determined by the (expected) skills of your project staff. A first pass can be made by simply working through your decisions regarding approach, techniques, tools, and environment, and by listing the skills implied by their adoption on the project. Comparison with the skills of the proposed staff (if known) will help you to compile a list of skills for which training will be required. If you do not have any particular staff in mind, you must make an intelligent guess when planning. It is not sufficient in this case to simply *omit* any budget for training.

Additionally, you should consider setting up formal coaching on the project. The project manager and senior technical staff can be tasked with giving coaching sessions to junior staff in various aspects of the project. This can be related to the on-the-job training identified for staff as part of their career development.

Step 2.2 – planning the development environment

Where and with what tools is the software to be developed? Decisions must be made about the development environment hardware and the supporting tools that will run on it.

The following factors will influence your choice of hardware and tools for development:

- the client's requirements or expectations
- the availability of tools to support the methods you have chosen
- the need for the development environment to be the same as or compatible with the target environment or the maintenance environment
- the availability of appropriate tools on your computing facilities
- the compatibility of the target environment with the systems available within your computing facilities

- the cost of buying the tools against developing similar of your own.

As far as is sensible, the reasoning that leads you to your decisions should be recorded in the Technical Plan.

Of crucial importance is the need to draw up a list of hardware and software to be purchased, a timescale for those purchases, and your requirements for any other computing facilities.

Step 2.3 – planning the client's maintenance environment

An important factor in the choice of development environment is how the system will be maintained after delivery.

If you are required to undertake maintenance and enhancement on behalf of your client, you will need to acquire and support the environment. These will possibly be integrated into your own computing facilities, and this would have cost implications that would need to be passed on to the client. Those costs could arise from the need to purchase extra hardware, tool licences and software licences, from rental or other charges for rented equipment, and from charges for the use of your facilities.

If your client is to take on the responsibility for maintenance, they might need to procure an environment sufficient for maintenance and enhancement, and this environment would, assuming it is all of, or a subset of, the development environment, need to be shipped to the client at delivery. If the development environment includes components of your facilities, replacements would need to be purchased by the client. Licences originally purchased by you for development purposes would have to be transferred to the client or the client would need to purchase new licences.

Determining the implications

Having made the choices of technology and planned for supporting those choices, the final step is to determine the implications in terms of timescales, finance and use of your computing facilities:

- Training courses, the delivery of development hardware, and so on, have implications for the timescales of the project.

- Training, software licences, hardware purchases etc, have implications for the costing.

- The tools chosen and hardware required to support them will generally have an impact on the your computing facilities.

All of these need to be recorded – especially at bid time.

2.5   WRITING THE TECHNICAL PLAN

A constant theme of this book is that planning is about *decision making* – not about writing plans. You record your decisions in a plan for a number of reasons:

- you want other people, such as your staff, to act on your decisions

- you want other people, such as your management, to know you have made decisions and to prove that you are not jeopardising your department's or company's well-being
- you want other people, such as the finance department, to take external actions as a result
- you want to make it possible for others to give an independent review of your decisions
- you have a bad memory.

Whilst the written plan is the end-product, it's the decision-making process you go through that counts. Nevertheless, at some point you are going to put pen to paper, so in this section we look at the form the Technical Plan takes, and how it can be produced without undue labour.

Writing the Technical Plan at bid time

We need a document produced at bid time that contains the information resulting from technical planning. Part of the aim is to identify the technical input to the bid before commercial considerations are brought to bear. Some of the deductions – the technical strategy and the resulting costs – may find their way into the proposal itself in some form, but there is a need to record the findings as quickly as possible at bid time so that they can be reviewed, and also so that they can form an input to the planning process when the project itself starts.

So, at bid time the Technical Plan should be produced in all but the smallest of bids as a separate document. The need for its production must be identified as early as possible during the bid and it must be appropriately resourced and timetabled. A contents list for the document is given below. It should be remembered that the primary motivation for technical planning at this stage is not just to increase the likelihood of obtaining the contract, but more to increase the reliability of the cost estimates and timescale estimates, ie to increase the feasibility and likelihood of success of the proposed project.

In some cases the bid team might, at the outset, decide that the Technical Plan is to be part of the proposal. This decision would result in appropriate sections – perhaps structured like the contents list below – being included in the contents list of the proposal.

Writing the Technical Plan at project inception

Here the situation is different, and there are three ways that you might present the Technical Plan, depending on the scale and nature of the project:

- If the scale of the Technical Strategy issue demands it – for instance, a complex process model is demanded – then a separate Technical Plan document should be produced as an input to the definitive Resource Plan. In this situation the contents list given below is recommended for it.

- According to your local conventions, your Resource Plan will probably include sections on technical strategy, development methods and tools, training, and the development environment. On a small development project which does not have a free-standing Quality Plan, the Resource Plan can be augmented with the material of a Technical Plan.

  In this case, a separate appendix in the Resource Plan might be the appropriate place to record the findings of the technical planning activity. If an appendix is used, it should contain the headings and sections given below.

- If the project does not have a full-blown Resource Plan (perhaps you are using an abbreviated work instruction of some form), then such technical planning as is required can be recorded in that work instruction. If necessary, an appendix with the contents list given below should be provided.

Recommended contents list for a Technical Plan

The following contents list is recommended. The contents of the sections derive directly from the work described above.

    1   Introduction and summary
    2   Constraints
         2.1   Risks and uncertainties identified
         2.2   Characterisation of the system to be developed
         2.3   Client expectations or requirements
    3   Choices
         3.1   Chosen process model
         3.2   Chosen development methods
         3.3   Chosen tool support
         3.4   Chosen target environment
    4   Implementation
         4.1   Planned development environment
         4.2   Planned maintenance environment
         4.3   Planned training
    5   Implications
         5.1   Timescale implications
         5.2   Financial implications

Mapping the output of the Technical Plan into a Resource Plan

One of the principal purposes of Technical Planning at project inception is deciding how the system is to be developed, in terms of the overall shape of the project, the deliverables to be produced and the activities that will generate them. The resulting decisions are clearly a major input to the Resource Plan. Below I indicate how the decisions recorded in the Technical Plan can act as input to the Resource Plan (Technical Plan section headings are in italics):

2   Constraints

   2.1 Risks and uncertainties identified

      This is the principal input to section *3.1* below.

   2.2 Characterisation of the system to be developed

      This is input to sections *3.1* and *3.2* below.

   2.3 Client expectations or requirements (regarding software engineering practices)

      These are unlikely to be a consideration at this stage as the contract should define any standards or practices which are obligatory; these become "automatic" choices in section 3 below.

3   Choices

   3.1 Chosen process model

   This, together with *3.2 Chosen development methods*, is the most important part of the Technical Plan. It feeds directly into the Resource Plan by determining the overall shape of the project and hence defining a basic shape for the project network. It also defines the activities to be carried out and the deliverables they will produce. This might be done in considerable detail.

   3.2 Chosen development methods

   This section, as well as simply identifying in general terms the methods to be used, might well go into considerable detail as to how the methods will be used, adapted and expanded for the project's particular requirements.

   3.3 Chosen tool support

   Tools not available on your existing computing facilities will have to be purchased and this needs to be timetabled and costed into the Resource Plan, so these choices are input to sections 4 *Implementation* and 5 *Implications* below.

   3.4 Chosen target environment

   This should have been established at bid time but might still be unresolved at project inception. Either way, plans need to ensure that the target environment or a substitute is procured and installed, and that integration on it is catered for.

4   Implementation

   This is input to section 5 *Implications* below.

5   Implications

   5.1 Timescale implications

   This is input to the network and activity planning done for the Resource Plan. Activities will be required for training, procurement of hardware and software, etc.

5.2 Financial implications

This is input to the costings that appear in the Resource Plan.

The completion of these parts of the Technical Plan is fully explained at the end of chapter 4 once I have described the process in detail in chapters 3 and 4.

2.6   THE LIFE AND TIMES OF A TECHNICAL PLAN

We have seen how a Technical Plan is designed to provide input to various other documents, as well as being a vehicle for guiding a project through the process of how it is going to undertake the development. In this section, we look at the likely life history of a Technical Plan, from bid preparation through project inception and on into the development.

When you plan the proposal process you will need to decide:

- whether the Technical Plan is to be a separate document or part of the proposal

- assuming it is to be a separate document, whether it is to be delivered as such to the client, and

- whether it is to be formally reviewed and by whom.

In an ideal world you would write your Technical Plan and review it before beginning work on your proposal. This is because the Technical Plan is designed to generate much of the input needed for determining the technical approach you will adopt, and for drawing up the plan and costs. We do not always have this luxury, however, and it might be necessary to prepare the Technical Plan and the proposal in parallel. Clearly, the Technical Plan should always be "ahead" of the proposal with regard to those areas which the Technical Plan impacts. In deciding to make this compromise, your proposal team needs to be clear of the risks being taken.

If the Technical Plan is to be delivered in some form to the client then you need to review it from this point of view (eg paying special attention to style and layout as well as to the technical issues) and this special review needs to be planned for.

Once you have won the project and started the new project, your bid-time Technical Plan can be resurrected and used as an input to the preparation of the project inception Technical Plan.

At project inception up to three plans need to be produced: the Technical Plan, the Quality Plan and the Resource Plan. The question arises, in what order should you produce them? Once again you can start from the ideal situation which is that you write a Technical Plan, then a Quality Plan, and then the Resource Plan. To some extent, of course, the Quality and Technical Plans interact, and you can therefore expect to produce them in parallel.

Delaying the preparation of the Resource Plan until this preparatory work is done can be difficult, as your client in particular might want to receive plans as early as possible. If this is the case, I recommend that you deliver an early "bootstrap" plan that covers only the production of the full plans. This will allow your client to see that matters are under control, and above all it gives the project breathing space to do good technical planning. If, for totally unavoidable reasons, a Resource Plan for the entire project has to be produced before the Technical Plan can be prepared, then clearly you are taking a risk and you must recognise this.

It might be the case that the approach being taken to development is of such importance to the client that the Technical Plan is to be issued to the client. This would mean that it needs additional reviewing as noted above, and this activity should be planned for.

At project inception a further question has to be answered: will the Technical Plan be a controlled document, in particular one that is kept up to date? If the decisions made at the start of the project are liable to change or are to be significantly refined during the course of the project, there may be good cause for you to plan to review the Technical Plan at intervals or at significant points during development. If this is the case, this work will need to be planned for in the Resource Plan. The aim should of course always be to be sensitive throughout the project to the risks and uncertainties that can appear at any stage. Those that are thought of at the outset might happen and they might not. You might manage them, or you might not. But you can be sure that new things will also appear as the project progresses. By this I do not mean non-technical Acts of God, such as loss of your development team from accident at sea, or a change of ownership of your client leading to a re-evaluation of the contract by the new owners. I am thinking more of things such as unexpected features of the DBMS you choose, difficulties with your chosen architecture, problems with the compiler. Being sensitive to these is something we will revisit in chapter 7. Whether you choose to handle these things in a revision of the Technical Plan or in, say, your monthly progress report and forecast is a small matter – more important is that you handle it.

Finally, a good Technical Plan can be used by your team members as a statement of how the project is going to operate technically – what approach is being taken, what methods staff are to use and what tools will be available. This statement can be transferred into or referenced from other documents such as detailed work instructions.

2.7 REVIEWING A TECHNICAL PLAN

Here is a checklist for reviewing a Technical Plan. You can use it not only when actually reviewing your Technical Plan at a Structured Walkthrough or inspection, say, but also whilst you are in the process of preparing the document.

1   Does the Technical Plan record the rationale behind the choice of process model for the project?

2   Has the level of understanding of the system been realistically determined and recorded?

3   Has the nature of the system been adequately understood and recorded?

4   Does the Technical Plan record the rationale behind the choice of development methods for the system?

5   Have all the client's expectations and requirements on the development process been extracted from the Invitation To Tender and other relevant documents?

6   Has an appropriate level of staff training been allowed for in the timescales of the project and in its budget?

7   Has an appropriate level of familiarisation with the chosen development method and the tools been included in the project costs and timescales?

8   Does the Technical Plan record the rationale for the tools chosen to support the chosen development methods?

9   Have all the software licences to be purchased been itemised and costed?

10   Have all the development environment hardware components been identified and costed?

11   Has the development environment been reconciled with the proposed maintenance environment?

12   If the development involves the installation of hardware on your premises or the use of the in-house computing facilities has the computing facilities team been involved in the review of the Technical Plan or consulted in its preparation?

13   Does the Technical Plan record all known, unresolved technical issues and has the resolution of these issues been planned for elsewhere?

2.8   CHAPTER RECAP

Software development is a risky endeavour that starts with many unknowns and uncertainties. Your choice of strategy for your software development project must therefore be determined by the risks you perceive and what you need to do to resolve or minimise those risks. That strategy will take the form of a process model that captures the level of commitment you are prepared to undertake given what you can reasonably predict, the points at which major decisions will be made, the activities that will generate the data you will need to make those decisions, any iterations expected to handle uncertainty, and any other specific activities you will undertake to tackle specific problems or answer specific questions.

Your choice of methods for the project is determined by what sort of system you are building and its quality requirements. You must match the strengths of the methods to the essential features of the problem to be solved. Your choice of tools for the project is determined by your choice of methods and by productivity issues.

Technical planning is a rigorous procedure by which you ask the right questions so that all these choices can be made. Your Technical Plan is a primary input into the remainder of your planning process.

2.9   How to Read the Rest of this Book

This chapter has given you an overview of the technical planning process.   The next two chapters, 3 and 4, take you into more detail on, respectively,

* how to plan for risk reduction

* and how to plan for quality achievement by choosing the right methods.

In both cases, the analysis you go through is designed to lead you to elements of your Resource Plan. These elements can take one of four forms:

* a process model for your project, eg a three phase project with two intervening review points

* single activities, eg *prepare a system specification using Yourdon analysis*

* decision points at which one of a number of alternative paths is chosen, eg *if a relational database will suffice use one, otherwise develop a purpose-built file-handler*

* dependencies between activities, ie *logic* for your plan, eg *agree interface definition before specification work.*

Taken together, all these components will be the key input to the construction of your Resource Plan – a topic which is the culmination of the process and which is described in chapter 7.

At the end of chapter 4 we draw the technical planning outputs together into the layout recommended above in section 2.5.

En route to chapter 7 we will look at what is meant by a *quality culture* in a software development organisation (chapter 5), and the forms that *quality control* can take in the process of developing software (chapter 6).

3

PLANNING FOR RISK REDUCTION

3.1   WHAT IS A PROCESS MODEL?

The term *process model* refers to what in the past has been called a *lifecycle*. It is
a description of the overall shape of development of a project, of the approach to
be taken to getting from the client's requirements to a system in use by the client.
A process model is not the same as a method. A project adopts one process model
and a number of methods within that process model. We shall see that some of
the more extensive methods such as SSADM imply the use of a particular process
model, but that is not in general true.

In the earlier days of computing, a major birth took place: that of the
stagewise model of software development, described by Benington in [Benington
1956]. In what was perhaps one of the first steps towards moving the activity
onto a more engineering-based footing, a simple formulation of the process was
defined that consisted of a sequence of phases through which development was
supposed to proceed. The names varied according to the author, but I'm sure the
following will be familiar to you:

1   analysis of requirements (what does the client want to achieve?)

2   system definition (what is the client going to get?)

3   system design (what architecture will the system have?)

4   system construction (building the actual system)

5   system acceptance and delivery (giving it to the user).

The recognition of this simple process really was quite a breakthrough, though we
might now look back at it and consider it rather naïve. But it was a model that
helped give structure to software development, and it still serves its purpose
today in many respects. An easy criticism that has been made of it is that it does
not recognise the need for revision, ie for returning to earlier phases and reworking
things in the light of information obtained during development: information about

what the user wants, or how the design might perform, or how the operating system gets in your way, or whatever.

Thus, we need to accept the possibility that we will iterate during the development, perhaps within a given phase (eg reworking a design until it seems that it will give the required performance), or from one phase back to another (eg to correct a faulty design decision that, during construction, is exposed by a failure to be able to implement it). The biggest iteration is the one where we complete the development and, when we see what we have produced, we decide we need to start again and redefine the user requirements in the light of what we have produced. Such iterations happen in the real world and we wanted to accept this fact and put it in our model. Royce first formulated this idea in what he labelled the *waterfall model* [Royce 1970] (see figure 3-4).

Another criticism has been that during development we have to make many decisions and those decisions can have a number of possible alternative outcomes. The simple model doesn't recognise this. For instance, depending on the analysis of the client's requirements, we might decide to implement the system from scratch, or to rework an existing one, or to buy packages that supply the functionality required. That single decision can have three very different outcomes.

Interestingly, we have seen above that any model of development needs to be able to capture a *sequence* of activities (define *then* design *then* construct), the *iteration* of activities (*do* some prototyping *until* agreement is reached), and *alternative* activities (*if* a package will do *then* buy that *else* build from scratch). Suddenly, we find ourselves wanting to describe software development as if it were a program with the traditional Dijkstra structuring units sequence, iteration and selection: perhaps a process model is really a program!

This notion is one that has recently received a great deal of attention, not least because if we want to automate more and more of the software development process – considered as a group activity of some complexity – then we need to be able to give our computers a model of the process we are using so that they "know" what we are doing and can "collaborate" in the process [Ould 1988].

3.2   WHY HAVE PROCESS MODELS?

Reducing risk

This business of process models might sound like a notion that would only entertain the software philosopher, but in fact it is vitally important for the software engineer.

> The purpose of a process model is to give risk-reducing structure to a software development project.

A project without structure is an unmanageable project. It cannot be planned, it cannot be estimated, it cannot be milestoned, its progress cannot be monitored, and you cannot give your client any promises about its cost or its outcome. A process model offers a structure which is designed to reduce risk, reduce uncertainty and increase manageability.

Different projects have different requirements. If you are developing a new product, the process you go through will, in general, be different from the process you go through to develop a one-off system. There will be underlying similarities of course but the differences are great enough to make it worth distinguishing between the two different sorts of development.

When you undertake a software development project you will want to ensure that your exposure to risk is kept to a minimum – this will in general be risk of failure of some sort: risk of over-running the budget, risk of producing the wrong system, risk of producing a system that does not do what was required, risk of producing a system that will never work, and so on. These risks all stem from uncertainty or a lack of knowledge about the system to be developed. The approach taken to software development – the process model – must therefore be designed to take into account the degree of uncertainty that is present at the outset and to give a structure to the project that reduces the risks or costs of failure.

To summarise: the process model used by a project is determined by how much is known and how much is unknown about the required system and what its likely future is. It is designed to reduce exposure to risks and uncertainties identified in the project.

Boehm's Spiral Model

Perhaps one of the most significant contributions to the understanding of the importance of risk in software development planning is Barry Boehm's *Spiral Model* of software development and maintenance [Boehm 1986]. Boehm first presented the model at the 2nd International Software Process Workshop in Coto de Caza outside Los Angeles in 1985. At that workshop we heard a great deal of discussion about whether or not we needed *meta-models* – models that would generate models. At the time I found such discussion amusing to me as a mathematician, but rather too esoteric and removed from the reality of project life for me as a project manager. When Clive Roberts and I started working on meta-models ourselves in 1986 as part of the Alvey *IPSE 2.5* project, the importance of a "driving force" in a model became clearer. In the Spiral Model that driving force is risk and its management.

In the Spiral Model, development and maintenance (which I shall abbreviate to just "development" here) proceeds by repeating a basic five stage process:

1   determine the objectives, alternatives and constraints

2   evaluate the alternatives; identify and resolve risks

3   develop and verify the next level product

4   plan the next cycle

5   review the outcome of the cycle.

Figure 3-1 suggests the operation of the model: development proceeds by moving clockwise round the origin, passing through the four quadrants that represent stages 1 through 4 above. The length of the radius at any one moment measures the costs we have incurred so far – the cost of a cycle will clearly be determined by the size of the problem being bitten off on that cycle. On each cycle some risks are removed, sufficient to proceed to the next cycle.

The process now becomes risk driven, rather than product driven. Boehm gives an example of the model at work in his paper. In [Wolff 1989] Gerry Wolff describes the model in use on an internal development at Praxis. The objective was to develop some form of management information system for the company. Gerry describes the first few phases that took place, and that were driven by the Spiral Model.

In cycle 1, the objectives had been defined concisely as "to develop an information system to meet the needs of the management" – step 1. To get the ball rolling, a first cut requirements gathering was carried out; this formed part of the process of defining the objectives and constraints on the project. A number of alternative solutions were then listed – subcontracting to another company, using DBMS *A*, using DBMS *B*, using a database machine *C*, and assembling a set of packages. Criteria for the evaluation were drawn up and the alternatives evaluated against them. As a result a decision was made to continue further with the option of using DBMS *A* and to do some further investigation of the solution using the database machine *C* which had other attractions.

The second cycle therefore consisted of developing a first version of the system on DBMS *A*. Since no major problems and/or alternatives were apparent, this cycle could be a fairly standard development: gathering detailed requirements, preparing the system with Fourth Generation Tools that came with the chosen DBMS, and evaluation of the result by prospective users.

As a result DBMS *A* was not found to be a good vehicle: performance was too poor even with the partial system that was put together as the first attempt. Perhaps this could have been seen beforehand as a risk that needed evaluation before the commitment to its use was made. However, the second cycle did produce useful information about requirements, even if the vehicle that supported it was not ideal.

The third cycle was planned to take a further look at the database machine as one way of handling the performance problem, with a new version being developed on it if the evaluation showed it to be a good solution. Unfortunately, other influences external to the project meant that further development could not be funded and the project remained incomplete. However the experience proved instructive and Gerry reported a number of observations in his paper:

- Although the Spiral Model moves step by step, with potentially quite short horizons, there may well be longer term objectives that need to be carried through successive cycles – for instance, an objective to use a particular technology once it was sufficiently mature.

- There can quite often be a need for spirals inside spirals – recursion, if you like.

- A cycle might not present a clear set of alternative solutions at the outset, and the aim of a cycle might well be to explore a range of alternatives, eg through a prototype.

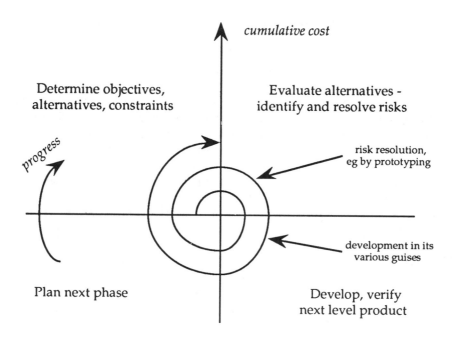

Figure 3-1. Boehm's Spiral Model

In a perfect world with clients prepared to proceed in the stepwise fashion implied by the successive cycles of the spiral, committing money in discrete lumps corresponding to the cycles, it would be possible to operate the Spiral Model by making each cycle a separate contract. We shall see that this is indeed what happens in many cases. However, we have to accept, as Boehm does in his paper, that this is not always possible. Very often the development of a software system is just a part of a much larger venture – building a new aircraft, offering new financial services to bank clients, reorganising a government department – ventures that have already been committed to. In such situations, the software development is seen as an "implementation detail" and not something open to discussion. The contractor who agrees to undertake the work is often asked for a single price for all the work, ie for perhaps several, or even an indeterminate number of turns of the spiral. Such a client wants to be assured of a system for a given price and, whilst being happy for the contractor to undertake to do the work in several stages, is not prepared to commit to several contracts of as yet unknown price.

In a recent example at Praxis, we prepared a proposal for a client for a system that was, in its final environment, to connect to a number of systems some of which were not at the time defined. We saw a risk in the integration of our system with these others and, to handle this risk, proposed a fixed price development to include testing our system against simulators of those external systems, plus a T&M (time and materials) contract to cover the integration with the other systems. This was unacceptable to the client who probably appreciated the risks but wanted a fixed price for the whole development. This particular case points up the importance here of separating commercial imperatives from technical judgements – a theme we shall return to frequently. We did offer a fixed price for the whole development after some rearrangement of contract terms, but knew explicitly the commercial risk we had introduced by letting in the technical difficulties of that final integration.

3.3 WHICH PROCESS MODEL?

In the same way that a program containing decision points and iterations can execute in many different ways depending on the input data, so the Spiral Model can unwind in different ways depending on the circumstances of the project. We can think of the Spiral Model as a meta-model – a model for models. The Spiral Model can unwind in a number of different ways and each of those ways is a process model itself. And each of those process models can unwind in a different way to give a piece of history so to speak. Although it is possible to use the Spiral Model directly on a project, I feel it is more useful to look at a number of possible unwindings of the spiral that frequently occur in software development. Subsequent sections of this chapter therefore look at a number of "set-piece" process models, but first we give a quick overview to set the scene.

- If the project is "well understood" in that it is well specified and a development route can be clearly identified at the outset then a single pass development will be appropriate: this involves using the *V process model*.

- If there are areas of uncertainty about the requirements on the system or its implementation but these are not "great" then the addition of small-scale prototyping activities to the simple V process model will suffice; we then have the *V process model with prototyping*, which will also be referred to as the *VP process model*.

- In the *evolutionary development process model* a sequence of systems is produced. Here each system in the series has full functionality but the aim is to evolve the system over time through a number of versions. The series might or might not terminate depending on whether the system and its environment stabilise with respect to each other.

- If only some of the functionality of the system is required (or clearly perceived and specifiable) initially and the remaining functionality can be delivered over a number of increments then the *incremental delivery process model* is appropriate. A sequence of systems is produced. Each is a partial system except the last (if there is one), but all are usable systems.

- Finally, if the purpose and nature of the system are very ill-defined then this can be recognised by using the *exploratory process model* on the project.

Figure 3-2 illustrates the first four different process models in diagrammatic form. Although they are treated as distinct models here for the purpose of clarity, it is useful to remember that we can think them all as particular unwindings of the Spiral Model – we return to this in section 3.9.

For each model covered in the following sections you will find discussion under the following headings:

- *The model described*

  We start with a description of the model and summarise the description in terms of the *deliverables* (or *products*) that the model produces, the *major review points*, and finally a *Work Breakdown Structure* (WBS) fragment that captures the structure and activities of the process model under discussion. This fragment will form the basis of your project plan as described in chapter 7. (If you are not familiar with WBSs quickly read the relevant part of section 7.2 before going on.)

- *Where to use the model*

  Knowing the situations where a model is appropriate is clearly key and so each section continues with this.

- *Running a project with this model*

  I have suggested that the purpose of a process model is to provide a project with a structure that makes it manageable. We need to look at the management impact of the different models. We cannot assume that a single management style can be used in all situations; moreover, the process model we choose will have a major bearing on the nature of the contract that can be undertaken with our client. The discussion of each process model therefore contains some guidance on these issues under the heading *Running a project with this model*.

  A natural outcome of the analysis of the uncertainties and risk of a project will be some understanding of what *commercial* risk is involved. In an ideal world we limit our commercial risk to what we can reasonably predict. So, under the sub-heading *Contractual considerations* I describe how the choice of that process model is related to the degree of commercial risk involved.

Warnings

All models are simplifications and should never be interpreted over-strictly. Their purpose is to give shape to a project and hence to make it manageable. The need to have a manageable and a successful project always overrides any apparent strictures implied by the process model in use.

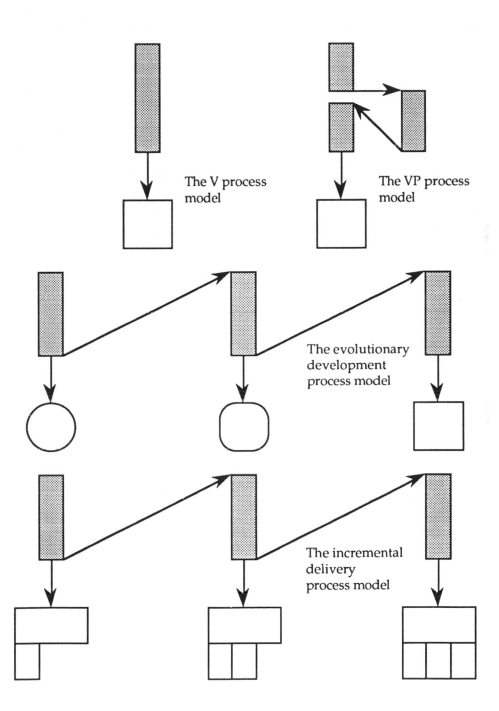

Figure 3-2. Four possible process models

There will also be situations where none of the particular models described here for illustration fits the bill well enough. There is clearly no obligation to follow one of the offered models religiously but in such a situation your Technical Plan would describe the model you have invented instead – for instance, some mixture of models – and would outline your reasons for adopting it.

In some cases, your client will wish to impose their own process model on the project. You will need to take this into account when you bid or undertake a project. You might agree to using their model, or prefer to convince them otherwise, or even adjust their model to be more in line with your approaches if you feel that they are preferable.

Finally, you must remember that the process model defines which deliverables should be produced for that style of development, but the format and qualities required of those deliverables are the concern of the project's Quality Plan.

It is with these points in mind that you should read the rest of this chapter.

3.4   THE V PROCESS MODEL

The model described

The V process model (figure 3-3) describes a project in terms of a progression of stages from requirements analysis, through system definition, system design and implementation, on through unit testing and system integration to system acceptance. It emphasises the fact that the activities in the latter half of the project are all about testing implementations of the specifications produced in the earlier half.

It is the V process model that underlies many of the methods used in the software engineering world at large: SSADM, MASCOT, Yourdon Structured Analysis and Design, and VDM for instance.

Development in this model proceeds via a sequence of phases that leads to the delivered system. The earlier phases constitute a design process leading from the user's ill-formed notions to code. Each of these early, downward-pointing phases results in a specification, each being derived from the preceding one. There is an implied decomposition from system, through subsystems, to modules – however you wish to define the terms *subsystem* and *module*.

The deliverables from the later, upward-pointing phases are (part-) systems that, through testing, have been shown to be implementations of the matching specifications on the other side of the V. Thus, the Delivered System, resulting from the Acceptance Testing phase, has been satisfactorily verified against the System Specification. In the process of verification, the Acceptance Test Specification defined the tests that would be carried out. The combination of a specification and the software that satisfies it, together with the specification of the test that established "satisfaction", is what I term a *system model*. We shall look at these in detail in chapter 4.

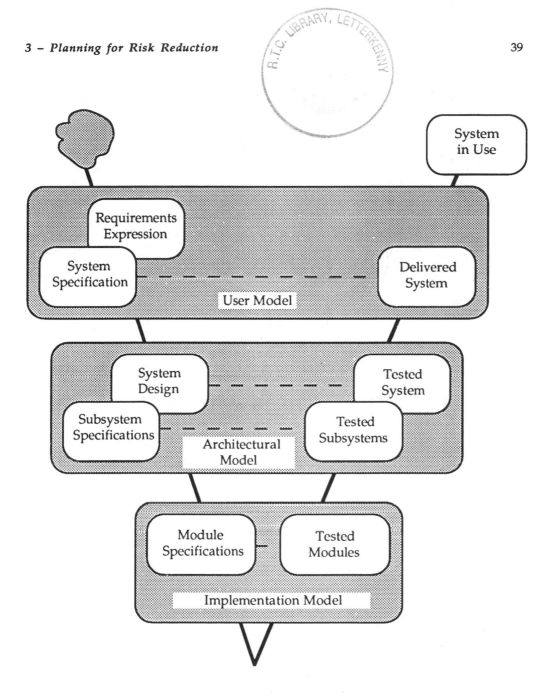

Figure 3-3. The deliverables produced in the V process model

The "oldest" process model is the *waterfall model* (figure 3-4) to which we return momentarily. This shows a similar progression from inception, through definition, the various stages of design, code, unit testing and integration to final acceptance. The fact that that progression is never smooth and monotonic is acknowledged by drawing little backward arrows suggesting iteration. This model has a number of advantages and disadvantages.

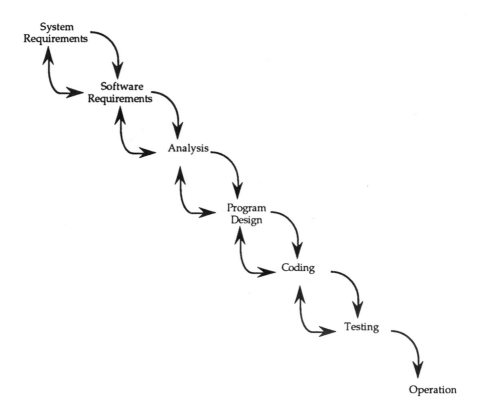

Figure 3-4. The waterfall model

The advantages are that it does give a structure to the whole of a project in the form of a well defined sequence of phases – well defined in that we can precisely define exit criteria for them. Whilst recognising the need for iteration, this sequence forces a pace through the project and does ensure that compromises are made to preserve that pace. It recognises that there is no perfect solution and that it is not commercially sensible to look for one. It might be commercially preferable to accept a sub-optimal solution in order to make a profit and/or to satisfy the client. As such the model makes a good management tool. The V process model preserves this advantage.

The disadvantage is that a compromise can, in the limit, become an error and a project can end up discovering, too late in the day, that it took a wrong turn earlier on. The V process model perpetuates this disadvantage. Because there is no explicit admission that there can be risks, their effects are always felt at the last moment rather than anticipated as early as possible.

Also, the simple notion of iteration is generally unsatisfactory. The V process model emphasises the true nature of iteration: the fact that, rather than being simply back to the preceding phase, it will more generally be back to the specification activity corresponding to the object in which a problem is found. This failing in the model tells us that it is not appropriate where there is a likelihood of significant iteration – something we return to in a couple of pages.

The major deliverables

The major deliverables can be read off figure 3-3:

- The *User Model* in the form of Requirements Expression, System Specification and Accepted System.

- The *Architectural Model* in the form of Technical Specification, Subsystem Specifications, Tested System and Tested Subsystems.

- The *Implementation Model* in the form of Module Specifications, and Tested Modules.

Note that we do not include here "minor" deliverables such as test specifications and User Manuals which do not affect the overall flow.

The generic Work Breakdown Structure

The overall shape of the project is of course simple and straightforward:

1000	Prepare User Model
2000	Prepare Architectural Model
3000	Prepare Implementation Model
4000	Prepare Build Model

The major review points

The obvious review points for the V model are the ends of the stages and the preparation of the Test Plans between specifications and implementations:

- review of the System Specification (part of the User Model) to definitive status

- review of the Acceptance Test Specification to definitive status

- review of the System Design and Subsystem Specifications (parts of the Architectural Model) to definitive status

- review of the Build Test Specification to definitive status

- review of the Module Specifications (part of the Implementation Model) to definitive status

- review of the Unit Test Specifications to definitive status.

The purpose of such reviews is, as always, to ensure that each succeeding stage can proceed on a firm basis and that the work of individuals is coordinated through a common approach and a common understanding.

Where to use the model

The V process model should be used when there is either a good System Specification and a "predictable" solution, or a good Requirements Expression and the prospect of a good System Specification and a predictable solution. Without even a good Requirements Expression it is impossible to choose a process model at all. The judgement about whether a given specification is good and whether there is a technical solution in sight is one that is largely based on experience.

In summary, if there is no major uncertainty as to whether there is a practical solution and there are no major uncertainties over what the system is to do or be like, then the V process model is quite appropriate.

Despite the criticism that this simple model has received in the past, it still has its uses and I have used it successfully on several occasions, including one where we were implementing a system to act as a communications multiplexer between terminal users and mainframes. The communications protocols to be handled were effectively cast in concrete by manufacturers and international standards, the loadings were not expected to be high, the switching was straightforward, and only the failure conditions gave us any real concern. The development proceeded absolutely classically: a system definition agreed with the client; a design completed before coding started; coding completed before testing and integration started. Since the risks were low we could plan and estimate with confidence and use a simple model for the project. I don't have any embarrassment admitting that I have used the simple V process model but, when I look back, I realise that it was successful simply because the problem and solution domains were so well understood by the team I had working for me! With a different team the situation could have been quite different, and, with the new risks and uncertainties, I would have been wise to have chosen a model that allowed more risk reduction en route.

Running a project with this model

Contractual considerations

The V process model assumes that the system is "well-understood" and that there are no major technical obstacles in view. The development of such a system is relatively risk-free and tolerably reliable estimates can be made of the cost and timescale. Under these conditions a fixed price contract for the entire development is possible.

However, there are often still good reasons for reducing risks as far as possible by splitting such a project into two phases, each being done for a fixed price: a specification phase leading to an implementation phase, as shown in figure 3-5. The price of the implementation phase can then be one of the outputs of the

specification phase and the initial contractual commitment will simply be to the
first phase.

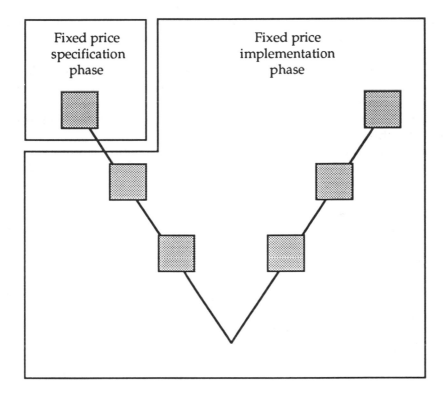

Figure 3-5. The V process model in two phases

This scheme can work to the benefit of both sides. The developer restricts any
exposure just to the first phase, which in most situations should be relatively
straightforward. The purchaser has the opportunity to steer the specification to
the system they want without being constrained by a total contract price, and
they can also potentially keep the overall price down since the developer should
be able to offer a price with a reduced contingency for the implementation phase
once the specification phase has revealed the full extent of the work.

Management considerations

Conceptually the V model is of course very simple and hence it should be equally
simple in management terms. However, because its success depends on everything
being straightforward, and because life generally isn't, it requires special
sensitivity from the project manager to changes in situation. At any stage,
assumptions that were true at the outset might become untrue. Suppose your

project is started with version 5 of your favourite DBMS, a version whose characteristics you know well, whose performance is understood and whose foibles are appreciated. Midway through the project version 6 is released and you are obliged to use it. Immediately you have an unknown: what bugs have been corrected? what new ones have been introduced? what is the performance now?

Significant changes might need a re-evaluation of the process model you are using. In extreme cases you might find yourself back at the negotiating table because of new risks or uncertainties that the client would like to introduce. This is not a criticism of clients: the system is *their* system and it's their right to want to change it, but such change will invariably mean a renegotiation of contract terms if the scope of the project is to be changed from what was originally negotiated – that is *your* right.

Project managers who have "come up through the ranks" from being software engineers invariably find the business of asking for a renegotiation of the price a difficult one. When the first change request comes in towards the start of the project – formally or informally – it is all too easy to say "yes, no problem, we can absorb that". After all, software engineers are nice people and they want to give their clients the systems their clients want. They want to oblige. Unfortunately, when the second change request comes in and then the third, a precedent has been set: small changes can be absorbed. But the changes get bigger and the project gets further into its budget and timescale and the room for manoeuvre decreases by the day. Finally the time comes that the project manager has to say "enough is enough – you'll have to pay more", and this can sour a good relationship.

In my experience the best policy by far is to ask for a price increase on the very first change request, no matter how small. The aim is to set a precedent. After all, as project manager, one has a responsibility to one's company and its profitability, as well as to the client. This is a policy I learnt on a fixed price project where we had bid an architecture designed to support certain of the features that the client wanted. Just as we were in the specification phase my client asked for a feature that at first glance looked like the others, but which, on closer examination, proved to be quite impossible with the architecture we had bid. Summoning up my courage I said we had not contracted for that feature and the cost would be another £30,000 (~$45,000) for reworking of the specification and the architecture, and possibly renegotiation of the implementation price. There was a silence on the other side for a while but, after some discussion and proof of the figures from me, the change was accepted and the project got off to a sound start. (I have colleagues who take an even stronger line and feel that in some cases one should even consider *prompting* for the first change request in order to get the precedent in place. But this is a little too strong for me.)

3.5   THE V PROCESS MODEL WITH PROTOTYPING

Why prototype?

The simple V process model works on the assumption that there are no major uncertainties that put the project at risk (particularly in terms of overrunning its budget or timescale). If there are uncertainties then prototyping is one of the ways we can reduce risk and so we introduce the *VP process model*.

When we build a prototype we are building something designed to help us establish some feature of a system we ultimately want to build, or, more generally, to get information. That information might be about the exact requirements to be placed on the system, about whether a particular design approach is actually feasible, about what the exact properties of the target architecture are or about the nature of a proposed solution. For instance, we can imagine:

- prototyping a user interface to chéck its ergonomics and acceptability to the user

- prototyping a scheduling algorithm to determine its performance

- prototyping a heuristic algorithm to check its behaviour

- prototyping an entire system to check its viability in terms of performance, size and so on.

Thus one sort of prototype yields information about some characteristic which is then fed back into the development process. There are many ways of getting such information – simulation, desk calculation, walk-throughs; a prototype is typically used where there are no adequate analytical ways of determining the characteristic. You perhaps know the behaviour you want but you cannot be sure from examining (say) your design whether it will exhibit that behaviour when implemented. A prototype allows you to expose the behaviour of your design so that you can check it.

Another sort of prototype helps in the situation where you are not even sure what behaviour you want – the ikiwisi syndrome (I'll know it when I see it). This is the sort of prototype that is built for evaluating user interfaces.

Prototyping is therefore experimentation designed to yield information for the development process. It is worth noting that – just as testing cannot prove the absence of bugs, only their presence, because it is a sampling technique – prototyping suffers from the same shortcoming: it cannot prove anything since it requires human induction to make any general conclusions from the sampled output from use of a prototype. Great care has to be taken that the conclusions drawn from the use of a prototype are valid, for instance because the prototype has been exercised in a thorough and systematic fashion and not simply "played with".

Adding prototyping to the V process model

We noted in the section on the V process model that one of its disadvantages was that a wrong decision made early in development might not be discovered until very late in the day. This can prove costly or even disastrous.

In the V process model with prototyping (what we are calling the *VP process model*) we make explicit the possible need to prototype some aspect of the system. Prototyping is seen as an investigative technique used wherever further information is required and can only be reasonably obtained by building a partial system or a model. Our progression of phases is still there but we add the possibility of prototyping at each phase as a way of reducing uncertainty, risk and hence future iteration. See figure 3-6.

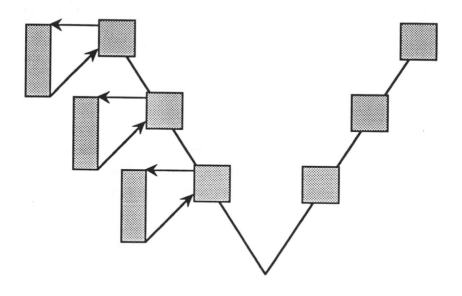

Figure 3-6. The VP process model

Where to use this model

The VP process model should be considered where there are minor uncertainties or risks that can be resolved with some sort of investigatory work, such as prototyping. For instance, during system specification, it could prove necessary, in order to resolve a feasibility issue, to experiment with a particular design approach; during design it might be necessary to implement a number of alternative codings to determine their relative performance in tandem with the target operating system; or a sample application might need to be built using a DBMS to check the understanding of the workings of the DBMS.

Indeed, prototyping of some form should always be undertaken where the project is to use a piece of software whose properties are not known – even though they might be "fully" written up in the vendor's manual there is no substitute for actually using the software to find out what it really does and to find out whether the way you intend using it is sensible (or even possible). I have a personal experience of this. A project for which I was system architect was using a bought-in package to draw on a graphics display. One program needed to ring the bell on the display and nothing more. A designer on the team innocently specified that the package's `ring bell` routine should be called to do this. Unfortunately, at integration this tiny routine dragged in so much supporting object code that it blew the address space of the program. This taught me that whenever your project is going to use a package as part of the delivered system, you should plan for someone to spend some weeks simply digging and hammering to determine what the package *really* does. This is an excellent task for a junior member of the team at a time when it is otherwise difficult to give junior staff useful work. Not only do you get facts to help you avoid future mistakes or to get the design right, etc, but that junior member acquires a new skill and a status in the team that would otherwise be hard to get at this stage.

The user interface is the commonest subject matter for a prototype. There are two clear reasons for this. Firstly, ease-of-use is a major consideration with any interface with the user – especially with the naïve user or the user not familiar with computers. A poor interface can kill an otherwise good system. Secondly, it's very often the case that what can be communicated across the human-computer interface defines entirely what the system does; the system only does what the user can ask for, so defining the user interface is the same as defining the functionality of the system.

When I was designer of the sonar system mentioned in various places in this book, we had the problem of defining an interface for a smart terminal that was to provide rolling real-time data at the same time as control facilities. The problem was how to combine these and how to make the system's functionality accessible to operators who were engineers. This was the first time I had ever experimented with presenting a client with a look-and-feel simulation of an interface and how it would behave. In little more than two weeks I wrote around 2,000 lines of Algol in two programs. The first allowed me to interactively create and edit a screen and store it on disc. The second allowed me to replay preprogrammed sequences of screens and, to a small extent, mimic inputs and the system's response. I used it to experiment with different screen layouts and to get the client's reactions.

In effect I wrote a screen painter – something common enough these days with our application generators and 4GLs. It was excellent value. I was able to run sample conversations and show how the real-time update would work too. This was before we had started to design the software that would drive the interface. We had already done some exploratory work to see just what this terminal could do (it was really quite smart for the time, with a memory that held several screenfuls and lots of display features such as locking areas and scrolling others). So by the time we had finished we could get on with the design confidently. Today, of course, screen painters and screen generators are the order of the day, but I hope I've demonstrated that the cost of even writing such things for yourself can very easily be paid off by reduced rework time downstream.

Prototyping in a sense occurs at many levels. There are uncertainties in all projects: it might be said that a project is entirely composed of the elimination of uncertainties, resulting in the delivered system. But for the most part it is straightforward to estimate for the resolution of such day-to-day problems and the work resulting from the chosen outcome will not vary much from outcome to outcome

We can expect therefore that a project could switch between the V and VP process models if a major area of uncertainty arises unexpectedly. In this situation estimates dependent on the outcome of the resolution of the uncertainty are themselves unreliable, so switching to the VP model can be (correctly) equivalent to a "no forecast" on future milestones except the conclusion of the prototyping activity!

Risks and uncertainties comes in two flavours: those to do with the problem and those to do with the solution. In the first case there is something about the problem itself that we do not fully understand; in the second case we might understand the problem perfectly well but have little idea how we will solve it. I have been involved in situations where there was a large measure of both: we were not clear about the problem that the client wanted us to solve and we certainly weren't clear what sort of solution we might want to apply!

In the case of the sonar tracking system, the problem was clear enough: using data coming from some sensors with certain data and failure characteristics, provide track data to the following accuracy under the following conditions. We didn't know of anyone else who knew how to do this and they probably wouldn't tell us how they did it even if they had! We were on our own. Fortunately we had a strong mathematician on the project who came up with some new applications of advanced filtering techniques, which, he decided after some experimentation with them, would do the job. I suspect I didn't realise at the time that there was ever any doubt that his algorithms and logic would work – I was very thankful for his competence – but I remember not being very enthusiastic about the idea that he would experiment with them. Like many a project manager, I wanted something that would work, period!

Let us suppose that you are more enlightened and recognise the need for prototyping and experimentation as an early activity in order to reduce downstream risk. Here is a list of some of the sorts of questions or uncertainties that you might decide you need some form of prototyping to resolve, divided into those two categories.

Risks and uncertainties about the problem

Some examples:

- If the system has an interface with humans, we will want to check that the syntax and semantics of that interface have the right feel and performance for each of the different types of user. We may be using new devices for the first time, or for the first time with this particular set of users – how will they react to using a tracker ball or a mouse? The only way of answering these questions might be to put the alternatives in front of the users.

- The general issue of performance is a traditional topic that is evaded when it comes to detail. What are the volumes of data involved? What are the response rates required? What is the throughput in numbers of transactions per second? How often must the processes be run? Answering these questions might require some calculations on the part of the customer, calculations that take into account larger requirements such as the quality of service to be offered overall, the communications costs to be incurred by some connected system, or the profile and size of their client base to be supported by their new system.

- What are the error responses of the system to be? How is the system to react to failures of various sorts? What are those failures? What might a hazard analysis reveal?
- Finally, there will always be uncertainty about straightforward functionality – should it do X or Y, or both? How you find out depends on the tools to hand, plus any constraints on the budget.

Risks and uncertainties about the solution

Some examples:

- The precise functionality of a piece of middleware is not fully understood. For instance, that middleware might be a database, an operating system, a communications protocol, a windowing system, or a filing system.
- The performance of a piece of middleware might be unknown or unstated by the supplier. For instance, with a database system we will want to know the speed with which it returns records for various types of search, for various configurations of files or relations, for various volumes of data, for various key structures, and so on.

  For an operating system that will underlie a real-time system we will want to know the speed with which it will perform a context switch. For the run-time package of a language we will want to know the speed with which functions or procedures are called; if the language is object-oriented we will want to know the performance characteristics of the message-passing mechanisms.

- The "performance" of one of the tools we plan to use might not be known. Typical of this is the compiler – will it handle name spaces as large as we expect to need on the project? Does it produce object code that is fast enough with the sorts of constructions we plan to exploit? To what extent does our configuration tool support the working of a large team?
- If we have chosen a particular design strategy for a multi-processing system, we will want to check that under various loading conditions it performs at the right rate.

The major deliverables

We have the same deliverables here as we had for the V process model except that now of course we add the output of any prototyping activity that we decide upon.

The prototype may or may not be a deliverable itself. I am personally against the idea of delivering prototypes for actual use in the case where a prototype is a functioning piece of software. There is too great a danger of preparing the prototype to non-production standards in order to get the fast turnaround one needs. As a result it might be "lashed up" with poor documentation – not the sort of product one typically wants to have to maintain, let alone deliver!

However, you might deliver prototypes that answered questions for you, simply because they might be needed for the same purpose at some time in the future. A prototype to establish performance will often be useful later in the life of a system when some major change is required that might significantly affect performance. The evaluation of the proposed change could be done with an adaptation of the old prototype quite cheaply. However, such re-use brings with it the requirement that the prototype is documented and developed in a way that makes such re-use both practical and economical – ie probably at an increased cost and timescale.

The generic Work Breakdown Structure

The WBS for your complete project will have a decision making segment in it for each prototyping activity. As we saw in the discussion of the Spiral Model, a prototyping activity might answer a question – resolve an uncertainty – by either exploring a space of possible solutions with a prototype as the means of exploration, or by actually listing alternative solutions and evaluating them against some predefined criteria. The WBS will vary accordingly. In the first case you will have a project fragment of the following shape:

n100   Define the uncertainty

n200   Define a means of exploring solutions (eg a prototype, or some experiment)

n300   Carry out the exploration/experiment

n400   Make deductions – ie answer the uncertainty

You might need to iterate during the exploration activity – perhaps trying several prototypes, or refining one prototype as you converge on the solution. There will then be a corresponding elaboration of the WBS to reflect this.

In the second case the project fragment will look like this:

n100   Define the uncertainty

n200   Identify alternatives and criteria for choice

n300   Evaluate against those criteria

n400   Choose the best-fit alternative

The major review points

Generally speaking, the completion of any activity that produces a prototype will be a sensible place at which to hold some form of review. Since the prototype was intended to answer some question or resolve some uncertainty, the natural expectation will be that the review will analyse the results of the prototyping activity and supply the necessary answer or resolution.

Managing a project using prototyping

Contractual considerations

There will be cases where the course of a project can be significantly determined by the outcome of experimentation with a prototype and in this case it might not be possible to give estimates or plans for the project as a whole; only ranges or alternatives might be possible. Clearly a project with such uncertainties could not be undertaken on a fixed price basis and one purpose of a prototype would be to help to establish the price for the actual system.

In the VP process model we recognise that there might be a need for prototyping to remove some uncertainties at certain stages of the project. For instance, some prototyping might be necessary during the requirements capture to tighten up some area of functionality, or some prototyping might be necessary during architectural work to help decide amongst alternative designs. The assumption of the model is that some aspect of functionality can be agreed or that a design can be found – it is just a matter of deciding which one – but which one is chosen will have a significant effect on the costs and/or timescales of the project. Here, it is clearly not sensible to undertake to undertake the entire project against a fixed price since there is so much uncertainty after a certain point. However, it is possible to undertake fixed price work on that part of the development before the decision is made. Once the decision has been made a new price can be estimated for the remainder of the project or up to the next major decision point if there is one. Alternatively, estimates can be made of the effect of the different outcomes and, simplistically, the maximum used.

The assumption throughout is that the result of the prototyping activity (or whatever investigation we are undertaking to solve a problem) will not vary much.

Given that prototyping reduces downstream risk it should be possible to make some calculations of the cost/benefit of the approach. Such calculations always rest finally on subjective assessments of risk but can at least suggest to what order of magnitude the risk is affected by prototyping. See [Tate 1990].

Management considerations

There are of course major implications for the project manager. A prototyping activity needs to be planned into the project and the relevant dependencies of other activities inserted. In the simplest case, the prototyping can be a simple matter – perhaps the use of a screen painting package to check out the layout and design of some forms – leading to a simple decision. Estimating such an activity is no more difficult than usual and the time limit established can help to guillotine what might otherwise become an endless, subjective debate.

At the other extreme, the building and use of a prototype can be a major project in itself – such as the prototyping of the entire user interface of a system. Here, the project manager must plan for a project within a project: the prototype must be defined, designed, built and used. In particular, it must be defined, otherwise no sensible estimate can be made of the time and effort required even to construct the prototype, and it must not be embarked on without a clear understanding (preferably written down) of what the prototype is designed to achieve.

So we can see four stages in a prototyping activity:

- *The establishment of prototyping objectives.* It is essential to establish why the prototype is being built and what aspects of the proposed system it should reflect. This can be ensured by writing down a list of questions to be answered through the construction of the prototype. It must be possible to decide whether a supposed "answer" does indeed answer the question so the phrasing of the questions is vital and should be carefully reviewed.

- *Function selection.* A prototype usually covers those aspects of the system from which the required information may be obtained. The selection of the functions to be included in the prototype should be directly influenced by the prototype objectives.

- *Prototype construction.* Fast, low cost construction is normally achieved by adopting less stringent quality standards except of course where this is in conflict with the objectives. This means that everyone – including the client – must be aware of the fact that the main purpose of the prototype is experimentation and learning rather than long term use.

- *Evaluation.* This is the most important step and must be planned carefully. The result of the evaluation should either be the information required in the original objectives or a recommendation to produce a further prototype, in other words, to iterate. The purpose of the prototype is to gain information. We must check that that information has indeed been obtained.

We are still left with the problem of how to *control* the prototyping activity, especially in the case where the prototype involves the user. Take the case where we have decided to use a prototype approach to decide on the structure and appearance of the user interface to our system which has a high degree of user interaction. This is a common situation. Users, being human beings, are capable of indefinitely many views on what is good, what is bad, and what might be better. Let us suppose we decide that we will show our prototype to the prospective users, then take comments on how things should be changed, then update it to accommodate those comments, and then go round again. We could be in for an indefinite amount of iteration. How do we call a halt? How do we say "enough is enough"?

This is a question that will probably be answered differently in different situations, depending on the amount of flexibility in the solutions possible, the whims of the users, and so on. One experiment that has been reported on is [Mayhew 1989] where the prototyping activity was controlled by classifying the changes requested and then allocating resources according to a prioritisation scheme. The dangers noted by Mayhew et al are:

- "In this more flexible environment [where prototyping is being done], the potential number of prototypes and hence the potential amount of iteration is uncertain at the time when the initial project estimation is carried out.

- Prototyping depends on active user involvement to succeed. Development that has such a high degree of participation is inherently less predictable than that which has a more passive level of user involvement.

- Project management are less likely to have experience in the estimation of projects that involve prototyping than those for the more structured approaches."

In summary, using a prototyping approach may reduce the risk of developing the wrong system, but can introduce plenty of new risks in making the project unmanageable! Their solution is as follows. They define three classes of change that users might ask for in the prototype:

- *Cosmetic* changes that can be made without any effect on the design. These will be cheap and risk-free to make.

- *Local* changes that have a relatively small impact on the rest of the system. The local nature of the changes means that they will cost only a "moderate" amount and represent a small technical risk.

- *Global* changes that impact other parts of the system. These will be quite likely to require substantial amendment to the design in some way. They will be correspondingly expensive and risky.

From their experience Mayhew et al then propose appropriate ways of dealing with these three categories:

- Cosmetic changes are implemented in the current prototype by the developers without seeking approval (by definition this is possible at low cost).

- Local changes are also implemented directly, but the last version of the prototype is archived against the possibility that the resulting prototype is worse. Since the changes necessary *do* affect the design – albeit in a locally contained way – some form of design review is held to ensure that they are being made correctly.

- A global change cannot be incorporated without a design review that looks at all the ramifications and decides how the change should actually be implemented.

With these categories in place, the prototype can be exhibited to the users who, in some way, experiment with it (this is a matter that one cannot pontificate on – it will vary too widely). All the changes the users propose during a session are logged and each is classified at the end of the session. Between sessions, changes can be made either to the existing prototype or a new prototype can be constructed, depending on the classifications of the changes proposed. Project management only get involved in the decisions as to what should happen next.

The benefits of this mechanism were found to be that progress towards the "right" answer could be monitored; cosmetic changes could be made without management involvement; global changes were only made with management's knowledge and approval, thereby ensuring that any side effects – and hence any impacts on costs and timescale – were sanctioned; and the impact of prototyping on the project as a whole remained visible to management. The technique also offers ways of deciding when prototyping should stop, though such criteria must be locally decided in the context of local budgets and timescales. Mayhew et al point out that in their experiment it was not unusual for global changes to appear well into a prototyping session, which probably reflects the notion that there is little correlation between the importance of features to users and the cost of implementing them. However, if only cosmetic changes seem to be coming out of the sessions then a simple guillotine would seem to be appropriate. Stay in control!

Further advice on organising and managing prototyping can be found in [Mayhew 1990]. Some other problems on the human side that have been reported [Livesey 1984] are

* the difficulty of estimating the resources needed for planning and preparing for prototyping, as well as actually carrying it out
* the way that the existence of a prototype can raise hopes (especially with users) that the system is almost ready
* the frustration that a development team can feel as change after change is requested
* the need for the developer to take on an analyst role to carry out the prototyping.

All of these need careful management.

3.6   THE EVOLUTIONARY DEVELOPMENT PROCESS MODEL

The model described

The *evolutionary development process model* can be likened to the VP process model in which the prototype is in fact an entire system. A whole sequence of complete systems is developed. Each system is complete in that it provides full functionality to the user. See figure 3-7.

Once a system has been built and used, features of it will be noticed that will require changes to be made to the system. Moreover, once the system is installed and used in its environment, that environment will itself change under the influence of the new system and, to some extent, make the system inappropriate – it was after all designed for the old environment! The changes identified are incorporated in the specification for the next system in the series, which is then produced.

The sorts of changes that might be made include changes to functionality, changes in the user interface, changes in non-functional characteristics such as reliability, and changes in implementation to, for instance, improve speed or performance.

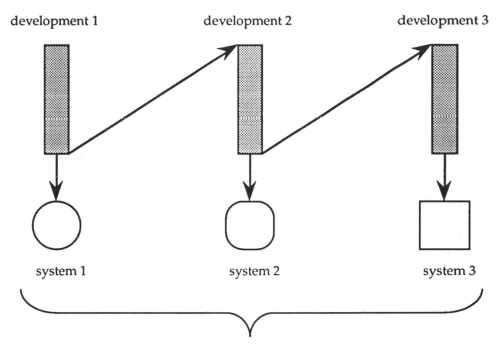

Figure 3-7. The evolutionary development process model

The approach to the way in which each system is built can itself vary; the V or the VP process model might be used for instance. The choice will depend on the nature of each system. It is quite possible that early systems are built using "rapid prototyping" tools and that at some point during the evolution a decision is made to move to a system that is engineered to higher standards of construction, reliability, performance and so on. However, it is important to remember that every system in the evolving series is of "production quality", ie fit for use and with full functionality.

You may have realised that the traditional development phase plus what we have always called "enhancement" together make up one form of the evolutionary development model. However, by showing it this way we emphasise that changes that turn out to be needed after delivery will often require a return to the definition of the system and its design before the code can be changed.

Where to use the model

What sort of uncertainty or risk in the project would lead us to use this model? Clearly, we know enough to build at least the first version of the entire system. But for some reason we believe that when it goes into the field there will be significant changes required. Those reasons could include the possibility that the system will so affect its environment – for instance, the working practices of its users – that it will in some way invalidate itself and thereby need adjustment; or the need for new areas of functionality will become apparent once the system is installed.

(Note that if, at the outset or during development, we identify small areas of functionality that are uncertain we should aim to prototype them there and then rather than leaving them until delivery.)

One place where this model is the natural one is in the development of software products. A product is developed with a complete set of usable functionality. Experience with it in the field leads to new functional requirements and amendments to existing functionality, and the vendor chooses which of these will appear in the next release. The product evolves.

The major deliverables

The deliverables are precisely those that are used on the development path, except that there might be a sequence of them. Thus, suppose we used the simple V process model for the first system to be developed. All the deliverables we would expect – User Model, Architecture Model, etc – will be produced here. Let us call them *UM1, AM1*, and so on. On the second evolution we will produce a new sequence: *UM2, AM2*, etc.

The generic Work Breakdown Structure

The WBS will clearly consist of a number of major units:

    1000   Plan overall development

    2000   Develop evolution 1

    3000   Develop evolution 2

    4000   Develop evolution 3

    ...

Each cycle will be composed of some planning activity, then the production, finishing with some form of review:

    n100   Plan this evolution

    n200   Produce this evolution

    n300   Review the evolution

Note the cyclical similarity with the Spiral Model. The precise WBS fragment in *n200 Produce this evolution* will of course depend on how you go about it –

perhaps with a V process model, perhaps with some prototyping or perhaps in a further evolutionary fashion.

The major review points

The major review points are of course after the production of each evolution. The sorts of decisions to be made include

- how does the result match user expectations or requirements?
- how might user expectations or requirements themselves change as a result of the new evolution?
- what changes should appear in the next evolution?

Managing the model

Contractual considerations

If the evolutionary development process model is being used there might be the implication that the future direction of the system's evolution cannot be determined until something – the first system – is in place and in use. Care should be taken therefore before any contractual commitment is made that extends beyond the production of the first system. Otherwise, managing this model is the same as managing the V or VP process model, whichever is used.

An initial version of the system may be delivered to the users very early in development and it is then essential that they are educated to understand the nature of the process: it will not be perfect, some things are going to change, it is a learning exercise in certain respects, and so on. On the positive side users will not be surprised when they see the "final" system and will also have the opportunity of training on the early versions. The successful use of the model requires that both developer and user are willing to communicate openly during the (possibly long) evolutionary process.

Management considerations

The success of the evolutionary development approach rests on the ability of the designer to build modifiability into the system from the start. The steady evolution can fail badly if at some point a change in functionality that is small in externally perceived terms in fact requires a massive restructuring of the software internally. This has implications for the methods chosen to build systems that will undergo evolutionary development. Object-oriented development and JSD are both strong in this area.

The secret is to decide what it is about the system that is unlikely to change and what is likely to change. The system should be founded on structures that are themselves built on those aspects that are least likely to change. Likely-to-change features then need to be implemented in a way that indeed makes them easy to change. A building should not need to have its foundations dug up to accommodate a change in wallpaper and the same applies to software systems.

The assumption in JSD, for instance, is that the entities that are the subject matter of a system are likely to remain constant whereas the functions that the system performs are likely to change. It also assumes that the organisation of the *external* system that the computer is to track is likely to change. For instance, a bank will probably always have clients. This entity type could underlie the system that handles the bank's business. But the information that senior management want about the bank's clients will change frequently, as will the different sorts of accounts. Finding these "foundation" concepts is crucial and a key question for management as well as for the technicians.

(Ironically, it appears that the technologies we have for the database systems that support organisations are in conflict with the way organisations change! If indeed the entities that are the subject matter of an organisation are the least likely thing to change (assuming the organisation stays in roughly the same business) then they should be at the centre of the system – and indeed if we use a relational database they are: the relational model of those entities is easily captured in the database. Incidentally, that model is also comparatively easy to change, if tedious. On the other hand however, what *does* change in organisations is their logic, that is, how they go about their business – their business rules. And the only tools we have to capture this are the screens, their triggers and all the logic we encode behind those screens in SQL, COBOL, or whatever. And such code is the devil to change! What we desperately need is tools that allow us to capture the business rules of an organisation in a way that they. are easily accessible and easily changed, rather than being buried in code that we cannot change without great pain.)

A further major consideration is the control of successive systems. Because we have a sequence of versions we will have a sequence of deliverables: a sequence of User Model, a sequence of Architectural Models and so on, as we have seen. As anywhere else in software development, if you've more than one version of anything around, you've potential problems unless you exercise strict control over identification of versions, and their release. With products you have the worst problem, with perhaps several versions in the field on many sites, perhaps on many different platforms.

Change control and configuration management are the techniques that you must exercise. They are big topics and not the subject matter of this book. For extensive systems see [Babich 1986] and [Buckle 1982]; for standards in the area see [IEEE 828] and [IEEE 1042].

3.7   THE INCREMENTAL DELIVERY PROCESS MODEL

The model described

It is sometimes the case that a system is to be delivered in a number of increments. Each delivery to the client is usable but will have only partial functionality. Each delivery is the same as the previous one but with some new functionality. This suggests the *incremental delivery process model*. See figure 3-8.

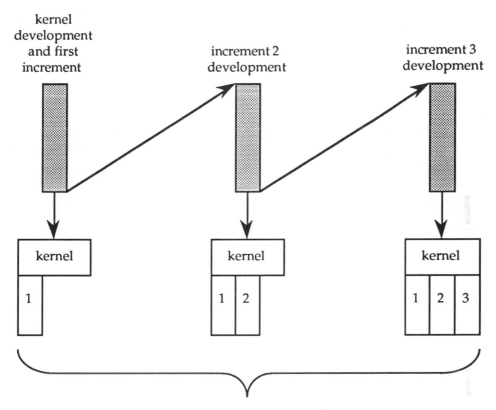

Figure 3-8. The incremental delivery process model

A typical situation is where a central core is delivered together with a small amount of functionality. Succeeding increments add further functionality to that core.

The success of the incremental delivery approach rests on the ability of the designer to create – from the start – an architecture that can support the full functionality of the system so that there is not a point during the sequence of deliveries where the addition of the next increment of functionality requires a massive re-engineering of the system at the architectural level.

The major deliverables

The major deliverables are now the initial system or kernel with its partial functionality and a sequence of increments. For each of these there will be new version of the various system models, much as with the evolutionary development process model.

The generic Work Breakdown Structure

The overall shape of the project for an incremental delivery naturally breaks down into the initial definition and design work, the implementation of the kernel, and then a sequence of separate developments of the increments. The development of the kernel or of an increment could itself take a number of different forms depending on the outcome of your analysis of the risks and uncertainty of the relevant part of the system. (I should emphasise again the need not to treat these models as in any way special or even normal – they are samples of basic schemes that you should adapt.)

1000	Plan overall development
2000	Produce User Model
3000	Produce Architectural Model
4000	Develop kernel

       4100   Produce Implementation Model for kernel

       4200   Produce Build Model for kernel

       4300   ...

5000   Develop increment 1

       5100   Produce Implementation Model for increment 1

       5200   Produce Build Model for increment 1

       5300   ...

       5n00   Revise Models for kernel

6000   Develop increment 2

       6100   Produce Implementation Model for increment 2

       6200   Produce Build Model for increment 2

       6300   ...

       6n00   Revise Models for kernel

The major review points

In addition to normal review points, note how we need to review the kernel during the development of each increment. (Although shown above at the end of the WBS sections, this review process could occur at any time, most probably during the early stages of detailed design of the increment, when the kernel's ability to support the next increment is most closely explored and tested.)

Where to use the model

This process model is often used where there is a risk (or even certainty) that the system in its entirety cannot be delivered by the date required by the client, but where the client can make use of a subset of the system at that date and then take larger subsets or the balance at a later date. There are a number of different ways this can appear.

Unknown increments

One form of uncertainty that can occur is where a significant amount of the system's functionality is in the form of many similar transactions or other units. The exact number of these might not be known at the outset, so that it is difficult to estimate the amount of work required to develop them. We might therefore choose to deliver the system in (at least) two increments. The first would contain the core of the system. Once we had produced that, we would, we assume, be able to estimate how many of them there will be and how long it will take to develop each.

Unknown difficulty

On the other hand, we might know how many there will be but not how long it will take to produce each; this might depend crucially on the architecture of the system chosen during development. In this case a first phase would produce the core of the system plus some small usable subset of all the transactions. From our experiences with that subset we would be able to estimate how long the rest would take and could then commit to delivering subsequent increments with them in.

I was once involved in a major project which delivered a whole sequence of partial systems to the client. The final system was a large transaction processing system that lived on a distributed database network. The system was intended to administer a major examination system involving hundreds of schools and thousands of students sitting many exams. Legal requirements meant that the system had to be in place by a certain date. As is often the case, the client's organisation had a considerable amount of work to do to get itself ready for the transfer to the new automated system from the existing manual system. At various points over the eighteen month development period, parts of the system were needed for early use – the take-on of basic data for exam syllabuses, the registration of schools, the registration of students for examinations, the registration of people who would mark papers, and so on. At each of these intermediate stages of preparation before the exams were held, a new tranche of transactions was required by the client. By the final date everything had to be in place and the system ready to take the marks and prepare the results.

Time was short and getting that sequence of increments defined was crucial to success. There was no way in which the whole system could be waited for, and so the incremental approach was necessary. As increments were developed it would sometimes prove necessary to rework old transactions to bring them in line with the new ones.

Product development

Perhaps one of the more obvious times when the incremental delivery model gets used is in product development. In the product arena there is generally a pressure to get something out on the market as quickly as possible, with enhancements in functionality coming along over a number of subsequent releases. The early version will offer a degree of functionality sufficient to get the market place interested and to sell sufficient licences to get the ball rolling. The product developer could not visualise everything that would be needed, develop it and then try to sell it. The economics and dynamics of the product world do not work that way. The first version will therefore contain basic functionality and – if the developers have been very lucky – will be based on an architecture that will support a number of subsequent enhancements. Unfortunately, those future enhancements cannot be forecast in the early days. As release follows release and the code undergoes further and further change, it gradually "decays"; in thermodynamical terms the disorder or *entropy* of the system increases.

Finally it becomes so disordered that further changes cannot be made without its collapse. The kernel or architecture of the product has served its useful life and here is a case where the foundations have to be replaced to support new parts of the building that were never envisaged at the outset. It is also not unusual for continual enhancement to have a continual deleterious effect on the performance of a system for similar reasons. The original architecture served the originally foreseen functionality, but with successive new layerings it starts to creak and only a complete overhaul will return the product in its enlarged form to an acceptable level of performance.

Provided we understand product development to have this sort of characteristic we can plan to deal with it: we should at least be ready to spot when entropy has reached unacceptable levels and act accordingly. Unfortunately, commercial considerations can again rule that the system must take "just one more release" before it is radically restructured for the future. But one release too many can kill the product.

Reducing interface risks

I have also used the incremental delivery process model when taking delivery of product from someone else. The case I have in mind was one where we were developing a digital framestore for capturing television in real-time. The framestore was to be controlled by a microprocessor that itself received commands from a minicomputer. The framestore was custom designed and built, and was being developed in the same time frame as the software. Indeed, the early design of the framestore was done at the same time as the design of the software – the two were intimately related and hence were married at an early age. But we clearly could not wait for the framestore hardware to be completed before we started integrating it with the software on the microprocessor, and the minicomputer with that. There was a major risk that – as at any interface – we had got something wrong in the specification of the hardware and/or the software. We couldn't wait until late in the day to find out whether we had it right.

The solution was to require from the hardware engineers a series of partial framestores – it turned out to be eight. The first hardware delivery was the core: the backplane (bus), the microprocessor, its memory and the I/O ports. As new boards providing new functionality came out of production the framestore was incremented in functionality and the matching control software was blended in. The first version of the hardware – and it makes me blanch to remember it – consisted of around four PCBs in a cardboard box, held apart and vertical by polystyrene packing material, with a power supply taped to the side of the box at one end. Nevertheless it worked perfectly well, though I guess it would not have pleased a safety inspector. The second and third increments added further PCBs, with the fourth version (or thereabouts) going to two "racks" made out of polystyrene. The major problem at this stage was preventing the whole edifice from collapsing in an untidy heap. Increment five was, I think, in a proper metal casing and new versions of the boards – without "cuts and straps" – started to appear.

That approach proved highly successful – we spotted problems about as early as we possibly could have. We had the continuing problem of bringing software and hardware together at the right times, but the advantage of moving in small steps. It wasn't a brilliantly innovative solution to a risky problem but it was very effective.

Managing the model

Contractual considerations

The straightforward incremental delivery process model, by its nature, presupposes that each increment – including the first – is well-understood and hence can be undertaken using the V process model or the VP process model. In the best case therefore, commitments can be made on the entire project.

Key to the success of the simple V process model is that there is a good specification of the system at the outset that can be agreed by client and developer. In the incremental model, if the specifications of all the increments can be agreed at the outset, the same considerations apply as apply to the V process model. But it can be the case that the precise nature of the increments is not known until the time comes to define the next. For instance, if you are building a system to process transactions coming from automatic bank tellers, early versions of the system might come with basic facilities such as the dispensing of cash and movement of funds between accounts, and future increments might be planned that add additional facilities for the customer. If a new increment is required that, say, handles transactions coming from customers' own home computers and offers home banking facilities, it might not be such a simple matter as adding the odd new transaction process.

In this sort of situation, it becomes necessary to (re)negotiate the contract increment by increment, with each negotiation being preceded by some sort of costing exercise. That exercise might perhaps be based on a preliminary design much as we might undertake in a two phase development consisting of a fixed price definition phase and a fixed price implementation phase, with one of the outputs from the definition phase being the costs and plan for the second phase.

It needs to be borne in mind, however, that, if the content of all the increments is not known at the outset (and this is probably the most common case), there is a high probability that the underlying architecture that is designed at the beginning does not survive beyond the first few increments. As a result increments after the first will often have part of their cost due to reworking necessary on the architecture. This is something not always considered by developers or understood by customers. But it is a fact of life: if you start out with a ship in mind and later want it to run on roads you'll be in for some reworking of the basic structure.

Managerial considerations

Clearly, the development of increments can overlap, but there are dangers with this, especially if the increments require concurrent changes to the kernel. In an ideal world such concurrent changes would not be necessary. But our world is not ideal, and the need to compress the delivery schedules of projects often forces project managers to take the pain of such overlaps in order to satisfy commercial requirements. The problem requires as a minimum a strong configuration and change management scheme, especially on the kernel.

A number of the managerial issues are discussed in [Royce 1990] in a description of TRW's *Ada Process Model*. In this model, increments are not necessarily delivered, but their use serves to

- resolve issues – especially the hardest ones – as early as possible
- keep the cost of change during the lifecycle more or less constant, rather than the traditional geometric cost growth
- give greater visibility of progress to both managers and users
- get testers involved from an earlier point in the development process.

For a discussion of incremental process models see [Graham 1989].

3.8   THE EXPLORATORY PROCESS MODEL

The model described

I include this model simply to show that the Spiral Model can unwind in small turns, with each turn achieving a small amount, and possibly with the whole process starting without necessarily a clear target in mind. We have to accept that, especially in the more research-oriented environments, this can happen and is often desirable.

As is suggested by figure 3-9, the small developments (each an unwinding) may follow one on another in an apparently unguided fashion. But it is likely that what a development should deal with will be decided as a result of the previous development: the work is exploring some domain or other.

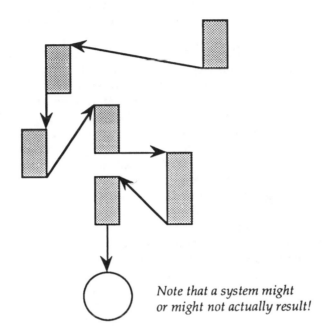

*Note that a system might
or might not actually result!*

Figure 3-9. The exploratory process model

The major deliverables

In this model they could be anything, large or small, related or unrelated – we can make no firm prediction. That's the nature of the work!

The generic Work Breakdown Structure

Since the work can only be planned from one small step to another an overall WBS is meaningless, though each development could itself usefully have some structure – it should at least be planned.

The major review points

A similar comment applies here.

Where to use the model

Clearly, this model should never be used unless conditions definitely demand it. I would consider it very uncommon outside the research environment. I have found it very useful in controlling a research project without unnecessarily over-constraining it. I feel that even in a research environment – especially if you have a client looking for signs of progress – it helps immensely to set and achieve individual targets.

At Praxis, a colleague, Clive Roberts, and I undertook some research work for a client where we were investigating ways in which we could write formal models of the development process. This was an area where – as far as we could tell – nobody had done any substantial work that we could start from. Additionally, we were but a small part of a much larger collaborative project that was investigating the construction of IPSEs for the support of formal software development, IPSEs that would moreover take an *active* part in development (in contrast to the passive environments of, for instance, UNIX). If we'd known the answer to the problem – just our problem – we could have got on with a normal development. But we only had some ideas about some useful-looking technologies and some very broad aims. No question here of agreeing with the client on a price for a delivered piece of software!

Instead we simply worked on a month-by-month timeframe. Each month we would agree with the client a small target of solving one problem, or investigating one topic and making a recommendation, or writing a small prototype, or developing some new ideas, or whatever. And we'd concentrate entirely on that, presenting our findings to the client in a report or verbally at the end of the month (or so). After a "free-ranging discussion" we would set and agree the next parcel of work that we all reckoned would take the topic another step forwards (or perhaps recover some ground lost as a result of the previous month's work). The project has continued in this way for nearly four years now and, as a result, has produced results that could never have been predicted or defined at the outset. Progress has sometimes felt slow but with research of this sort we should not expect the same rate of delivery as on a "straightforward" project.

Managing the model

Contractual considerations

Naturally, on the principle that we should only commit to what we can reasonably predict, no-one is going to take a fixed price contract on anything more than the next small unwinding. In a true research environment of course, the client may let a research contract for a period of time, during which a number of developments might or might not take place, according to how things went. But that sort of project is outside the scope of this book.

Management considerations

The exploratory process model implies that the direction of the project is effectively unknown and unestimatable. A research project of this sort must be run as such, budgets being set according to the price the organisation is prepared to pay for possible results. But naturally those results cannot be guaranteed. The management of the project must be appropriate to research activity, setting goals for but not constraining creativity.

3.9   BLENDING PROCESS MODELS

At the beginning of this chapter I stressed that the process models presented above are not the only possible models and they are not to be followed rigidly. They are simply particular examples. I also stressed that, according to the project being undertaken and the areas of risk and uncertainty within it, some blend of process models would be necessary.

A major project in Praxis used a combination of the VP and incremental delivery process models illustrated in figure 3-10. The first phase of the project did some preliminary experiments – some prototyping – to establish the right overall design, and then proceeded with a series of increments.

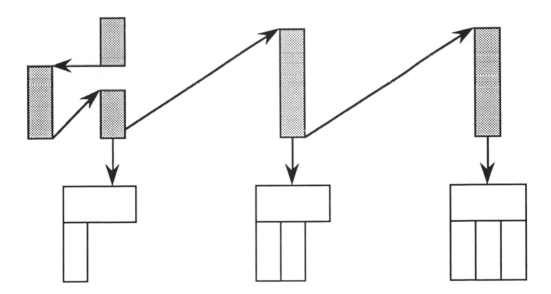

Figure 3-10. A mixed process model

It is worth looking back to the description of the Spiral Model and to observe how each of the basic models described in this chapter is, in some way, just a different "unwinding" of the Spiral Model:

- The V process model is a single unwinding in which the whole system is addressed in one go and there are no significant risks or uncertainties to be resolved.

- The VP process model is an unwinding in which each prototyping activity is a separate cycle designed to resolve some risks or uncertainty.

- The evolutionary development process model unwinds to allow a re-assessment of how the system should be at the end of each cycle; as unwindings occur, the system evolves.

- The incremental delivery process model has an unwinding for each of the increments, which might or might not be known at the outset of development.

- The exploratory process model unwinds in a more or less unpredictable manner, entirely determined by the results of each development.

3.10   DETAILED RISK REDUCTION MANOEUVRES

So far in this chapter we have looked at major variations that are possible in the overall shape of your project – various "unwindings" of the Spiral Model if you like. But there will often be far less major structural variations, risk reduction manoeuvres, that can help to handle and reduce downstream risk.

For instance, suppose that at some point during development you will have to connect your system to someone else's. Everyone knows that when this is done the combined system won't work. You can be as careful as you like with the specification of the interface, but, as sure as eggs are eggs, something will be not quite right. A lot of time will then be wasted establishing where the fault lies – typically, on which side of the interface the fault lies!

Recognising that this risk is a fact of life means that you can plan to manage it when it happens. A simple and natural thing to do is to develop a simulator of the system on the other side of the divide and to use that simulator as a test input generator for your own system before you get to the point of integration. We can then imagine the following elements of a plan – *plan fragments* – that will help you manage this risk:

- design a simulator based on the interface specification once the interface has been agreed

- construct the simulator before the start of system integration

- test the system against the simulator before integration with the other system.

Here we have three simple activities – *design, construct* and *test* – together with some logic: *this before this*, or *that after that*. If the interface is complicated or the integration with the other system is likely to be expensive (because they are deeply embedded or remote or whatever) then we can imagine some elaborations.

For instance, we might additionally design the simulator to work with real responses from the other system if that already exists. We could capture data from the other system with some additional software and drive the simulator with it so as to test our system with some realistic data, as well as with data concocted from the interface specification. The plan fragments would now look as follows:

- design a simulator based on the interface specification and able to accept recorded live data; do this once the interface has been agreed
- construct the simulator before the start of system integration
- prepare software to capture live data from the other system and collect that data before the start of integration
- test the system against the simulator using recorded data before integration with the other system.

Other examples of plan fragments designed to handle specific risks are:

- experiment with a database to check out its behaviour in certain situations before committing to certain parts of the design
- conduct a review of a specification that has been sourced outside your group, before starting any design based on it
- determine the performance of peripherals prior to design
- measure the efficiency of a search algorithm once it has been coded but before integration.

To summarise, for each detailed risk or uncertainty for which only a detailed manoeuvre is required (as opposed to a major process model feature), we can expect to come up with what I would call a *risk/risk reduction pair*:

1 a statement of the risk or uncertainty

2 one or more plan fragments designed to manage that risk downstream, where each fragment takes the form of a list of activities together with a piece of plan logic that places them in context. That logic will indicate sequencing (typically *before* or *after*), iteration (*repeat until* something is true), or selection (*if* this is true *then* do this *else* do that).

(For a tutorial on risk management see also [Boehm 1989].)

3.11   PREPARING THE INPUT TO YOUR PLAN

At the end of chapter 2 we observed that technical planning would lead to various inputs to your Resource Plan:

- a process model
- single activities
- decision points at which one of a number of alternative paths is chosen
- dependencies between activities,

in other words, a process model and a set of risk/risk reduction pairs.

At the end of chapter 4 we'll see how the various decisions you have made so far fit into the Technical Plan (whose contents list you'll find in section 2.5). Then in chapter 7 we'll see how these inputs are used in resource planning. Briefly, the process model gives you the overall structure of the work and the overall logic of it. The single activities can be added to the list of all the other work items that will be necessary. And the decision points and dependencies will provide detailed logic for your plan in its network form.

3.12   CHAPTER RECAP

A project without a plan is an unmanageable project. All projects have risks and uncertainties and it is these that cause projects to go wrong, ie to overrun in time and/or budget. The easy part of planning is the bit you understand, but the hard part is knowing what you *don't* know and planning to find out. A central part of your planning process must therefore be the analysis of risks and uncertainties.

Some risks and uncertainties are so major that the overall shape of your project itself can be completely determined by them. Such project shapes – *process models* – are designed to ensure that (commercial) commitment can be limited to what you can reasonably predict. Typically this means some sort of phasing, with each phase being determined or steered by the previous one. Different process models can be seen as different unwindings of Boehm's *Spiral Model*.

Other risks and uncertainties are less extensive in their effect on your project's shape. For these you need only devise activities that will remove or sidestep a risk or that will resolve some uncertainty. You must fit these activities into the overall project in such a way that they happen early enough to reduce or remove exposure to risk. This results in some plan logic saying when in the project they should take place. Each activity together with this piece of logic forms a *plan fragment*.

Typical areas in which risk and uncertainty can be found are

• user interfaces

• performance

• the use of new software

• the use of new hardware

• interfaces to other systems

• poor requirements

• novel problem domains.

You will use your chosen process model and your chosen plan fragments later on in the construction of your Resource Plan.

4

PLANNING FOR QUALITY ACHIEVEMENT

4.1   INTRODUCTION

In the software arena we can identify three aspects to the notion of *quality* – a term that is more fully explored in chapter 5. Those aspects are

*   quality achievement
*   quality control
*   quality assurance.

Quality achievement is about *methods*, ie about how we engineer quality into something (eg a design) during its development. *Quality Control* (QC) is about checking at the end of some development process (eg a design activity) that we have built quality in, ie that we have achieved the required quality with our methods. *Quality Assurance* (QA) is about having an overall development and management process that provides the right environment for ensuring the quality of the final product, in particular through quality achievement and Quality Control. Quality Assurance is addressed specifically in chapter 5 and Quality Control in chapter 6. In this chapter we are concerned about quality achievement, about the process of development, about choosing the process that will allow us to engineer quality into our software – in short, about the choice of *methods*.

Within any organisation there is a need for a common framework for software development within which different development approaches, methods and tools can be viewed. Approach, methods and tools must always be chosen to match the needs of the project in hand.

The purposes of this chapter are therefore

*   to describe a general framework for system development in terms of the production of a set of *system models* which is independent of the approach taken

- to give you criteria for choosing the most appropriate methods for the problem in hand
- to illustrate how different methods and standards can be used to produce the different system models.

4.2   MODELLING A SYSTEM

The need for a development framework

The two problems facing the software engineer at the start of a project are firstly to choose the process model appropriate to the development of a particular system, and secondly the methods that are appropriate – the two key questions involved in technical planning.

In chapter 3 we looked at the different process models for software development and did it in the context of the Spiral Model. But there are also numerous software engineering techniques: VDM, SADT, JSP, MASCOT, Yourdon, Ward-Mellor, SSADM and so on. Whichever process model is chosen, there are a number of deliverables that can be expected to come out of development and different software engineering methods are designed to produce different deliverables concentrating on different aspects of the system being built. In order to be able to choose methods for a project it is therefore important that we understand the relationship between system characteristics and methods. The framework we look at in this chapter allows us to identify the sorts of systems that the different available methods can be applied to and to identify their deliverables. This means that during technical planning the choice of methods can be made rationally and recorded in the Technical Plan.

The framework concentrates not on the process (ie the approach or method) but rather on the product (ie the deliverables). It asks the question "what sorts of things can we expect to produce during system development?". Once we have an answer to this question we can then ask "what aspects of my system do those deliverables need to cover?", and then "how do the different development methods help me tackle the different aspects of the deliverables?".

In other words, the development framework offered is intended to give you a framework for choosing a development method, rather than prescribing a particular development method. Within your organisation you might have a number of preferred methods – preferred because they are appropriate to the sorts of system you develop and preferred in that they are supported by training and tools.

In this section we look at the two principles on which the framework is based:

- There are a number of different views or *system models* of our system that we should construct when we develop it, independent of methods or process models.
- There are a number of different aspects of a system that can be represented in a given system model; these concern the dynamic and static structure of control and data.

"What is a module?"

Some possible definitions

By way of introduction to the framework we look at a question that is asked in most projects as part of the business of deciding how the system and its documentation should be structured: what is a module? Frequently a module is defined as (or is confused with) for instance

- the contents of a file of source code
- a compilation unit
- a group of compilation units plus their data areas
- a functional unit that has a "module specification"
- a language entity such as a C procedure
- a group of procedures
- a recovery unit
- a package
- an abstract data type
- a process, activity or task ("schedulable unit")
- a linked unit.

Most of these things are different from each other in the average system. A system may be logically decomposed into a number of functional units (sometimes called *subsystems*). The functions of a functional unit might be implemented by different parts of a number of tasks or by code replicated amongst tasks or shared by tasks. The running system operates as a number of communicating tasks, some replicated dynamically and geographically. Each task is made up of a number of procedures and data structures. The source of these procedures and data structures will come from various source files and their linkable object code will reside in various libraries.

In other words, there will not necessarily be simple 1-1 mappings between functional units, schedulable units, editable units, compilable units and linkable units. We would prefer it if there were. In a system consisting of a single program there most likely will be – if we arrange things properly. But in a multi-process and/or multi-processor system there may not be such simple mappings for very good reasons, for instance to do with the fact that we have to build our systems on non-ideal hardware and software using incomplete and/or incompatible development tools with their own idiosyncrasies.

It's because there isn't a 1-1 mapping that we have complex build mechanisms that transform directories of source files into the executable binaries.

The system models introduced

The different types of units address different problems:

- *Functional* units are about making sure that everything in the System Specification is carried forward into the design and they are chosen to give conceptual integrity to the design (to help development and ease maintenance inter alia).

- *Schedulable* units are chosen on performance grounds and to achieve the right system dynamics, and they are often constrained by the capabilities of the target operating system.

- *Editable* units are chosen to make the business of maintaining and editing source a manageable task and one within the capabilities of the editor.

- *Compilable* units must be compilable (eg must not blow the symbol table) and must be chosen to support the hiding of names.

- *Linkable* units must be linkable (ie not blow the linker) and must be chosen to avoid name clashes, to fit in with libraries and so on.

Since these units are so different in the purposes they serve and we cannot always make a neat 1-1 correspondence between them, we know that in general we have to separate them out. Clearly then, we must look at any system in a number of quite different ways.

I like to identify the following four different *system models* of a system:

- the *User Model*
- the *Architectural Model*
- the *Implementation Model*
- the *Build Model*.

These four system models underlie the development framework presented in this chapter. Recognising their existence and the equal importance of the different purposes they serve is central to understanding the framework. They are described in detail in section 4.3.

In what follows it is important not to think of the system models as "levels" in some form of decomposition. They are parallel and complementary views of the system. The strongest structuring that we could place on them would be "weak precedence". For instance we generally need to know what the system is to do (the User Model) before we can engineer it (the Architectural and Implementation Models) and then put it together from its parts (the Build Model). But what the user wants might well be tempered by what is feasible and we might experiment with software to see what can be achieved, perhaps through some form of prototyping.

Why these models are needed – we have poor technology

It is important to remember firstly that in an ideal world these four system models would be in a simple 1-1 relationship, and secondly that the fact that they are not is due to the shortcomings of our hardware, operating systems, databases, languages, compilers and so on. There is a *structure clash* (in Jackson's terms [Jackson 1975]) between the structure of the real-world and the structure of the target environment on which we build systems. The need for different system models reflects this structure clash.

In the future I believe we should aim to use techniques that reduce the number of different transformations we go through from problem statement to problem solution. This will mean using target environments onto which we can more easily map the structure of the real-world and development techniques that handle the structure clashes effectively when they are necessary. Also, it is frequently the case that an implementation that models the real-world exactly (the ideal situation) or even closely would not have the necessary performance characteristics and it becomes necessary to transform the ideal structure into a structure that does.

I would like to illustrate this idea with a simple example from my own experience. I once did some experiments with Prolog, a logic programming language in which one expresses a problem in terms of logical statements. In plain English we might have the *rules* "Jane likes an animal if the animal has four legs" and "all dogs have four legs"; and we might have the *facts* that "Rover is a dog", "Tricia is a dog", and "Fido is a cat". Give this to a Prolog system and ask "which things does Jane like?" and you would get the answer "Rover and Tricia". (We didn't say that cats have four legs so we can't tell that Jane likes Fido.)

There is an old problem relating to how one can ship an equal number of missionaries and cannibals across a river in a boat. You start with N missionaries and N cannibals on one side of a river, and a boat with a rower that can take one person across or back at a time. The problem is to devise a sequence of boat passages that ensures all the missionaries and all the cannibals are ferried across the river without deaths: the catch is that deaths ensue if there are more cannibals than missionaries on one side of the river. In particular, one can ask for a program that devises a schedule of passages for an arbitrary value of N.

I'm not sure how I would develop such a program in, say, C or Pascal. But I would need to devise an algorithm that could try out sequences of passages and backtrack if there was bloodshed. I would guess I would need several pages of C, simply because the control structures of C do not in any way match those of the problem. In particular we would not be able to model directly the "rules" of the problem: what are "safe" situations, what happens as a result of a passage, etc.

Prolog allows you to say things like (what would read in English as) "a position is safe if on both sides of the river the number of missionaries is no less than the number of cannibals or is zero". This can be stated directly, with no need for loops, checks, decisions or any of the *procedural* constructs of a language like C. Similarly we can define the start state directly ("there are N missionaries and N cannibals on the south side, none on the north side and the boat is on the south shore"), the end state directly ("there are N missionaries ..."), and what states can be reached from a given state by a boat passage ("increase the number of missionaries on the north side ..."), and so on.

I wrote a Prolog program of about ten lines that solved the problem. The reason I could do this was simply that there was *no structure clash* between the problem space (safe positions, movements by boat) and the solution space (logic statements). Moreover and most importantly, Prolog works by manipulating logic statements and backtracking where necessary; you can ask it to see if one logic statement is derivable from another given a set of transformations. In our case the question is "can one get from the start state to the end state using allowable boat passages?".

Computational models

We can be sure that all methods have at some time been inappropriately used, in other words used on systems where they simply "weren't right". When this happens the developers spend time trying to force square pegs into round holes: either they try and mangle the problem to make it fit the method, or mangle the method to make it "work" on the problem. Neither of these is a terribly satisfactory approach to software development. Either results in a poor system and/or a bad reputation for the method – with one development team at least. I think that this mismatch can come about because the people choosing the method haven't looked at what we can call the *computational model* of the method and compared it with the characteristics of the problem they are solving. (My thanks go to Clive Roberts for introducing me to this term.)

Let's take some examples.

The object-oriented computational model

If you are developing a system using object-oriented principles, in particular an object-oriented programming language (see for instance [Cox 1986]), then the computational model is the object-oriented model. In this model, at run-time, objects are created and have an existence of their own. And to make things happen they interact by passing messages to each other: "redraw yourself in the current window", "tell me how many items you contain", "divide into three equal parts", or whatever.

In other words, the computational model is one in which independent objects, each containing its own private data, pass messages to each other, and in which there is no global data. This is quite different from the situation with a traditional procedural language where the computational model equivalent is one where functions (procedures, etc) call one another, where global data (shared memory or files) is often used for inter-procedural communications, and where code and data are separate and there is a very loose connection between the two.

The computational model of JSP

The computational model that underlies JSP (Jackson Structured Programming [Jackson 1975]) is quite different. Here, the model is that the structure of a program should be based on the structure of the data that it is processing. To over-simplify, the input data that is processed by a program can be defined in terms of a grammar that allows sequence, selection and iteration of data items.

For instance, data coming into a program that processes transactions at a cash dispenser might have the format opening transaction from the dispenser *then*

{transaction from users of the dispenser} *then*

closing transaction from the dispenser

where the curly brackets represent repetition (ie *iteration*). The *then*s (traditionally replaced by semi-colons) represent *sequence*. A transaction from a user would itself have the structure

carry out identification *then*

[funds transfer *or* cash withdrawal *or* balance enquiry]

where the square brackets contain options (ie *selection*). (For simplicity, in this example we assume that only one of the three options can be exercised by the customer in any given transaction.) A funds transfer would itself have a structure:

specify account to be debited *then*

specify account to be credited *then*

specify amount to be transferred

So we could describe the incoming data as a grammar thus:

opening transaction from the dispenser

then

repeat until time to stop

transaction from users of the dispenser *ie*

carry out identification

then

do funds transfer *ie*

specify account to be debited *then*

specify account to be credited *then*

specify amount to be transferred

or do cash withdrawal

...

or do balance enquiry

...

end repeat

then

closing transaction from the dispenser

It only takes a little imagination to see how this can be turned directly into a program with the same logic. (Clearly, I have simplified away issues such as multiple input streams, error handling etc, but the principle remains the same.) The computational model of a JSP-designed program is based on sequence-selection-iteration derived from the syntax of the incoming data. We know a lot from Dijkstra about such well structured programs.

The computational model of MASCOT

Let's take an example at the design level. If you are using the MASCOT method for the design of real-time systems [JIMCOM 1987] then you will design your system as a number of asynchronous communicating processes. Communication between processes is achieved through two sorts of pipe: a *channel* which is a buffered queue, or a *pool* which is a simple global data area.

For each channel and pool you define *access mechanisms* that handle potentially asynchronous access by asynchronous and independent processes. To support your MASCOT design you can use a MASCOT kernel that supports a set of predefined primitive operations on which you build your communications and synchronization as necessary. This is quite a different scheme from the computational model used in Ada. Here, all inter-process communication is synchronous and quite a different architecture results. The design ideas underlying MASCOT and Ada have different computational models. Attempting to build a MASCOT design on Ada requires a certain amount of contortion to make things fit – something that is very undesirable.

The computational model of JSD

A related technique is that of JSD (Jackson System Development [Jackson 1983]). The principle is similar to that of JSP. Firstly a model is constructed that models the real world. So for each entity instance in the real world - for instance, a particular bank account – a process in the system tracks its history. A bank account is opened, undergoes a number of transactions, and is closed. A process in the system tracks each account's status as real-world events occur to it. Such processes are called *model processes* and they can communicate with one another in reflection of such communication between the real world objects.

Into this real-world model we now insert new processes – *functional processes* – that generate outputs from the model. The overall computational model here is one of a network of cooperating processes each of which has a status reflecting that of something in the real world or which uses that status information to produce outputs.

The computational model of VDM

Finally, let's take an example from the specification area. If you specify a system using VDM [Jones 1986] you specify it in terms of a *state* – generally expressed in terms of a set of data elements and their values – and a set of *operations* that can act on the state and change it. Thus, a library system might be defined as a state consisting of the set of books (characterised by their titles and accession numbers say), a set of borrowers (characterised by their names and addresses, and the number of books they are allowed on loan at any one time), and a set of borrowing relations between books and borrowers. Operations on the state such as *borrower X borrows book Y* cause changes on the state – in this case a change in the relationships between books and borrowers.

Before specifying a system with a method like this we would want to be sure that this computational model (operations on a state) was an appropriate one. I was once involved in a system in which we wanted to specify that an airborne system had carried out a certain set of manoeuvres on a given mission. This was tried in VDM but became difficult because VDM does not easily support the idea of "history" – a notion that was crucial for what we wanted to describe when we defined this system.

Understanding the computational model implicit in the methods you are using is absolutely key if you are going to choose the best methods for your problem.

Views of a system

Let's look at all this in a little more detail. When we define or describe or construct a software system we are building a model. A model concerns itself with some views of the thing it is modelling and not with others. A model of a building built to sell the plans to a buyer will concentrate on capturing the building's aesthetic qualities, showing how brilliantly it will fit in the existing cityscape, and suggesting a bold statement about the buyer's place in this world. A model of the same building constructed to analyse how well that design will stand up to earthquake or to high winds will not be in the final colours that the buyer was so interested in.

When we build a software system we will want to concentrate on those aspects that are the most important to us as modellers. If the performance of the system is critical, our design models had better allow us to represent and measure the performance properties of our design. If the safety properties are important then we had better have ways of expressing and establishing the presence (or otherwise) of those properties. If the integrity of data or its distribution are important then those aspects must be brought out by the methods we use. And so on.

Now, at a general level, a software system can be defined in terms of its data structures and its control structures. We can take static and dynamic views of each of these. Static views show the fixed aspects of the structure of the data or control. Dynamic views show how the data and control structures change in time or in place.

We thereby end up with six different viewpoints that we can take when looking at the different system models. Each of these viewpoints is served by a number of different methods as suggested in figure 4-1.

In particular we can see that,

- an entity-relationship model (ER model) shows the static relationships of one data entity to another

- a data flow diagram (DFD) captures the movement of data around a group of processes but does not show the logic (ie *when* movement or processing happens) – extensions such as those devised by Ward and Mellor [Ward 1986] add this to simple DFDs

- a module calling hierarchy shows the static (ie coded) inter-relationships between the modules in a program – what calls what, but not when
- VDM captures how the system state is affected by operations on it
- a Finite State Machine (or state transition diagram) shows how control changes in time (in particular the movement from state to state according to input)
- a Petri Net shows how concurrent control moves around a network over time (ie the *where*) and the logic of that network, and captures the logic (ie the *when*)
- an entity life history (ELH) shows how data (an entity) changes over time
- and so on.

		data	*control*
static		JSP ERA model	Module hierarchy
dynamic	*temporal*	ELH VDM Z	Process map Petri Net FSM, CSP, CCS
	local	DFD ACP diagram JSD/SSD	Petri Net CSP, CCS

Figure 4-1. Six views of a system

In a given system one or more of these viewpoints will be more important and need emphasis. In a concurrent system, control aspects are crucial and we tend to concentrate on them: how are the processes organised? how do they synchronise? etc; in an administrative system for an organisation we will concentrate more on the data aspects: what are the entities? how does data about them flow between agents? where is the data located? etc. Particular methods have particular strengths in particular areas so we can see that choosing a method (or methods) is a matter of matching strengths against critical aspects. SSADM uses ELHs, DFDs and an ER model as its three principal modelling techniques and can be seen quite clearly to concentrate on the data aspects of a system.

This will sometimes lead us to choose several methods to cover a number of aspects. The matrix can help us avoid the danger of relying on one method to do everything and is designed to assist in the choice of methods as part of the technical planning process as we shall see in more detail soon.

In section 4.3 we describe each system model in turn. In section 4.4 we go on to examine the interplay between them.

4.3   THE SYSTEM MODELS DEFINED

The User Model

The specification side: Requirements Expression and System Specification

As a minimum, the User Model consists of a System Specification agreed with the client. In the general case, a preceding Requirements Expression might form part of this system model or at least provide input to it.

The Requirements Expression describes what the user wants to achieve with a system. This might be to do with organisational, financial or technical matters. It might say "any system that we buy must generate benefits X, Y and Z". It might say "we actually need a system that does this or that because they are the benefits we want or because they are needed if we are to get the benefits we want". The Requirements Expression specifies a class of systems by describing a need (the *what*).

The System Specification describes one system (a *how*) that would satisfy the requirement in the Requirements Expression, and in turn specifies a class of implementations of it.

(Subsequent system models in the development process describe one of those implementations from a number of different viewpoints.)

The User Model in the form of the System Specification must satisfy two criteria:

- it must be a sufficient basis for design and implementation (this is the internal view of the System Specification)

- it must be a sufficient basis for the preparation of an Acceptance Test that the client can agree to as a determining test of the system supplied (this is the external view of the System Specification).

The System Specification will contain three types of statement:

1   descriptions of the functionality to be exhibited by the system, ie how it will respond to specified stimuli and conditions

2   constraints that the system must satisfy, such as use of a given hardware infrastructure

3   properties that the system must possess, such as the various -ilities: portability, maintainability, and so on.

(In the terminology of chapter 5, type 1 statements are *functional quality features* and type 2 and type 3 statements are *non-functional quality features*.)

The components of the User Model

Given that the User Model covers all those aspects of interest to the user (or client in general), we can expect it to include

- a Requirements Expression
- a System Specification
- the Acceptance Test Specification
- the System ready for operational use, having satisfactorily "passed" the Acceptance Test
- any User Guides, User Manuals, User Training, or other materials required to make the system usable by its users.

The Architectural Model

The Architectural Model captures the software architecture of the system in terms of the logical structure of its control and its data. It describes how the functional structure of the system is mapped onto the target environment or local infrastructure, be it naked machine or sophisticated transaction processing system.

In broad terms we can describe an architecture as one structure built on another: the functional structure built on the infrastructure. Any non-trivial system will have a number of components identified in its architecture, and we can arrive at the decomposition of the system into those components in a number of ways that vary from method to method. So our discussion of architecture and the choice of methods for the Architectural Model will centre on *decomposition criteria* and *target infrastructure*.

Decomposition criteria

A useful way of classifying architectural design methods is to look at the criteria they use for decomposition. This takes us back to the question asked earlier: "what is a module?". The question we shall ask here is "what are the units of decomposition and what characterises them?". Deciding which method is appropriate becomes a matter of deciding which method uses the most "natural" criterion for decomposition, ie which has the computational model closest to the world being automated. Some examples are:

- Units in the architecture might correspond to units in the part of the real-world that is being monitored or controlled. This is a criterion at the heart of JSD, JSP, and the *model-view-controller* notions used in object-oriented design, as we saw earlier.
- Units in the architecture might correspond to security units so that levels of security, security boundaries, authentication, etc can all be reliably controlled.

- Architectural units may be chosen in a way that reduces communication between them. The *high coherence and low coupling* notion introduced by Myers [Myers 1975] was an early formulation of this criterion whereby a decomposition is chosen that keeps architectural units (*modules* in Myers' terms) as independent as possible.

It is not unusual for two or more of these criteria to be important in any one system, depending on whether data and/or control is the most important part of characteristic of the system, whether dynamic or static aspects predominate, and whether time or place is more important.

Target infrastructure

All architectures rely on some infrastructure (what is sometimes know as a *virtual machine*) that supports facilities to do with control structures and data structures. The lowest level infrastructure available will be that provided by the target environment: the hosting operating system together with such things as graphics packages, DBMSs, comms systems and TP systems. In other words, the target architecture has its own computational model. But it is generally unwise to couch the architecture directly in terms of the lowest level available. This typically produces designs that have little internal coherence and no central dogma other than the simplest offered by the operating system (OS). So we often define higher-level infrastructures that provide architectural constructs closer to our needs. It is an important function of the Architectural Model to record what facilities are assumed in the underlying infrastructure. The architecture is then expressed in terms of this higher-level infrastructure.

For example:

- We might produce an architecture for a simple control program in the form of a Finite State Machine. The average OS does not provide mechanisms for FSMs but our Architectural Model expresses the architecture in terms of such mechanisms. In the Implementation Model we will actually describe how those mechanisms will be implemented in terms of the facilities that are offered by the OS or whatever.

- We might design a concurrent system as a number of processes operating as a Petri Net. Again this will presuppose some mechanism that supports a Petri Net style of operation. The Architectural Model will give the architecture of the system in terms of a Petri Net and specify the presupposed infrastructure necessary to support it.

This case demonstrates that an important aspect covered by the Architectural Model is the control aspect and particularly the dynamic control aspect if the system is a concurrent system. Here the system is divided into logical tasks. These are functional units that could operate independently of each other. They communicate data between each other by various means that will be supported by the underlying virtual machine.

The ideal network is one that maximises the amount of potential concurrency and decoupling between the logical tasks. The potential dynamic structure of the system is thereby captured. Not all this potential might be exploited – exactly how much will be determined in the Implementation Model.

- We might define an architecture for our system in the form of a number of free standing programs that operate independently on a database through a database management system (DBMS). Such an architecture thereby presupposes a supporting infrastructure in the form of the facilities provided by the DBMS and the local operating system.

- If we have been "given" a transaction processing system as part of our target infrastructure, our architecture is going to be very much decided for us, as the authors of such systems generally provide hooks onto which serial code can be hung. Again we take the supporting infrastructure and the implied architecture as givens.

- In an object-oriented design each object would be a logical task and the dynamics of message exchange between the object processes would be the basis of the control aspect. This architecture could be implemented in a number of ways depending on what mechanisms were available in the target infrastructure. It is the job of the Implementation Model to describe that choice.

The components of the Architectural Model

Summarising, the Architectural Model will include

- an architecture expressed in terms of one or more explicitly defined computational models, based on a specified infrastructure itself based on the base underlying infrastructure; this architecture will identify the major components ("subsystems", "processes", "activities", etc, according to the decomposition criteria of the computational models), will identify their logical relationships within the terms of the computational models, will (in the case of a concurrent system) show all possible concurrency, and will define the logical data structures that support the architecture

- specifications of the major components

- Build Test Specifications that define tests for the major components against their specifications

- versions of the major components that have passed the Build Test Specifications.

The Implementation Model

The Implementation Model captures the way in which the (possibly ideal or logical) architecture is actually implemented. It takes into account the limitations of the target environment (operating system, hardware, database, file system etc) on which the system must run. It is a record of the "compromises" made in order to implement the ideal architecture of the Architectural Model on the un-ideal target system. In particular, it says

- which real tasks/activities/processes (schedulable items) will exist to implement the potentially concurrent activities identified in the Architectural Model; they might for instance be compositions of logical tasks, combined into one real task for performance reasons
- how each resulting inter-task communication path will be implemented (global data areas, message queues, comms package, service subsystem, OS services, language constructs, etc)
- the structure of each task in terms of procedural (ie language specific) units, typically in a module hierarchy
- how data will be passed between the procedural units (parameters, messages, global data (not recommended!), etc)
- how logical data structures will be implemented physically
- which code will be re-entrant and which will be single-thread.

Once these have been established, procedural units can be coded and tested. The tested code forms part of the Implementation Model, being the final "compromise" of the ideal architecture. The Implementation Model therefore contains the following items:

- a definition of the physical process structure, its logic and data flow
- a module/component calling hierarchy for each process, showing the data passage mechanisms
- specification of physical data structures (memory and peripheral based)
- specification of functional and non-functional features of each module
- a test specification for each module
- tested modules.

The Build Model

This system model describes how the system of communicating programs or processes and their data is actually built from the source code using the tools available (compilers, linkers, make files, command files, etc). It might exist in several forms if more than one system is to be delivered, or in parametrised form if a range of systems is to be configurable.

A Build Model contains the following items

- files required to construct processes/programs from source code
- scripts for installation of infrastructure components such as comms, operating system, database, screens and forms
- scripts for system start-up, process initialisation, and system control.

Where does prototyping fit in the models?

It doesn't. Prototypes, you will remember, are used to answer questions. Once a question has been posed, the prototype developed and used, and the question answered, the prototype is not of further immediate interest. The information generated by using the prototype finds its way into one or more of the deliverables listed above.

4.4   THE SYSTEM MODELS IN PRACTICE

In a subsequent section we look at the methods that can be used to construct the different system models but here we look at how the system models are used in practice.

When are the system models produced?

It is easy to concentrate on one of the system models to the virtual exclusion of the others. This is easily done if a single development method is chosen: for instance an SADT model concentrates principally on the software functional model aspects, and a MASCOT model on the architectural and implementation models; one project in Praxis found that SSADM covered much of the system models but gave no help in the establishment of the system architecture in cases where it was not a straightforward transaction processing system supported by your friendly local DBMS. An aim of this chapter is to stress the need to give all the system models their correct weight and to select methods appropriately.

It is worth repeating here that the system models are not levels in some form of decomposition. They are different views of the same system. Like models in general, each of the four system models concentrates on some aspects and ignores others. The relative rate of development of the different system models at any one time will depend on the sort of software being developed and the process model that has been adopted.

At one end of the spectrum is the development of a system with little "speculative" content. In other words, the required functionality can be written down and a solution looks possible; the functionality might be contentious and the solution difficult but progressing from the User Model into the Implementation Model and Build Model in one sweep is an appropriate development process – our V process model. As we have seen, a frequent (perhaps mandatory) requirement is to establish design constraints imposed by the target virtual machine early on during the project. This will result in some details and/or broad brush material in the Architectural Model or the Implementation Model.

At the other end of the spectrum is the exploratory process model typical of AI work. Here, the functionality is only expressible in the most general terms and development takes place by direct experimentation with algorithms and programs, the results being fed back into better understood functionality, an extended architecture and further experiments.

As we saw in chapter 3, between these poles is a whole spectrum of development processes involving more or less iteration, more or less experimentation and more or less feedback. The choice of which is to be used depends on where the areas of uncertainty and risk are in the project. But whichever approach is used, a major problem is always that of maintaining conceptual integrity of functionality, architecture and construction, in other words maintaining a well structured User Model, Architectural Model and Implementation Model throughout development.

Typically, well defined systems with low technical risk can be developed in the single pass fashion. The management of their development can make use of traditional planning leading to relatively reliable time and effort predictions. Ill defined systems with high technical risk require a different form of management that reconciles iteration and experimentation with the need to plan to a schedule. This may require making use of an ability to set functionality to what can be achieved or using techniques of incremental planning, development and delivery so that a potentially unmanageable development is broken down into a sequence of manageable increments.

It has been emphasised that the four system models are not levels in a hierarchy. However, each system model will often be recorded in some hierarchical fashion: a hierarchy of data flow diagrams, a hierarchy of procedure calls, the logic of a procedure expressed in a structured PDL, and so on. Such hierarchies allow good structuring and the definition of useful layers of abstraction, of virtual machines and so on. How a hierarchy is developed is largely personal matter. Some prefer stepwise refinement, others working from the lowest level machine to the highest, others still from both ends. What is most important is that the resulting hierarchy should be well structured with levels of abstraction clearly preserved and a conceptual integrity permeating the structure.

Interaction between the system models

In a typical system, getting from one system model to the "next" is not necessarily a refinement – it can be a major jump. We have seen that this is principally because there is not necessarily a one-to-one relationship between the units of one system model and those of the next, a structure clash. Thus, the functional structure as perceived by the user will not necessarily bear any relationship to the process structure of the system. This mis-match can make the transition from one system model to another very difficult particularly that from User Model to the Architectural Model.

In fact, of course, this transition is precisely what we call *design*! And design is the hardest part of any system development simply because it requires this creative leap from one structure to another in a way that preserves all the requirements expressed in the former, yet is feasible in the computational model of the latter. No cook-book technique will ever make this design process mechanical. All methods "avoid" it – most without saying! A good, honest design method will make clear exactly what step is left to the creative skill of the designer.

The difficulty derives from the mis-match between "function" as expressed in, say, the User Model and "function" as expressed in the Architectural Model. To avoid this difficulty, object-oriented methods (eg object-oriented design and JSD) have concentrated on producing system architectures that mirror the object structure of the external real-world. With object-oriented definition and object-oriented design we can thereby avoid the mis-match between a system's functional structure and its process structure – the two become the same.

The resulting object-oriented architectures, like all architectures, presuppose some supporting mechanisms for the concepts they use. That support must finally derive from the target infrastructure. If that infrastructure can be supplied through a suitable object-oriented language such as C++, Objective-C, Simula or SmallTalk, then the Implementation Model can also be in 1-1 correspondence with the Architectural Model and another structure clash is avoided. If the target infrastructure is, say, COBOL and a DBMS, then the Implementation Model will need to "invert" the architecture in some way so that it can be supported sensibly and efficiently – this is what happens in the latter stages of JSD.

The fact that we have identified a series of system models does not imply that there is a corresponding strict ordering of development (or indeed maintenance) activities. Work on any one system model will require two forms of iteration: *intelligent look-ahead* and *controlled reworking*.

Intelligent look-ahead is the action of looking ahead to the subsequent system models to check that what is being proposed is feasible. The distance of look-ahead will be inversely proportional to the degree to which lower levels are under the control of the project. If the project intends using a supplied graphics package or DBMS it is clearly vital to establish the precise nature of that package (probably by experimentation) before committing to design based on the package.

The distance of look-ahead will also be determined by the perceived risk in the implementation of the proposed system model. Technically difficult or innovative solutions will require a greater amount of look-ahead than normal. We have already seen in chapter 3 that this sort of look-ahead should come out of a consideration of the risks and uncertainties that are in our system or its development. This sort of look-ahead is what underlies the VP process model.

Controlled reworking is the process of reworking earlier system models in the light of work on a particular system model. It can turn out that the earlier system model was difficult to implement, did not lead to a "good" implementation or was actually impossible. This will require adjustment, perhaps under configuration control.

One area where we have already seen a possible need for controlled reworking is in an incremental (or even evolutionary) process model, where a kernel that survives/supports, say, the first four increments might prove not up to the task of supporting the fifth. The system model of the original kernel will need reworking. You will remember that the Work Breakdown Structure for an incremental process model included that reworking of the Implementation Model for the kernel.

Methods for producing the models

Over the last decade, there has been an explosion of methods for producing the different models, ie for doing system definition, system design, and system implementation. For surveys of methods see [Birrell 1988] and [STARTS 1988].

4.5   TECHNICAL PLANNING AND SYSTEM MODELS

Now that we have developed our framework of system models within which to choose the right methods for the system we have to build, we can go on to look at how we use this analysis during technical planning.

Choosing the appropriate method(s)

The process of choosing the most appropriate method is, put simply, one of finding the method that offers the most appropriate computational model. In other words, the computational model of the method must reflect some structural feature of what you are trying to capture in the real world. If the real world (or the part you are automating) is about data and how it moves around, then a method with data flow underpinning its computational model is the right method.

The simple matrix in figure 4-1 classifies computational models in a coarse way that should help you determine appropriateness at a coarse level. To take extreme cases by way of illustration, SSADM is unlikely to be suitable for embedded systems because of its emphasis on the data aspects of a system, whilst MASCOT probably wouldn't make much sense for a database-based system using supplied forms and reports tools. However, what can be missed without an analysis such as this can be, for instance, the possibility of using VDM to give precise definitions of the effect of database updates, the use of a Finite State Machine (FSM) to give precise definition to the logic of a user interface, or the use of an ER model to provide input to an object-oriented design.

We saw above how different computational models in methods can match different structural features in the real world. If the real world is about serial files with a regular grammar then JSP has an appropriate computational model that helps you abstract the real world easily and fully. If the real world is one in which data moves between functional units then DFDs can capture that movement – they can abstract it out of the rest of the detail. And so on.

The above guidance should make it clear that it is perfectly possible for one system to need a number of methods for a full attack. It is for this reason that some of the larger and all-encompassing methods pull together a selection of techniques that give good coverage of my classification matrix, and hence the possibility of covering all angles on any one system. They also run the danger of course of suggesting that the developer should throw all methods at every problem – an equally pointless and potentially dangerous act. The SSADM method favoured by the UK government for administrative system development combines DFDs, ER, and ELH models in the specification phase alone: the concentration is on data from three viewpoints which are then pulled together.

Ward-Mellor and similar extensions of Yourdon add control logic in the form of FSMs to the data-oriented techniques of "traditional" Yourdon: DFDs and data dictionary.

In summary, the choice of methods goes thus:

1   Decide which which are the most important aspects for the system or its subsystems: control or data, static or dynamic (temporal and local).

2   Choose the method(s) that promise the best fit.

3   Check that the computational model of the method matches that of that part of the world you are trying to capture.

4   Determine the criticality of the system or its subsystems: low criticality means that methods with less formality can be used; high criticality means methods with greater formality should be used, thereby allowing greater V&V potential (see section 6.3).

Fitting the system models into your process model

In chapter 3 we examined a number of possible process models – possible unwindings of Boehm's Spiral Model – and we identified the major steps in terms of their deliverables through the generic Work Breakdown Structure (WBS) of each. Those deliverables were of course the different system models that we have introduced in this chapter. When you sketch out your process model at the macro level (as in figure 3-10 for instance), you will therefore be sketching out what sequence of what models you will produce (as well of course as all the minor and supporting intermediate deliverables).

Now that you have chosen the methods you will use to produce those models you can make your Work Breakdown Structure (WBS) much more specific: instead of writing an activity such as *1200 Prepare User Model* you will be able to make a more explicit expansion such as

> 1200   Prepare User Model
>
> 1210   Prepare layered DFD for entire system
>
> 1220   Prepare Data Dictionary for all entities
>
> 1230   Prepare VDM model of secure transactions
>
> 1240   Prepare FSM model of secure transaction processing
>
> etc

We shall see in chapter 6 how this will help us to decide what verification activities to incorporate in our development: having identified clearly what we will produce and how, we can make decisions about how to define and then verify the *quality* of those deliverables and hence of the system overall. In chapter 7 we shall also see how the more such detail we can provide the more likely our estimates are to be "right", ie achievable and minimal. These are not just thought games!

4.6   PREPARING THE TECHNICAL PLAN

In chapter 3 we looked at how many of the basic features and structures of your project come from a consideration of the risks and uncertainties in the project and how they can be either avoided or managed downstream. In this chapter we have looked at how analysis of the system to be developed leads us to a choice of methods and hence additional activities and structure for the project plan.

In this section we look at how the results of these two analyses come together in the Technical Plan structure recommended in section 2.5. Here is that structure again:

1   Introduction and summary
2   Constraints
    2.1   Risks and uncertainties identified
    2.2   Characterisation of the system to be developed
    2.3   Client expectations or requirements
3   Choices
    3.1   Chosen process model
    3.2   Chosen development methods
    3.3   Chosen tool support
    3.4   Chosen target environment
4   Implementation
    4.1   Planned development/host environment
    4.2   Planned maintenance environment
    4.3   Planned training
5   Implications
    5.1   Timescale implications
    5.2   Financial implications

Let's look at it section by section.

Section 2: Constraints

Section 2.1: Risks and uncertainties identified

This section takes the form of a simple numbered list of all the risks and uncertainties identified during the analysis described in chapter 3.

Section 2.2: Characterisation of the system to be developed

This section takes the form of a list of the main characteristics of the system or parts of the system that are pertinent to the choice of methods for those parts. This will come from an analysis of the system aginst the matrix in figure 4-1 and a consideration of what would be an appropriate computational model.

Section 2.3: Client expectations or requirements

Be sure to record the expectations or indeed requirements of the client in matters of how the system is to be engineered, whether or not you have decided to take them on board.

It is increasingly common for the purchaser of a bespoke software system to demand that it be built using a particular method or with certain tools. The reasons for doing this are varied but very often it is the case that the buyer intends to do subsequent maintenance and enhancement using their own staff. They will often have house standards for development which you will have to fit in with so that their staff will be able to take over future work on the system without extra training or knowing about two development techniques, two sets of tools and so on. It is this reason that underlay the US Department of Defense's push for Ada, and the UK Government's development of the SSADM development method for administrative systems.

In some cases you might find that your client wants to specify methods or tools that are really not appropriate, or that are even going to be counter-productive in some way. How you handle this will clearly be a matter for careful consideration. In some cases I have convinced a client of the benefits of doing it the way that I believe would be most cost-effective (not only for the development itself but also in the longer term). But this can look like arrogance. Step carefully.

Section 3: Choices

Section 3.1: Chosen process model

For each risk or uncertainty in section 2.1 of your plan describe how you plan to manage it. Describe the process model you are adopting to handle the major risks and uncertainties. Describe any detailed plan fragments required to handle the minor risks and uncertainties.

Section 3.2: Chosen development methods

Identify the methods or parts of methods that you have chosen for the parts of the system or entire system. If you choose a brand-name technique such as SSADM or Ward-Mellor you should try to be explicit about whether you are doing it in its entirety or just those parts that make sense. If you are only using parts, say which parts.

For a comparative survey of methods across the development cycle see [Birrell 1988].

Section 3.3: Chosen tool support

List the tools that you want to use to support the methods you have chosen. The choice of tools is a non-trivial exercise in itself but it is not one that I go into in this book. For guidance, see the various surveys such as the STARTS Guide [STARTS 1988].

These choices will have implications for training, licence costs and so on that you must take into account. When you have prepared your Quality Plan (as described in chapter 6) you might want to add further tools to this section to specifically support verification and validation activities.

Section 3.4: Chosen target environment

What system (hardware, operating system, DBMS, etc) will your software run on when it is operational? This may well have been decided for you, or you might have a free hand. The reason for recording the decision here is that the choice will have implications for not only the delivery of that hardware and software (if it is your responsibility) but also for the development and maintenance environments, which in turn have further implications on procurement which will have time and costs repercussions in your final plan. Easily forgotten, but frequently expensive.

Section 4: Implementation

So much for the analyses and the resulting choices. We now come to the point where we must look at second-order effects from those choices.

Section 4.1: Planned development/host environment

First a reminder by what I mean by an *environment*:

- hardware: processor and peripherals perhaps with communications facilities
- software: operating system, file system or database management system, comms software, any bought-in middleware such as TP systems or real-time support packages.

The *target environment* – the actual hardware and software that your system will run on – can be related to the *development environment* – where you develop the software – in a number of different ways, all of which have implications for your project costs and timescales.

- Firstly, the environment you develop on might become the target environment. There may be some complications here that you will need to take care of, such as the need, during development, to have the operating system etc set up in a way that suits development, whilst adjusting it to suit operational running when delivered with your system. There might also need to be slightly different amounts of memory, or disks, or comms bandwidth in development and in operation. Check these out and record your findings here.

- Secondly, the two environments might have the same "brands", ie the same hardware components and the same software components, but be physically different. This is the case when, for instance, your software is going to run on a system that already exists and is operational, but on which development work cannot be allowed at the same time, for security or performance reasons perhaps.

Here, you will need to provide for the purchase, rental or loan of your development environment, with the corresponding cost and timescale implications.

- Thirdly, the two environments can differ in the brands of components, sometimes quite radically. For instance, your software might be designed to run in a custom processor in a portable telephone – not an ideal development environment. In this case you will use a completely different development environment, and cross-develop from that onto the custom processor. There are many products available to help you do this. They have a price in money and time. Record your implementation here.

Section 4.2: Planned maintenance environment

It's important to consider at the earliest stage possible where you are going to do further enhancement and maintenance of the software after it has been delivered. How you handle this depends on the three situations listed above.

- The development environment becomes the target (ie operational) environment. You might be able to use the operational environment as the maintenance environment. But this is not always possible, for the same sort of reasons that the development cannot always be done on an operational system. In the latter case, you will need to make provision for a new environment for maintenance, perhaps smaller than that used for the original development.

- A separate but similar environment was used for development. It is highly likely that the development environment will continue to be used for future enhancement and maintenance.

- The development and target environments are radically different. There is probably no escaping the need here to retain the original development environment – perhaps scaled down – for future work.

Section 4.3: Planned training

For each of the methods chosen in section 3.2, for each of the tools chosen in section 3.3 and for the environment components that appear in sections 4.1 and 4.2, you will need to consider what training is going to be necessary for which staff. At project inception this should not be much of a problem, as you should have some idea of the staff you will have. At bid time it can be a less exact science, but not knowing precisely who the team will be and their skills is not a reason for putting no provision in the plan for training. Murphy's Law says that if you include a provision for training you will get suitably skilled staff, and if you don't you won't. So put it in!

Section 5: Implications

The implications you list in this section are those that derive as second-order effects of the implementation of your choices. Implications arising directly from the choice of process model etc need not be relisted here.

Section 5.1: Timescale implications

The timescale implications that you should pay particular attention to are

- the time required for training
- the time required for familiarisation with methods, tools, hardware and software
- the effort needed to procure, install, set up, maintain, decommission and so on the different environments.

All these implications will take the form of activities in your Resource Plan when you come to draw it up as described in chapter 7.

Section 5.2: Financial implications

The financial implications arising from the implementation in section 4 of your Technical Plan will include

- the costs of training courses
- the costs of the various environments: hardware costs, maintenance contract costs, software licence costs, and so on.

An example

In chapter 10 you will find a complete worked example of a Technical Plan prepared for a fictitious system and a fictitious requirement.

A note of reassurance

It would be easy to imagine that the process of technical planning and all the analysis that is necessary to get to the above plan contents involve a massive undertaking, and an undertaking that is being called for at those moments when management time is in shortest supply, namely at bid time and at project inception.

Firstly, however, it is my experience that many of the decisions do not require significant prior analysis – they are obvious. Many choices might have been made for you, such as the methods you will use or the environments you will use. Others will be clear because you have done such a system before. In these cases, noting the decisions is a speedy affair. *But*, importantly, the process then asks you to check out the implications of these "obvious" choices – it might still be the case that, although you are being asked to use a certain method, you have a team that is not fully trained, for instance. Miss this and you will have a project with a timescale that is inadequate and a budget that has no provision for training and familiarisation.

Secondly, when I have watched people (including myself) going through the bidding process, I have noticed how they very often deal with many of the sorts of issues that I have discussed above. But they address them in a relatively haphazard way and do not always follow through their thoughts by carrying the implications on into the Resource Plan for their bid. Where they don't, they end up with an unrealistic plan. The technical planning process is designed to make sure you address all the issues and follow them through to their conclusion in a systematic way. The process should speed up your work and not slow it down. It should also make your bid or your Resource Plan more thorough.

Above all, however many times you have done something, the risks and uncertainties are invariably different from one development to another. If there is one part of the technical planning process that I think is important above all others it is that analysis of what you don't know or don't have full control over. Handling the known is relatively easy and is what an inexperienced project manager will concentrate on. To be a better project manager you should concentrate more on what you don't know and what you are going to do about it. It's what is *not* known that kills projects.

4.7   CHAPTER RECAP

For successful software development you must pay attention to three aspects of quality: *quality achievement, quality control,* and *quality assurance.* Quality achievement is about building quality in, ie having the right process (methods) that ensure that you get things right first time. Since you have to assume that some defects will get through, you will follow up with Quality Control (the subject of chapter 6); and to make sure things happen you will carry out quality assurance.

The right choice of methods – ie the methods that lead efficiently to a correct system – requires you to match the strengths of your methods to the key characteristics of the problem you are trying to solve. This is the second step in technical planning, after the analysis of risks and uncertainties.

Every method is about *modelling.* Most methods model in terms of data and/or control, and model their static and/or dynamic aspects; the dynamics of data and control relate to how things change over time (the temporal aspect) or in space (the local aspect). Every method assumes some form of *computational model* in terms of these aspects. Choosing the right method then becomes a question of matching the modelling "language" and computational model of the method against the characteristics of the problem you are trying to solve. The method with the best fit is the method most likely to give you an efficient solution to your problem.

During development, whatever the process model you adopt, you will generally produce four different models of a system: a *User Model* which expresses the system in terms of what the users see; an *Architectural Model* which expresses the overall architecture of the solution system in terms of some abstract computational model; an *Implementation Model* which expresses the system in concrete terms related to the target environment; and a *Build Model* which expresses how the system is built from its constituent parts. Different methods produce different (parts of) these models. Your development path should therefore have methods addressing *all* models in some measure if the system is to be developed according to any sort of plan.

Your choice of methods will determine what sort of verification you will be able to do (as discussed in chapter 6) and will provide detailed input to your Resource Plan in terms of the deliverables that you will produce and the activities that you will need to produce them.

5

ESTABLISHING A QUALITY CULTURE

5.1 A DEFINITION OF QUALITY

We have seen how one of the key determinants of how we will build the required system is the degree of quality required. We cannot go without first defining the notion of *quality* and in this book we shall use the standard definition of quality given in ISO 8402 [ISO 8402]:

> The totality of features and characteristics of a product, process or service that bear on its ability to satisfy stated or implied needs.

In other words the *quality* we require of our software is simply the set of whatever features we wish it to have, so if we want to control quality we must start by finding a way to define each *quality feature*. Quality features come in all shapes and forms and it is useful for future discussion to view them under two headings:

- *functional features* – these typically apply to pieces of software, from modules to entire systems. Examples might be

    - "when the pressure sensor reading climbs through a pressure level of 3.2bar, the relief valve control line shall be set to *open*"

    - "at the request of the user from a menu, the account status shall be printed with the following data displayed as shown in figure n.m: ..."

    - "all data shall be secured to disk before any transaction is cleared"

- *non-functional features* – these can apply to any product of the development process: specifications, code, manuals, etc. Examples might be

    - "with no other load present the system shall complete any type transaction within 1.5s, the duration being that time from the operator's pressing the ENTER key to screen acknowledgement"

    - "the system shall be capable of operation on a computer with one megabyte of memory"

- "the system shall give uninterrupted service despite any power outages of up to 2s in duration"

- "the system shall have a failure rate not exceeding one in 10**4 demands under all conditions"

- "a warehouse employee shall be able to use the system confidently after two hour's tuition"

- "the system shall be designed so that the addition of new transaction types does not require changes to type A software"

- "the system shall be constructed so that the language of screen messages can be changed without change to procedural code".

So, when someone places an order for a software system, they can therefore expect to describe the quality they expect of it as a collection of features, some functional (what they want it to do), some non-functional (how well they want it to do it, and how they want it to "look").

When we, as software engineers, deliver the system, these *user related* quality features will be checked for at some form of acceptance test to make sure we have delivered the quality we contracted to deliver. They are therefore our ultimate target. However, to achieve them we must make sure that every step we make from the start to the end of the development keeps high our chances of successful delivery. So we can expect to be defining *developer related* quality features for all of the intermediate products of the development process: high level designs, low level design, test plans, project plans, build schema, and so on.

Thus we might require that the code of a particular module is of particular quality in the form of features such as

- its functional features must be such and such

- it must occupy less than 550 bytes of memory

- it must in the worst case execute in less than 3ms

- it must have been successfully tested on data from all combinations of single samples from the following ranges: ...

- the level of annotation must be at least the following: ...

- its McCabe complexity must be less than 12

- and so on.

Defining quality features

Quality features – both at the user level and at the developer level – would be meaningless if we could not test that they had been achieved, so it is important that, when we state what level of quality something should have, we should be able to express that level in a testable form. Features such as "the design must be extensible", "the code must be easily maintainable and well structured", "the manual must be easy to to use", "the test plan must be complete", and "the performance must be acceptable" are all quite useless. We must be precise enough to be able to devise a test that the feature has been achieved. In the example above, the word "confidently" in "a warehouse employee shall be able to use the system confidently after two hour's tuition" is clearly not precise enough (did you notice that?), and we would want to replace the vague notion of *confidence* with something such as "without more than one error in twenty transactions over three hours' use with the agreed standard profile of work".

All this is potentially easier with functional features: provided we can express those features in a precise and unambiguous fashion (not a trivial matter) we shall be able to check that the item in question possesses them and is therefore of the requisite quality in that respect at least. Some other quality features can be made precise with numerical values, such as "the software must occupy less than 320 kilobytes when delivered". In such cases, the necessary precision is there and we simply have to be certain we can actually make the measurement – something that is not always easy with, for instance, performance figures that require the construction of quite elaborate environments to check them out, or with a system in which functions are only loaded when they are called.

So, we can see that the specification of quality features is a non-trivial problem. Indeed, it remains a research topic but in the next two sections we shall look briefly at two practical approaches that have been proposed in the past.

The TRW 1973 study

In *Characteristics of Software Quality* [Boehm 1978], Barry Boehm et al report on a study done at TRW for the US National Bureau of Standards in 1973. The work is now (1990) somewhat dated, and the authors themselves saw it as only a first step, but it still has validity. A number of later authors have offered alternative views but, as this is not a survey of such work, it is sufficient for us to illustrate the notion of quality by using the TRW study's findings. See figure 5-1 (reproduced with permission from [Boehm 1978]).

The study was principally concerned with the delivered software, although we are interested in this chapter in all the outputs of the software development process. One of its results was a hierarchy of "well defined and well differentiated" features. The top level features relate to the *use* of the software whilst their refinements at the lower levels relate to features that can be measured in the software itself. A feature such as self-descriptiveness could be defined/measured through a checklist of questions such as "are variable names descriptive of the physical or functional property represented?", and "where there is module dependence, is it clearly specified by commentary, program data, or inherent program structure?". An algorithm can then be defined to score the module on the answers to these questions. The required quality of a module can then be defined in terms of a minimum score. This clearly requires some experience of the metrics that allows the pass marks to be set, and this calibration – as in all metrics work – requires prior experimentation.

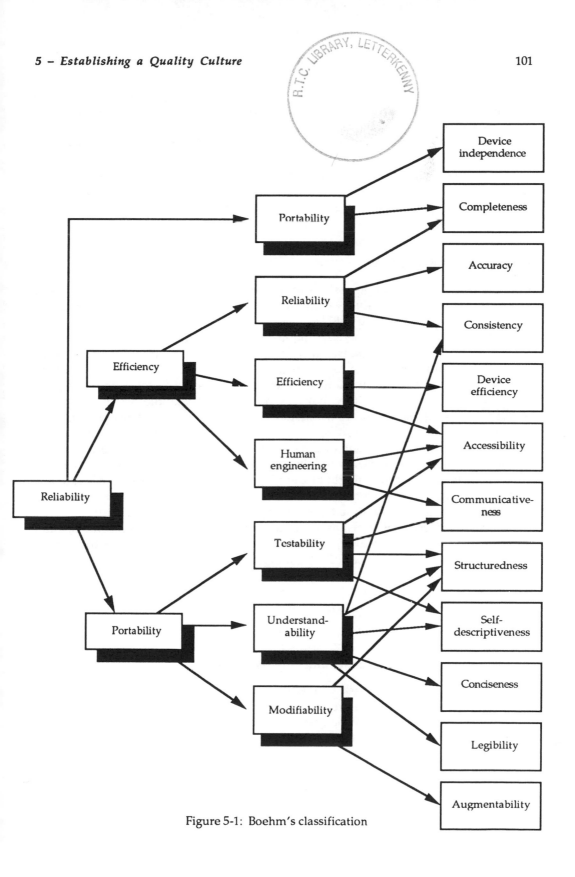

Figure 5-1: Boehm's classification

The degree to which numerical values are given to quality features is a matter of taste. In some cases it might be very appropriate such as performance features. In other cases, such as the quantity and quality of annotation of a piece of code, some degree of subjective judgement as to the "worth" of the comments is almost inevitable, though some minima can be set such as the requirement for a positive "yes" to questions such as "is reference made to the corresponding issue of the specification?", "are the units and scale of all floating point variables défined?", and "are all loop termination conditions explained?".

Gilb's Design by Objectives

Possibly one of the most pragmatic approaches to the definition, measurement and achievement of quality features is that of Tom Gilb in the techniques he refers to as *Design by Objectives* [Gilb 1987].

Gilb uses a technique whereby unquantifiable and untestable features (such as *the system shall be secure against intrusion*) are made testable and qualifiable by refinement. Thus, one measure of a system's security might be in terms of the number of unauthorised intrusions achieved by an "assault" test team in a certain period *and* the amount of effort that was required to make the first intrusion. A feature such as *it shall be easily maintainable* might be first decomposed into the ease with which the system can be changed in the event of an error's being found *and* the ease with which an enhancement can be made. The first of these might be further decomposed in terms of the time for the first ten errors found in operation to be corrected. The second might be decomposed in terms of the time taken to add a new transaction and screen to the system *and* the time taken to add a new field to a screen enquiry *and* the time taken to add a new data item to a report.

Once the decomposition has proceeded as far as quantifiable and testable features, Gilb recommends that, for each one, the following should be specified: a measuring concept (eg number of intrusions in one week), a measuring tool (eg the test log), a worst permissible value (eg five), a planned value (eg two), the best (state-of-the-art) value (zero?), and today's value where meaningful. Gilb provides a number of guidelines for steering this process.

Definitions of Quality Assurance and Quality Control

Now that we have a clear idea of what quality is and how we can go about defining quality features, we are in a position to define how we will ensure that the required level of quality has been achieved, ie that we have the required level of the quality features. Let us start with the ISO 8402 definitions of Quality Assurance and Quality Control.

Quality Assurance is

> that aspect of the overall management function that determines and implements the quality policy

where a quality policy is

the overall quality intentions and objectives of an organisation as formally expressed by senior management.

So Quality Assurance includes firstly the determination of quality policy – typically through the establishment of a Quality Management System as we shall see – and secondly checking that pre-determined Quality Control activities are being properly taken. It is useful to note the emphasis in the international standard on the need for the quality issue to be addressed from the top of an organisation. Whilst an individual software engineer might take steps to ensure the quality of their own work, the concept is only truly meaningful if all team members coordinate their quality activities, and if the surrounding corporation is setting targets for all of its teams. The importance of corporate level commitment to quality is stressed further in ISO 9001 (see section 5.2 below).

Quality Control is

the operational techniques and activities that are used to satisfy the quality requirements.

So, in particular, we are doing Quality Control whenever we check that a given item has a pre-determined value or amount of a certain feature. Anything that could be considered to be "testing" is a form of Quality Control, provided it is done against a definition of the features being checked for. Checking that a design covers all the requirements in a system's specification, testing a module against its specification, running a spelling checker over a user manual, measuring the response time of a transaction processing system – these are all Quality Control activities. See section 5.3 below.

We can see from the ISO definitions that, whilst we plan for both of them, Quality Assurance and Quality Control are retrospective actions that in themselves are not enough to produce "quality software". Quality always has to be built in at the point of production, and modern methods of software development are largely designed to ensure that the right quality is achieved in the first place (see [Birrell 1988] for a survey). Quality Control comes along close behind to check that those methods have been successful and to discover where they have not so that corrections can be made. Quality Assurance gives us added assurance that the whole producing/checking process is being properly planned and executed and hence is keeping high our chances of producing software of the required quality. In the next two sections we take these two concepts in some detail.

5.2   QUALITY ASSURANCE

Remember that Quality Assurance covers firstly the determination of a quality policy and secondly the checking that pre-determined Quality Control activities are being properly taken.

It is what happens at the corporate level of the organisation, and it sets the framework within which the software development team defines and carries out Quality Control activities. The policy defined by the organisation is normally described in a document somewhere – typically a corporate *Quality Manual* (see section 5.3 below) – and is generally implemented in the form of a *Quality Management System* which we now go on to describe.

Quality Management Systems

ISO 8402 defines a Quality Management System (QMS) as

> the organisational structure, responsibilities, procedures, activities, capabilities and resources that together aim to ensure that products, processes or services will satisfy stated or implied needs.

A QMS is something that is set up by an organisation to cover a group of projects or departments, on one or more of its sites. It is a statement by management of the strategy and tactics that will be used across the organisation to achieve the required quality in whatever is produced.

A great deal of work has been done in industry in general and in the software engineering industry in particular in defining what constitutes a QMS and this has culminated in national and international standards for them. They are of increasing importance to software engineering organisations as many purchasers of software are starting to realise the benefits of requiring that some form of accredited QMS has been used in the development of the software they are buying.

Perhaps the most important general standard for QMSs is ISO 9001 [ISO 9001] (which is identical to BS 5750 [BS 5750] and the proposed European standard EN29000). Because of its importance we look at it in some detail. (It is important to note that ISO 9001 covers any QMS in any industry, so its requirements need to be carefully interpreted for the software engineering industry. In the UK this interpretation is provided in part by British Standards Institution (BSI) *Quality Assessment Schedules* which we cover below.)

ISO 9001 defines 20 major requirements on a QMS:

- *management responsibility* – the organisation must "define and document management policy and objectives for and commitment to quality" and must "ensure that this policy is understood, implemented and maintained at all levels in the organisation". In particular the responsibilities of all staff who perform and verify work affecting quality have to be defined, and the senior management must systematically review the operation of the QMS to ensure it remains suitable and effective. Again, there is this emphasis on the need for quality to be addressed from the top of the organisation down.

- *a documented quality management system* – this system must cover Quality Control of all activities in development, and documentation of all the procedures. The documentation will generally take the form of a corporate Quality Manual (see below).

- *contract review* – this is included to ensure that a contract (in our case to produce a software system) starts out with a mutually agreed set of requirements for the system and that the developer is capable of delivering it to the purchaser. Without these safeguards, all else is futile!

- *design control* – the standard requires that the developer has and uses procedures to control and verify the quality of the design of the system to ensure it meets its requirements. These procedures should cover planning, identification of the inputs to the design process, identifying what form the design should take and what properties it should have, the verification of the design against the requirements, and how changes in the design will be handled.

- *documentation and change control* – this is an especially important area for software development where so much of what is produced takes the form of documents or data in some form: specifications, designs, code, test data, etc. Control of all these generally comes under the heading of "configuration management", "change management/control". ISO 9001 calls for procedures for document approval and issue, and for the handling of changes.

- *purchasing* – if you plan to incorporate someone else's work in your own system it is clearly important that you satisfy yourself of its quality in some way, and the standard requires, for instance, the assessment of sub-contractors' ability to meet quality requirements, what records should be kept about purchased items, and the verification that bought-in items satisfy the requirements on them.

- *purchaser supplied product* – this section of the standard requires procedures for the verification, storage and maintenance of bought-in items. At first sight this has little relevance to software engineering, but it is increasingly common for third party software to be included in a delivered system, and for that third party to issue a stream of new versions, part updates, patches and the like – you need to ensure that you have ways of handling these properly so that the right version is included in the system you release to your client.

- *product identification and traceability* – this has always been an important issue for software developers who, like other engineers, build their systems from many small components. "Configuration management/control" and "build control" procedures are once more required.

- *process control* – this is a general requirement that the production process itself be planned and monitored.

- *inspection and testing* – the standard requires that inspection and testing should take place during the development process, and once the system has been completed and before it is delivered for use, and on bought-in items before they are incorporated. It also requires here, as in most other areas, that records be kept of the results of tests.

- *inspection, measuring and test equipment* – equipment can here be taken to mean software tools in particular. These must themselves be properly controlled with respect to quality, version, etc.

- *inspection and test status* – so that the quality of all items at all stages of their development should be clearly known, the standard requires that their test status should be shown in some way at all times. As examples, the design specification of a system should say whether or not it has been reviewed or is only at draft status; a code module should say whether it has been successfully compiled, has passed its tests successfully, or has been frozen as "definitive" for integration purposes, and so on.

- *control of nonconforming products* – this is a requirement that items that do not meet their requirements cannot be inadvertently used.

- *corrective action* – if an error is found in an item when a Quality Control check is carried out on it there are two things that must be done: firstly the error must be removed from the item, and secondly the processes involved in its production need to be checked to see if they should be changed to avoid such an error appearing in future items of that type.

- *handling, storage, packaging and delivery* – again this is not obviously of concern to the software engineer but an organisation that makes and sells a software product will need to consider its procedures for replicating the software reliably, for ensuring that the correct versions are reaching the correct buyers, that magnetic media – especially those with the product on them – are correctly stored to prevent corruption, and so on.

- *quality records* – here the standard requires the developer to ensure that sufficient records are maintained to demonstrate that the required quality has been achieved and that the QMS is itself operating effectively. The first requirement effectively says that – as far as the purchaser is concerned – unrecorded quality actions never took place; the second requirement ensures that a poor QMS is not followed, lest it become a potential cause of poor quality itself.

- *internal quality audits* – this continues the theme that the QMS itself must be subjected to review to maintain its effectiveness, and requires a system of quality audits whose findings are followed up and reported to management.

- *training* – if staff are not adequately trained to do their jobs it is unlikely that their work will be of the necessary quality. This requirement covers the identification of training needs and the training itself.

- *servicing* – an area that must be subject to the same care as production itself

- *statistical techniques* – the developer is required to "establish, where appropriate, procedures for identifying adequate statistical techniques required for verifying the acceptability of product characteristics".

It should be clear from this short coverage of the ISO 9001 standard for QMSs that, taken this seriously, quality requires considerable investment and commitment from the software developer and management.

QMS accreditation

As in many areas of standardisation, the effectiveness of a standard for QMSs comes from the existence of bodies able to certify that a given supplier's QMS conforms to the standard: so-called *accreditation*. Each country has its own national accreditation bodies able to assess QMSs and issue certificates of conformance. In the UK the BSI is amongst such bodies. Accreditation generally requires that the QMS itself is examined against the standard by independent assessors, and that the operation of the QMS is observed to be running effectively over a reasonable period – having a system is not enough: it must be in use and be shown to be effective.

As we have seen, the interpretation of the ISO 9001 standard – which covers QMSs in general across all industries – requires some careful handling. In the UK there are a number of *Quality Assessment Schedules* prepared by the BSI that provide that interpretation. Of these, QAS3302/79 [BSI 1979] provides interpretation in the software engineering field. It is worth noting its requirements:

- management codes of practice requiring the production of a detailed development plan before development starts

- the use of development change control procedures on all development

- design reviews to highlight and resolve outstanding technical issues

- progress reviews to ensure the adequacy of planning and of resources

- software design to be traceable back to specifications and requirements

- the design to be properly documented and under change control

- suitable test plans, specifications and records to be produced.

Once a certificate of conformance has been issued, the accrediting body will make periodic checks to ensure that the QMS remains in force and remains effective. Such a check done by the BSI for instance can result in the assessors making *observations*, or noting *minor discrepancies* or *major discrepancies*. Major discrepancies are raised if the QMS or its operation is in some way sufficiently non-conformant to require withdrawal of the certificate unless immediate action is taken to remedy the situation. A minor discrepancy requires the organisation to take corrective action before, say, the next visit of the assessor. An observation is precisely that – an observation.

Other QMS standards

For completeness we should note that there are a number of other standards for QMSs.

AQAP-1 [NATO AQAP-1] is the current NATO standard for Quality Control Systems in general, and AQAP-13 [NATO AQAP-13] is the standard for Software Quality Control Systems. Two further documents – AQAP-2 [NATO AQAP-2] and AQAP-14 [NATO AQAP-14] – give guidance on their use. (These share a common origin with ISO 9001 – ie BS 5750 [BS 5750] – namely an earlier UK defence standard, now no longer used, so there is in fact considerable similarity.) However, the policy of the military regarding these and the international ISO standards may change.

The nuclear industry typically has its own standards, and in the UK the relevant BS is BS 5882 [BS 5882]. This covers all quality aspects of nuclear power plants – not just software – in the same way that ISO 9001 covers all industries.

A cautionary note

This constant and independent assessment of an organisation's QMS and its operation gives the certificate of conformance a strength that is important to those buying from the organisation. It clearly engenders confidence in the latter's commitment to quality. However, it is worth sounding a cautionary note here. An accredited QMS does not itself guarantee quality, nor does the possession of an accredited QMS allow an organisation to claim any particular quality in its products. The QMS is a means that still has to be used. Moreover, a QMS is typically a prescriptive thing, telling developers what steps they must take to satisfy the organisation's policy on quality. The standards forming the Quality Manual (see below) should, if they are to be effective and testable, be prescriptive, and this can be counterproductive if certain measures are not taken. As we have stressed, possession of a QMS does not guarantee the quality of the product – the system must be used and used constructively. Following it by rote without an understanding of what it is trying to achieve may not produce any improvement in quality. This is problem of attitude and culture, rather than a technical problem.

5.3   QUALITY CONTROL

What does Quality Control look like?

Let us start with a recap of the ISO definition: Quality Control is

> the operational techniques and activities that are used to satisfy the quality requirements.

For our purposes we can view it as the action of checking that a given item has a pre-determined value or amount of certain feature(s).

From this we can see straight away that Quality Control is best carried out on *products* (things produced during software development) rather than on *processes*. It would be possible to define the quality of processes: we could check that predefined actions had actually been taken and had been taken in the right order, but this would only tell us we had followed the "rule-book" so to speak. Checking the quality of the product of those actions is likely to be far more effective in bringing to our notice any errors introduced by the process.

Of course, we can (and should) use the errors in the product to trace an error in our process: if something keeps coming out wrong it is probably to do with the way we are producing it. (This is a second order effect, albeit one required by standards for a QMS.)

We can also see that the definition of Quality Control applies to any product. So we need in what follows to try to see what Quality Control means for system specifications, program specifications, test specifications, code, user manuals, database schema, and every other product produced during software development. We will return to this point later.

For each product – say, a Pascal module – we will want to apply Quality Control. What does this mean in practice? We can view it in the general case as a five step process:

1   define the feature(s) and level(s)

2   define the feature check procedure

3   carry out the check procedure

4   record the result

5   take and record any corrective action taken.

Steps 1 and 2 are planning steps that we would carry out before the product was ready for Quality Control operations on it – they say what we will do. In step 3 we carry out the planned actions and in step 4 we record them. Step 5 is vital: it closes the loop by ensuring that, if the product fails the check, the error is traced, corrected and the corrective action recorded as having been taken. It is all too easy to spot problems and then never quite get round to solving them and correcting the errors. Step 5 ensures that they are solved and that a trace is left to that effect.

As with the corporate QMS (see above) and the project's Quality Plan (see below): say what you will do, do it, record it, take any necessary actions.

How much Quality Control?

There might of course be several non-functional features that we would wish to check against. For our Pascal module, these might include memory occupancy and execution speed. The required level of the feature could take a number of forms. Thus: "the memory occupancy of the module must not exceed 2000 bytes", "it must execute always in less that 250ms". Such features are relatively easy to define, and we have a simple method of checking that a given module satisfies them: compile and assemble it to measure its memory occupancy, and time its execution on worst case data to measure its execution speed. Carrying out those methods is straightforward, and checking the actual value of the feature against the required value equally so.

Conformance to the functional part of the specification is another matter. This problem – the major part of what is normally referred to as *verification* – is hard and in general we have no guaranteed methods of checking for perfection. That is why the above definition in step 1 is so important. We know, for instance, that we cannot in general *prove* by testing that a module conforms to its specification. So, if we cannot achieve perfection, it is even more important that we define what level of checking we feel will be sufficient for our purposes.

The decision to be made by the software engineer here is "how much testing should I do to ensure the quality of this system/subsystem/module/procedure?". There is no simple answer to this question, but the responsibility remains with the engineer to decide, at the time that the Quality Control operations are defined, what level of checking (ie testing) is deemed to be sufficient and to record that in the Quality Plan. Systems with a high quality requirement, in the sense that they must not fail to behave as specified, will demand more extensive and detailed testing than, perhaps, a test tool for a non-critical system. So, the questions we must ask are: How critical is the quality of this product to the overall quality of the final product? How critical is the quality of the overall product? Can the quality of this product be most cost-effectively established in this way or that?

Thus, the quality required from the user interface of a test tool being developed for a project is likely to be less than that required of the final product. Central database functions in an administrative software system are likely to be more thoroughly tested than a little used report facility. Stringent user related quality requirements will generate stringent developer related quality requirements, as we saw above.

How to do Quality Control

Now that we have an understanding of what sorts of activities constitute Quality Control, we can see that Quality Control is something that takes place throughout the development of a software system, and, of course, beyond into the maintenance and post-delivery development work that takes place once it is in service. We can generalise this by saying that we should identify Quality Control on every product at every stage; every activity should culminate in a Quality Control activity that establishes – to the degree necessary – that the activity has produced products of the desired quality. This step-by-step approach to Quality Control underlies the "building quality in" notion, as opposed to "building quality on", and is brought out in *Testing in Software Development* [Ould 1987] for instance.

Since we would therefore like to be able to define a Quality Control activity for every activity during development it makes sense to look at how the development methods we use for each activity can themselves contribute to Quality Control. Some methods are good in that they offer us built-in Quality Control opportunities. Others do not and we must then apply general Quality Control actions to make up for this deficiency. Let's look at these two situations.

Method specific Quality Control actions

Methods that specifically support Quality Control are generally those that are more formal in nature, since that formality means that the semantics of the product are well defined and hence properties of the product can be more easily checked for. As an example, let us suppose we are using a Finite State Machine as a method for describing how our system will respond to an arbitrary sequence of events. An FSM model describes a system in terms of the different states it can be in and the transitions that occur between states in response to incoming events. With such a model we can easily check that the proposed system has desirable features such as not reaching certain states under certain input sequences, and not getting into a loop of states. We can also check that we have specified the system's response to the arrival of every event in every state, ie that there is some sense in which the model is "complete".

Many Quality Control checks can be automated if the meaning, ie semantics, of the representation we are using is well defined. At the very formal end of the spectrum there are formal methods that use mathematics and logic. Such methods offer mathematical proof as Quality Control steps on the products, for instance allowing the proof that a refinement of a piece of code preserves its functionality. Simpler cases include the use of static analysis tools (or some compilers) to check for anomalous code: sections of code that cannot be reached, variables that are never used, or that are read before they are written, and so on. Such analysers rely on the fact that the "meaning" of a piece of code is formally defined.

In chapter 6 we look at how methods can contribute to the degree of Quality Control that is possible.

Non-method specific Quality Control techniques

In many activities in software development, the way we produce the product does not offer us clear and reliable Quality Control actions. This might be either because the method of production we use is not formal (eg when writing a User Manual) or the resulting product is not amenable to such checks. In these situations we have to fall back on more general, less formal and hence less powerful Quality Control actions. They generally involve close human analysis of the product (so-called "eye-balling"), relying on individuals to use their experience and perhaps ingenuity to find errors in it. A number of variations on this common theme have been proposed in the past, and we cover two of them here, referring to them generically as *reviews*.

Structured Walkthroughs

In his book *Structured Walkthroughs* [Yourdon 1979], Ed Yourdon describes a general purpose review technique which has been adopted by many organisations over the years in forms tailored to suit their purposes.

A Structured Walkthrough is an organised event at which a particular item – a design, a code module, a chapter of a user guide, a test plan, or whatever – is scrutinised by a group of people looking at it from different perspectives and trying to find as many errors as they can in the item. The action centres on the producer of the item who presents it to the other participants who jointly look for errors. Any errors – or possible errors – found are recorded by a coordinate. The group concentrates on *error detection* rather than error correction, as it is the producer's responsibility after the walkthrough to take the record of errors found and make sure each is corrected in the item.

Yourdon identifies the following roles as appropriate:

- *the presenter* – the "owner" of the item and probably the person who originally produced it

- *the coordinator* – someone to organise the walkthrough and chair it

- *the secretary* – who will ensure that the material is issued beforehand and that the records are taken and presented to the presenter

- *the maintenance oracle* – who represents the people who will one day be responsible for maintaining the item

- *the standards bearer* – who scrutinises the item for adherence to the local standards that apply to items of that sort

- *the user representative* – who checks that the item conforms to the views of its user (who might be the final user of the system or, in the case of a specification say, the "user" of that specification, namely the designer)

- any outsiders who can contribute to the scrutiny.

Crucial to the success of a walkthrough is the prior preparation done by the participants. It is the presenter's responsibility to choose the other participants who could most usefully contribute, to nominate a coordinator who will be able to run the walkthrough effectively, and to choose a time and place. Copies of the item to be reviewed are given to all participants sufficiently in advance for them each to do their own scrutiny of the item. The more individual work done by participants the more productive the walkthrough will be. Participants will take their comments and queries to the walkthrough and, with the guidance of the coordinator, will present these and discuss them sufficiently to decide whether there is an error or likelihood of an error that demands further analysis by the producer of the item.

At the review, the item is scrutinised in whatever way makes most sense: a piece of text can be taken page by page, code procedure by procedure, design diagram by diagram. These are the "natural" and obvious ways of tackling the problem. However, a number of problems can arise.

Firstly, this serial approach to the walkthrough can lead people towards scrutinising what is there, and hence away from what is not. In other words it makes it difficult to see deficiencies and gaps. This can in part be handled by the use of checklists. Many users of walkthroughs and related techniques maintain lists of specific questions that are always asked at such reviews (or, better, by participants during their preparation). Such checklists will generally be specific to particular products: system specifications, module code, test plans, etc. For instance, a checklist used to check the completeness of the coverage of a system specification might contain the following questions:

- have all inputs to the system been defined?

- have their sources been identified? (human agent, other machine, comms lines, peripheral types ...)

- have their types been specified? (analogue, digital, electrical, acoustical, optical etc)

- have the range, scaling, format, byte layout etc been specified?
- have validity checks been specified?
- have the accuracy levels been defined?
- have all outputs from the system been defined?
- have all aspects of system performance been defined?
- what is the throughput of the system under different loads?
- what are the response times in different circumstances?
- what must be the system's response to failures of software, hardware, power etc?

Such a checklist is designed to help check for completeness – an important quality of any item. References [Birrell 1988] and [Ould 1987] contain extensive checklists for most of the major items produced during software development. These can be used as starting points for your own.

An important aspect of a good Quality Management System is that it is constantly refined by looking to see how it has failed to find errors in past items. This feedback loop helps to reduce the likelihood that similar errors will creep through in the same way in the future. Thus, you might discover as development proceeds that an interface with another system does not operate as expected – this could happen as late as system integration when correction will be expensive. On investigation you find that the error lay originally with the System Specification which failed to specify the period for which data on an interface remained valid, and that this was not noticed when the System Specification was originally reviewed. This would lead you to add to your checklist a new check for completeness:

- for how long does the data on the input channel remain valid?

A second problem that can arise from a serial approach to reviewing is that it makes it difficult for errors in the *overall* approach being taken to be spotted – high-level errors so to speak. This is a particular danger with text which, although it might be divided into chapters and sections is still a serial thing. Hierarchies of diagrams are less prone to such problems. This can in part be overcome again by the use of checklists that can, for instance, prompt reviewers into checking for the presence of a clear description of the overall strategy in a design, for a single diagram showing the interaction of programs, or for a summary timing diagram of the system's operation.

During the walkthrough it is the coordinator's responsibility to keep the discussion away from possible solutions since it is generally found to be a waste of time if six people argue over what should be one person's job, namely the producer's! It is also the coordinator's job to prevent the discussion from degenerating into arguments about style – all too easy, especially in the area of code!

Once the participants have covered the item in full, it is customary to agree on whether it should be re-reviewed after the producer has corrected any errors detected, or whether the corrections are likely to be minor enough to allow the item to be accepted as having passed its Quality Control checks without a further walkthrough.

In addition to noting the importance of good preparation for walkthroughs if they are to be successful and cost-effective, we should note two other guidelines that have been adopted by most users of the technique.

Firstly, the item being reviewed should be small enough to be reviewed in no more than, say, two hours. Opinions vary according to people's stamina and concentration span, but this is probably around the limit of the period over which a group can operate effectively. It corresponds to perhaps ten pages of text, five to ten diagrams, or of the order of 200 lines of annotated code.

Secondly, the item being reviewed should be considered complete by its producer. Finding errors is impossible if the item is incomplete. A participant might spot a problem, but is it just that such and such a section is missing at the moment? This is not to say of course that incomplete documents should not be reviewed informally.

Fagan Inspections

Fagan Inspections [Fagan 1976] are a general inspection technique developed within IBM. The overall principles are similar to those of a Yourdon walkthrough, but Fagan set his inspections in the wider context of planning, measurement and control. They serve two purposes: to find errors in a product, and to give greater control over error detection through the collection of error statistics. As with walkthroughs, the aim is detection and not correction, but errors are now classified in the record by type and severity so that profiles can be maintained to show up the commoner errors and to suggest how they can be avoided in the future. The emphasis as so often in this area is on feedback into the development process – learning from our mistakes.

A number of "checkpoints" are defined during the development path. A checkpoint corresponds to the completion of some product or other: a design, some code, a test plan, and so on. For each checkpoint, "exit criteria" are defined. These are quality levels that need to be reached by the product before it can pass the checkpoint. The inspection is the activity where the Quality Control check is made.

The original Fagan Inspections do not have the strong social emphasis of Yourdon's book [Yourdon 1979], but an important role is still there: a *moderator* is responsible for arranging, chairing and following up the inspection, much like Yourdon's *coordinator*. Around three further participants will be involved including the person responsible for the item being inspected. Fagan describes a four phase process. Let us suppose that an inspection is to be carried out on a piece of design.

The procedure would then be as follows:

1   The designer presents the entire inspection team with an overview of the product and distributes the design documentation and any other relevant material.

2   The participants do their own preparation using the material supplied. Besides bringing their own knowledge to bear on their analysis of the design, they use the accumulated experience of past inspections of designs in their part of the organisation – in the form of *inspection guidelines* in order to concentrate on looking in the areas where errors have most frequently been found in the past. This is designed to optimise the effectiveness of the inspection by concentrating on "high yield" problem areas.

3   The inspection itself now takes place. Someone nominated by the moderator walks through the product as for a Structured Walkthrough, and errors or potential errors are pointed out by the participants. Detection rather than correction being the order of the day, the moderator simply notes things found, and, importantly, assigns it a severity and classifies it by type. As in walkthroughs, strong moderation is necessary if the inspection is not to waste effort and temper on the solution of problems, on issues of style, and so on.

4   After the inspection, the moderator produces the inspection report which then goes back to the item's producer for action. All the issues raised in the report must be resolved, and the moderator has the job of checking that their resolution is complete and satisfactory. Fagan recommends that if the level of reworking involves more than 5% of the item then the moderator should require another inspection of the item.

Formal review report

Item under review	Code for module QQT13T issue 3.1
Date	17th May 1990
Participants	Pode (author), MAO, ASD, JITB
Re-review required by	none required
Project reference	P723.14.7

No.	Location	Severity	Description of problem	Person resp	Correction Approved
1	line 63	major	loop bounds incorrectly calculated	Pode	ASD
2	line 71	minor	possibility of invalid data not handled	Pode	ASD
3	line 122	style	variable name in non-standard format	Pode	ASD
4	line 133	major	incorrect flag returned if SSAW>0	Pode	ASD
...					

Figure 5-2. A sample Formal Review Report

The notion of feedback is important. The records of errors found, together with their severity and type (see figure 5-2), allow the organisation to refine the inspection guidelines used at step 2 above.

Like walkthroughs, inspections have a number of beneficial side-effects that do not concern us directly here but that are worth noting as part of the justification for installing one of these techniques in your Quality Control system:

- they spread understanding and knowledge around the team

- they allow easier transfer of ownership should staff leave or change responsibility

- they build team strength at the emotional level (if properly managed!)

- and they increase the level of shared ownership of the system by the team, without removing personal responsibility for the individual products.

Organisations often take the good points of Yourdon's and Fagan's techniques and combine the social aspects of the first with the feedback aspects of the second. As always this is an area where an organisation can set its own Quality Control procedural standards.

5.4   QUALITY PLANNING

Now that we have our QMS in place – in other words we have defined our (corporate) policy on how we will achieve quality in what we produce – and we have an idea of the range of Quality Control activities available to us, we have to look at the issue of planning Quality Control at the outset of the project. It is customary to draw up a *Quality Plan* to describe the Quality Control policy of the project. This is a plan that will define quality features and levels and will do this by drawing on quality standards from various sources. The QMS has set the framework and the basic procedures. The project must now take that policy and turn it into actions. There are three central notions: say what Quality Control actions you will take, take them, record the results. We take them in turn.

1: Say what you'll do – the Quality Plan

ISO 8402 defines a *Quality Plan* as

> a document setting out the specific quality practices, resources and activities relevant to a particular product, process, service, contract or project.

When a project is started it will begin by doing a great deal of planning work to ensure that development takes place in an ordered fashion. Your Technical Plan will identify the products (or deliverables) that the project will produce during development – specifications, designs, code, manuals, prototypes, etc – and the activities that will produce them. The Quality Plan will follow on by identifying what quality features and levels are expected from all these products and what Quality Control actions will be taken to check that the required quality has been achieved for each.

2: Do it – Quality Control

For each activity in the development process, we have now defined a Quality Control action that we will carry out on the product of that activity to check it has the required quality features to the required level. When the deliverable has been finished it is then submitted to those checks. For example:

- the system specification is reviewed in a **Structured Walkthrough** using a checklist drawn from the organisation's Quality Manual, together with additional questions specific to this project

- the design is simulated to check that process interactions are correct and that overall timings meet the system requirements; it is then checked to ensure that all the system requirements have been translated into the design in some way

- the module design is checked to ensure that it satisfies the specification

- the module code is tested against the predetermined test cases; and statically analysed to check that there are no anomalous data usages

- a subsystem is constructed from modules and its memory occupancy checked against the preset maximum

- the entire system is timed for the speed of transaction processing on a test database of predetermined size and with a predetermined set of transactions

- a novice user is given a preset amount of training and practice and their performance measured to ensure the required usability of the system.

3: Record it – Quality Control Records

Once you have checked an item's quality – and taken any corrective action if it is lacking in some way – you might feel that the job is complete. It is not. It is important that you then record the results of the check and the fact that the corrective action has been taken. There are two main reasons for this.

Firstly, Quality Control actions – reviews, module tests, whatever – frequently generate a large number of discrepancies. Each and every one has to be corrected. If a discrepancy is not listed then there is considerable danger that it might be forgotten and hence not corrected, thereby allowing an error to creep through into the next stage of development where it will be much more expensive to correct.

An important feature of any QMS is that it is visibly being used – ie that it is auditable. That audit might be carried out by the local Quality Assurance function who will be checking firstly whether the QMS itself is working effectively, ie to the organisation's benefit, and secondly whether the organisation is carrying out the company's quality policy. An audit might also be carried out by an external assessment function with the task of checking that the certificate of conformance is still justified, ie that the QMS is still being operated.

Secondly, the Quality Control record is formed from the definition of the check and the required results, the actual results in some form (paper or electronic record), and a record of any corrective action that was required. It is customary for such records to bear signatures (in some form) of those with the authority and responsibility. For instance, a moderator will sign off the report from a Fagan

Inspection indicating that all the problems noted were satisfactorily resolved; or a team leader might sign off the record of a successful module test indicating that the module satisfactorily passed the planned test cases and could proceed to, say, integration.

Quality Standards and the Quality Manual

We have seen how, at the outset of each software engineering project, we will want to identify in the Quality Plan for the project what quality levels we will require from the various products we will generate during development. Because such levels are often the same from project to project it is possible to define *quality standards* which we can reuse. Such standards are available from a number of sources including national, European and international standardisation bodies, trade and professional associations, major purchasers, and other interested groups. Some industries, especially those with stringent quality requirements such as the nuclear power industry, specify their own standards. (Note that we are concerned here with quality standards such as those for test plans, as opposed to standards to do with, for instance, communications protocols, languages, or interfaces to graphics packages. These latter standards are more concerned with standardisation to reduce barriers to trade and to increase commonality, than with quality.)

The national standards making body in the UK is the British Standards Institute (BSI). It is DIN in West Germany, ANSI in the USA, and AFNOR in France; at the European level CEN/CENELEC makes standards on behalf of the European Commission; and at the world level the International Standards Organisation (ISO) and the International Electrotechnical Commission (IEC) publish standards. The trend is increasingly for European and international standards to take precedence, and to this end standards at one level are often simply renumberings of standards at another. For instance the ISO standard for QMSs – ISO 9001 – is simply the UK standard BS 5750 with an ISO number.

One of the leading bodies in the software engineering scene is the IEEE in the USA. This body supports a number of projects involved in standards making and standards revision. IEEE standards are frequently adopted as US standards by ANSI. The IEEE publishes all its current standards relating to software engineering in a single volume [IEEE 1987]. Those standards include:

- ANSI/IEEE Std 729-1983: *Software Engineering Terminology*
- ANSI/IEEE Std 730-1984: Software Quality Assurance Plans
- ANSI/IEEE Std 828-1983: Software Configuration Management Plans
- ANSI/IEEE Std 829-1983: Software Test Documentation
- ANSI/IEEE Std 830-1984: Software Requirements Specifications
- ANSI/IEEE Std 983-1986: Guide to Software Quality Assurance Planning
- ANSI/IEEE Std 1008-1987: Software Unit Testing
- ANSI/IEEE Std 1012-1986: Software Verification and Validation Plans

- ANSI/IEEE Std 1016-1987: Software Design Descriptions
- ANSI/IEEE Std 1028-1988: Standard for Software Reviews and Audits.
- ANSI/IEEE Std 1042-1987: Software Configuration Management Guide
- ANSI/IEEE Std 1058.1-1987: Software Project Management Plans
- ANSI/IEEE Std 1063-1987: Software User Documentation.

For a comprehensive list of software engineering standards from many sources see [Hall 1988].

Because of the broadness of the area they try to cover, standards from international and national bodies are frequently general and hence somewhat weak. Many organisations take these standards and then adapt them for their own use, customising them to their own situation, and thereby giving them a sharper edge. A collection of such local standards typically forms the bulk of an organisation's Quality Manual, complementing descriptions of the overall statement of policy, quality management structures and responsibilities, and so on.

A typical Quality Manual would contain standards covering all the major products of concern to the organisation in question, such as

- System Specification
- System Design Specification
- Module Specification
- Pascal code (or whatever languages are used locally)
- Test Plans
- Acceptance Tests
- and of course standards themselves!

Additionally, a Quality Manual could contain standards on related topics such as:

- Project Plans
- Project Progress Reports
- Reviews, Walkthroughs and Inspections
- Project Debrief Reports.

The Quality Manual defines the QMS in force in the organisation. It is like a top-level Quality Plan for that organisation, which is then refined as necessary for each development project when it draws up its own Quality Plan.

5.5 CHAPTER RECAP

Quality is the totality of features and characteristics of a product, process or service that bear on its ability to satisfy stated or implied needs. Quality features are ideally defined in a quantitative fashion and certainly in a way that allows compliance to be checked.

Quality Assurance is that aspect of the overall management function that determines and implements the overall quality intentions and objectives of the organisation as formally expressed by senior management. The corporate Quality Assurance policy sets the framework within which each software development team defines and carries out Quality Control activities. The policy is generally implemented in the form of a Quality Management System (QMS) and is normally described in a corporate Quality Manual. Perhaps the most important general standard for QMSs is ISO 9001.

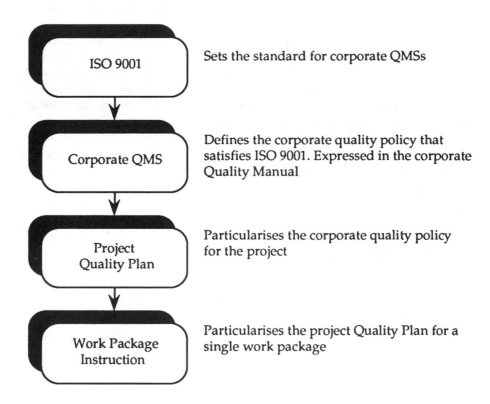

Figure 5-3 The hierarchy of standards and plans

There is therefore a hierarchy of standards: ISO 9001 is a quality standard for QMSs; a QMS sets a quality standard at the corporate level; a Quality Plan specifies quality standards for a project; and a Work Package Instruction can be used to specify standards applying to a piece of work.

Quality Control is made up of all the operational techniques and activities that are used to satisfy the quality requirements of any product. We can view Quality Control in the general case as a five step process:

1   define the quality feature(s) and level(s)

2   define the feature check procedure

3   carry out the check procedure

4   record the result

5   take and record any corrective action taken.

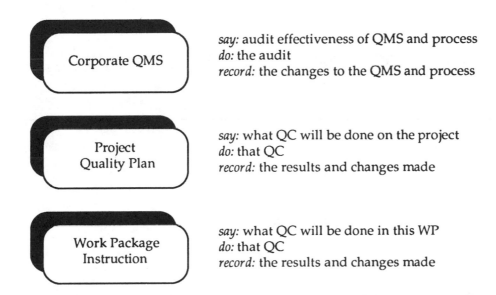

Figure 5-4. Say-do-record at the three levels

Techniques that specifically support Quality Control are generally those that are more formal in nature since that formality means that the semantics of the product are well defined and hence properties of the product can be more easily checked for. Many Quality Control checks can be automated if the meaning, ie semantics, of the representation we are using is well defined. In other situations we have to fall back on more general, less formal and hence less powerful Quality Control actions, such as Structured Walkthroughs and Fagan Inspections.

Each development project should have its own Quality Plan identifying how each of the (final and intermediate) products of the project will be checked for quality. The Quality Plan will often call upon existing standards in the organisation's Quality Manual.

At corporate, project and activity levels the rule is : say what you will do, do it, record it, take any corrective actions. (See figure 5-4.)

6

PLANNING FOR QUALITY CONTROL

6.1   WHAT IS QUALITY CONTROL?

Introduction

In chapter 5 we analysed what constituted *quality* in software production. With that understanding we can now go on to look at how we can check for that quality in the deliverables coming out of the development process. Let's look more closely at the concepts involved.

Verification and Validation

In traditional manufacturing industries, Quality Control involves the checking of the finished article to see if it has the quality required. Suppose you are in the business of making ball-bearings. You receive from your customer a specification of the ball-bearings required in terms of (non-functional) quality features such as weight, hardness, and size, plus tolerances on all these at piece and batch level, say. You turn on the ball-bearing maker and out come ball-bearings. To be certain the customer will pay, you check that the ball-bearings meet the specification before you ship them: you carry out Quality Control on them. All well and good – your client will get the ball-bearings they want.

But you could have a large amount of below-spec ball-bearings that you will have to scrap. So you decide that rather than wait to see what comes off the machine you will carry out Quality Control checks at various intermediate stages. So you will check the quality (ie composition) of the steel going into the top of the process; you will check that the dies in the forge remain correctly aligned over a production run; you will check the weight of the billets being cut off the steel wire you are using as input; and you will check that the temperature of the steel is correct at each stage.

For each of these intermediate Quality Control checks you will need to define quality features of some intermediate "deliverable" or process: the allowable range of composition and weight of the steel billets, the allowable temperature range of the steel, and the allowable distortions of the die. Each of these factors affects the quality of the final product. Indeed we can factor the required quality level of the final product into these intermediate quality levels for intermediate products.

Software production is no different. We cannot afford to go through the whole construction process before checking to see whether we have achieved what we set out to achieve, ie before seeing whether our software "works". We need to carry out Quality Control checks at each stage of the life-cycle, ideally on all the intermediate deliverables: definitions, specifications, designs, code, user manuals, documentation – everything. And to do this we will need to define quality features that we will look for in each of these intermediate deliverables. Following the analogy to the last, *we can expect to factor our final requirements for the system into .requirements on each and every intermediate deliverable.*

In software development we shuy away from old-fashioned engineering terms like Quality Control, that smack of white-coated Quality Control staff walking around with micrometers. We have borrowed two words – *verification* and *validation* – and we use them to mean *Quality Control*. Verification is checking that we have built the system right. Validation is checking that we have built the right system. This is a neat characterisation but let's go into the definitions in more detail.

When we verify something, say *B*, we do it by checking *B* against its specification, say *A*. We "verify *B* against *A*". *B* might itself be (or contain) a specification for *C*. The obvious examples are verifying a coded module against its specification, verifying a module specification against the specification for the subsystem of which the module is part, verifying a completed system against the system specification. In each case we are asking "have we built this thing right?", ie "does it meet its specification?".

Behind the notion of validation – "have we built the right thing?" – lies the assumption that, despite all the specifications in this world, what the user or purchaser wants is ultimately only something in their head that can't be checked out in any other way than by showing them something. In other words, the only way we can validate something is by going to someone and saying "is this what you wanted?". There is no objective test in the way that there would be if we had a specification against which to check out the delivered item. Validation is almost a special case of verification in that it is the act of checking that the final system complies with the requirements. The difference is that those requirements can only be found in the mind of the user and might never have been expressed explicitly – even though a full specification of a particular system to *satisfy* those requirements might have been produced.

Now, the assumption that, finally, we have to ask people if what we've done is what they want is quite valid. I personally find this unsettling as a project manager because, whilst I can agree to a written specification, I find it hard to say that I'll satisfy whatever is in someone's head! Anyone who has done any amount of specification knows that if offered two options a user will want both, with a facility to choose between them!

Finally, let's just note the IEEE definitions which summarise the above discussion. ANSI/IEEE Std 729-1983 [ANSI/IEEE 1983] has three definitions for *verification*:

1   The process of determining whether or not the products of a given phase of the software development cycle fulfil the requirements established during the previous phase.

2   Formal proof of program correctness.

3   The act of reviewing, inspecting, testing, checking, auditing, or otherwise establishing and documenting whether or not items, processes, services, or documents conform to specified requirements.

The definition for *validation* is

The process of evaluating software at the end of the software development process to ensure compliance with software requirements.

What should be verified?

Traditionally (and now I hope I'm referring to the distant past), verification was limited to testing, and testing was limited to the testing of code, at module, subsystem or system level. But over the years the industry has realised that verification could and should take place on *all* the items produced during development. It was this premise that underlies a book called *Testing in Software Development* [Ould 1987] that Charles Unwin and I edited for the British Computer Society's Working Group on Testing. In that book the Working Group designed a simple graphic to illustrate how verification could be carried out throughout development. We called it the *rolling hexagons model*. It is shown in figure 6-1 (this and related figures reproduced from [Ould 1987] with permission).

We chose to use a simple model of software development – a more elaborate process model wouldn't invalidate the idea. Each hexagon is a deliverable. Rolling left to right along the top, from the User's View we develop a Requirements Expression, then a System Specification, and so on to Module Specifications. The hexagons now roll right to left under their respective specifications, with a Test Plan connecting each specification to its code implementation. (We looked at the deliverables as part of three different "views": the User's View, the Designer's View, and the Programmer's View. These correspond effectively to what I call the User Model, the Architectural Model and the Implementation Model.)

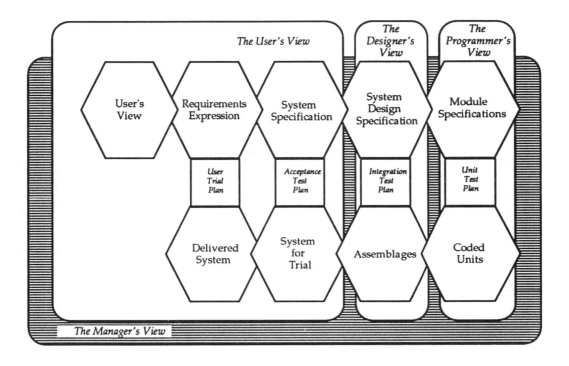

Figure 6-1. The Rolling Hexagons Model

We can test

- any specification with respect to itself – internal consistency (figure 6-2)
- any specification (except the first) with respect to its preceding specification – completeness, functional equivalence (figure 6-3)
- each code object with respect to its counterpart specification – functional equivalence (figure 6-4)
- each code object with respect to itself – internal consistency (figure 6-5).

We can then draw figure 6-6, the arrows on which show all the testing that we can do in this general model. Note that this covers more than the simple V process model in figure 3-3 as we have now shown more than the straightforward specification-implementation testing.

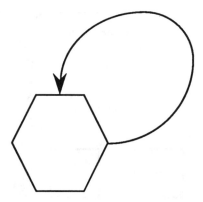

Figure 6-2. A self-consistency check on a specification

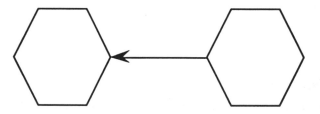

Figure 6-3. Verifying a specification against a previous specification

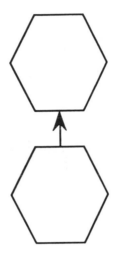

Figure 6-4. Verifying software against its specification

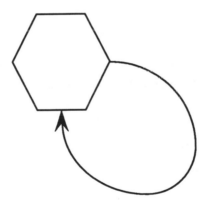

Figure 6-5. Verifying the self-consistency of code

In summary,

- everything you produce you should verify
- the purpose of planning Quality Control is to specify all such arrows in your own process model in terms of actual tests that can be carried out.

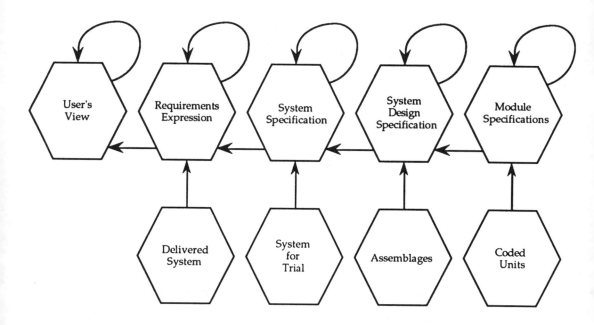

Figure 6-6. All possible verification in the simple model

So what is Quality Control?

We are now in a position to answer the question set in the heading of this section: what is Quality Control? Quite simply it is any form of testing done on anything produced, against its specification. We can expect to apply Quality Control to practically everything we produce. But let us go one step further and ask: what is *good* verification? We can summarise good verification in two characteristics:

- it should be *reliable*: it should be likely to expose (all) errors
- it should be *economical*: for instance, in the case of module verification/ testing, we want to generate as few redundant test cases as possible, ie test cases unlikely to expose different errors.

Where exhaustive verification of something is impractical we have to make do with a small sample of test cases. We would like that number to be as small as possible and yet still expose the errors in a deliverable. In an ideal world we would also like our techniques for test case generation to detect the more "important" errors with greater certainty – eg those that would cause loss of life before those that would cause an occasional need to repeat an input message. In general we don't know how to do this yet.

The next question is: how do we define the tests we should carry out during verification? To answer this let's first look at a number of background ideas that are often poorly understood:

- the importance of knowing how something was built in order to do strong verification, ie understanding the *V&V potential* of methods, the degree to which methods support verification of what they build

- the *factoring of quality*, whereby quality features required in the final deliverable define quality features in intermediate deliverables

- the *verification chain* from system specification to delivered system.

6.2   OVER-THE-WALL TESTING

Current testing practice can be caricatured as *over-the-wall* testing. Let's take the case of module testing. A software module is deemed ready for testing and then tossed over the wall to the testers. These poor folk have no knowledge of how the software was developed and hence cannot make use of any formality in the development method. They thereby throw away any chance of exploiting the potential the development methods might offer for helping in the verification and validation.

It's often said that the worst person to test a piece of code is the person that wrote it: they "know" what it is supposed to do because they know what cases they wrote it to handle. So those are the cases that they test it on. An outside person doesn't know how it has been written and hence is less "blinkered". That this is true is probably best demonstrated every time you give someone a program to use that you have written. No matter how much testing you have done, it seems that they will always break it within the first ten minutes of use. And this is generally because they use the software in some way that you did not think of and hence did not test it on.

So, I am not advocating that there is no need for independent V&V teams or for techniques of test data generation such as error guessing. Both of these techniques are of course needed. But we should not throw away opportunities to do really strong testing (ie testing that is both reliable and economical) by ignoring the methods that were used to develop the software.

Traditional code testing techniques as described by Myers [11] and others all assume that an arbitrary piece of code has arrived for testing. The techniques apply irrespective of how the software was developed: error guessing, domain analysis, structural analysis etc. One's first reaction to this is pleasure that they are so generally applicable. But, as in so many situations, a generally applicable method can be so broad in its generality that it becomes all but useless in individual cases. It might cover all cases that one might want to consider when those cases are considered as a group, but when we try to apply it to one case we discover that its generality is actually its weakness: universally applicable – yet specifically inapplicable.

But we know that if, for instance, we prepare programs that are Dijkstra-structured (ie consist only of sequence, selection, and iteration) then we have a much easier task when it comes to using structural analysis to determine the test cases we will apply. It becomes a great deal easier to traverse all "long" path segments (eg LCSAJs of length up to three). In a sense this is because the meaning of a program that is Dijkstra-structured is easier to determine than one that is stiff with `got os`. We also know that deciding test cases by analysing the input domain of the module (so-called equivalence partitioning for instance) is much simplified if we have specified the module in terms of the different states that the module and its data can be in – the very basis of formal specification methods such as VDM and Z .

In summary, a shortcoming of traditional verification methods is that they do not use information about the way something was developed or constructed. Moreover, we don't build for testing; ie we don't build for testability. The next section looks in more detail at the ways that our development methods can strengthen our verification practices.

6.3   V&V POTENTIAL OF METHODS

Using development knowledge

The point I want to make here is that every development method can, to a greater or lesser extent, help us in the verification (or validation) of the deliverable that that method is used to produce. The extent to which it does is what I call the *V&V potential* of the method. This idea is best illustrated with some examples.

Verifying a specification

Let's suppose that we are writing program specifications using a formal (ie mathematical) specification method such as VDM or Z. The specifications we produce can be analysed mechanically or at least systematically. In particular we can check for certain features such as consistency of operations and system invariants.

This is extremely powerful. A traditional module specification consisting of an informal description of the inputs and an informal description of how the outputs are to be derived from the inputs can rarely be checked for things like consistency – at least not with any degree of rigour worth speaking about. Let us take an example.

Suppose we want to specify a library system (a great favourite with VDMers!). We could define it informally in terms of the transactions that members of the library can carry out: registering as a member, borrowing a book, and returning a book; and transactions that the librarian can make: registering a book, withdrawing a book temporarily for repair, and deleting a worn-out book. We might add some rules such as a limit on the number of books that any member can have out at one time.

But we would probably not – in an informal specification – put down "obvious" rules such as the fact that a member cannot borrow a book already on loan to someone else, that a book cannot be borrowed until it has been registered, or that books cannot "disappear" from the system. But these are all properties we would want our library catalogue to have – and they are of course the sort of checks that programmers (might remember to) put into their code without being asked by the analyst via the specification.

But with a formal specification we can express those "invariants" of the system (such as the fact that any book must either be available for loan, on loan, or being repaired) in a mathematical and hence very precise way. By also describing the transactions as mathematical operations on the catalogue (itself described in an abstract way) we have all that we need to carry out rigorous, mathematical checks that each of the transactions *preserves* all the invariants of the system. (And, incidentally, those invariants can be used by the programmer to build defensive code into the software; this is no longer left to chance or their discretion.)

The crucial point is that *because* we have used a formal method (like Z or VDM) to write the specification, we have straight away given ourselves very powerful techniques for verifying the specification itself, or, to be more precise, to verify certain quality features in our specification. It would not be difficult to write an informal specification that defined transactions that in fact violated "obvious" (and perhaps unrecorded) properties of the system. In this way, fewer specification errors are likely to be correctly coded up by the programmer. Quality is ensured at the earliest possible moment in development.

Verifying a system design

Suppose we are designing a real-time system which consists of a number of independent but communicating processes which trigger each other. (This was the problem I faced when designing the sonar system I mention in chapter 2.) Such a system might be represented by the diagram shown in figure 6-7. Each square represents a process, and each arrow represents the occurrence of an event detected by the process at the beginning of the arrow. When a process completes, it places a "token" in the "place" (circle) on each of its outgoing arrows. As soon as the place on each incoming arrow to a process has a token in it, that process can be activated and all those incoming tokens are deleted (they are "absorbed" by the process). Such a model can be "run", and one can watch the tokens moving around and the processes firing as they do. This is a simple form of Petri Net (see [Peterson 1981]). (In Petri Nets the processes appear as "transitions" as, strictly speaking, they actually represent the transition of the net from one state (ie set of token positions) to another.)

In a multi-process system of this sort it is is not unusual for us to be able to define certain states of the system which we cannot permit. For instance we might want to ensure that there are no conditions under which two particular processes are running at the same time. To be able to do anything other than a very rigorous demonstration that our design does not let this happen would be very unsatisfactory. It would certainly not be enough just to try out a couple of sample firings of the net – we would want to have better proof than that. And a Petri Net model allows just such a proof. It is easy to write an algorithm that generates all the possible states from a given starting state and checks whether any of them has the two processes concerned active at the same time.

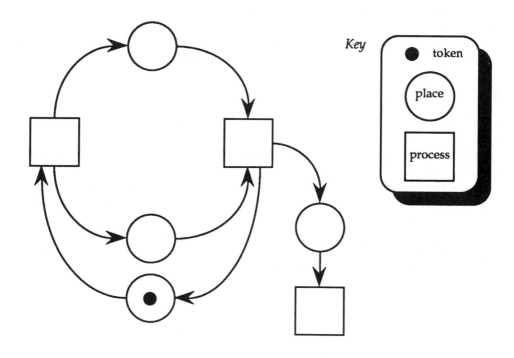

Figure 6-7. A simple Petri Net

Because we have expressed our design in a formal way, very strong verification of this important feature becomes possible. We do not have to wait until the system has been integrated and all the processes put together for the first time to find out that there is indeed one strange situation in which the unthinkable happens and our system goes down. Similarly we could check that there is no undesirable loop in the running of the system, perhaps one from which the system cannot escape, such as some form of deadlock.

Verifying a program design

One of my favourite examples of how a well-chosen method can assist directly in the verification of a deliverable is that of the use of Finite State Machines, and I owe it to Nick Birrell with whom I wrote a book on methods [Birrell 1988]. We were building a system that was to capture television in digital form in real-time so that it could be image-processed (for reasons we need not go into here – see [Ould 1982]) and then replayed in real-time from the processed digital form. At the time (around 1981), sinking 18 megabytes of data a second in a form that could be addressed pixelwise for processing – which is what we had to do – was not an off-the-shelf facility.

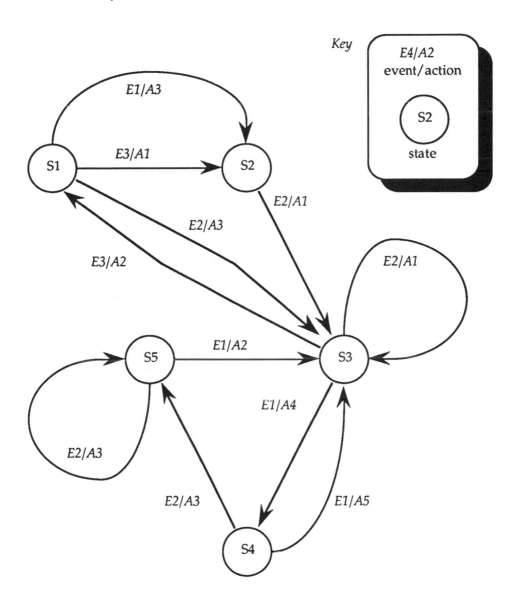

Figure 6-8. A simple Finite State Machine

As part of the solution the team built some digital framestores that could capture frames of TV and pass them to the controllers of a pair of very fast discs. These framestores were controlled by a microprocessor that was itself attached to a minicomputer. The software in the microprocessor had to run quickly as the gaps in TV signals when you can get things done are quite small and you have to be quick to catch the various synchronisation signals. The user controlled matters from the minicomputer which sent signals over a simple serial link to the microprocessor.

state \ event	E1	E2	E3
S1	A3/S2	A3/S3	A1/S2
S2		A1/S3	
S3	A4/S4	A1/S2	A2/S1
S4	A5/S3	A3/S5	
S5	A2/S3	A3/S5	

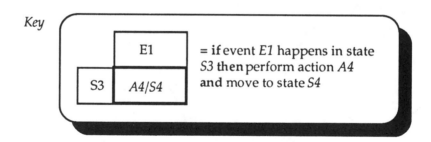

Key

	E1
S3	A4/S4

= if event *E1* happens in state *S3* then perform action *A4* and move to state *S4*

Figure 6-9. A tabular form of figure 6-8

The problem was to design the program in the microprocessor so that it could handle any sequence of synchronisation signals, commands from the minicomputer, and other spontaneous events. I suggested to Nick that a state transition diagram or Finite State Machine (FSM) solution sounded sensible. In an FSM, the system moves from one state to another depending on what events occur. Thus, in figure 6-8, the system can be in one of five states, represented by circles, and can move from one state to another along the arcs between the circles. For instance, if the system is in state *S4* and event *E2* occurs, it moves to state *S5* and carries out action *A3*.

After doing some research, Nick came up with a paper by Chow [Chow 1978] describing a technique for generating sequences of events that would test an FSM design rigorously. We decided to use it.

Now, an FSM is a very simple design technique that has been used for decades in a host of different applications. Yet it offers a number of important V&V possibilities to the designer:

- If it is drawn up as a table, as in figure 6-9, we can check that we have defined the effect of every event in every state. Thus in the diagrammatic form of figure 6-8 we do not define the effect of event E3 on state S4. But in the tabular form of figure 6-9 we would see from a gap in the relevant cell in the matrix that our design was deficient. So we can verify *completeness* in our design.

- By using Chow's technique for deriving test sequences we can generate all sequences of states that the system can pass through and check that its action is what we want. In other words we have a rigorous evaluation procedure made possible by the design method. (This is touched on in Nick's paper [Birrell 1984].)

- A simple analysis of the FSM allows you to check what cycles there are in the design. Thus the system in figure 6-9 has a number of cycles. In most software, cycles are of great interest. In particular, we are very often concerned with whether they are infinite or not, and whether they should be.

We used all these verification opportunities. The software in the microprocessor required a state table of some thirty or so inputs and nearly twenty states – not a trivial thing to define. But the method allowed us to verify the completeness of the definition and to validate the definition by using Chow's technique to generate test sequences of events. To do the validation, we wrote some software that took the definition of an FSM in textual format, generated the test event sequences, and then printed out the corresponding state changes and actions that the system would go through. By eyeballing the textual results we were able to check that whether sequences looked right – we were after all looking to see that the design carried out our intuitively understood requirements.

The success of the verification was considerable. During these simulations of the system driven from descriptions of the design (remember we had not yet written a word of the operational code), not only were we able to tidy up the design safely, but we discovered in an early version of the design that there was in fact one sequence of events where the system could lock up and get into an undesired cycle – "hang" in other words. It only occurred when a certain sequence of commands coincided with a certain sequence of hardware events (synchronisation signals and so on) – something that we would never have stumbled on in any amount of testing, but that we could be certain would have happened on the first day of live running of the system after delivery to the client!

Verifying code

As I have mentioned, traditional code testing techniques such as those described in [Myers 1979] are very much over-the-wall techniques. Both the black-box testing and white-box testing techniques described by Myers assume you know nothing of where the software has come from or how it was produced. Let us look at techniques of code production that allow us to verify the code in a much stronger way than the selection of a few test cases from the (generally) vast number of potential cases.

The reason that we use dynamic testing – where we apply a number of well chosen test cases to the module and compare its action with that expected from the specification – is that we have no other way of comparing the specification with its implementation, except in this trial and error fashion. Ideally then, we would like to preserve the link between the specification and the code so that we could verify that we had achieved a correct implementation *in general* rather than on a small fraction of the possible cases. This is where the techniques of *semantic analysis* and *compliance analysis* come in.

In outline, these techniques work as follows.

During the construction of the code, we use a formal approach. For instance, we specify the module in VDM or Z. Our specification now takes the form of a set of *preconditions* for the module (assertions about the state of the system on entry to it), and a set of *postconditions* for it (assertions about the state of the system on exit). Typically, the preconditions limit the range of input variables, whilst the postconditions describe how the values of the output variables are related to the values of the input variables. These assertions are embedded at the start and end of the code respectively. As we develop the code, we derive new assertions about the state of variables at various points in the code such as at the "entry" to a conditional statement. Loops are proved to be correct constructions through the use of so-called *loop invariants*. These are assertions that are true before every iteration of the loop. They are also embedded appropriately in the code.

As development proceeds, the assertions which result from the reasoning about its correctness are embedded at various points. If the process is carried out properly there will then be a chain of assertions along each path through the program. A tool known as a *semantic analyser* can be used to traverse the program. By taking the embedded assertions on a path and by interpreting the actual instructions on that path, a semantic analyser can construct a number of theorems which must be proved to be true if the code is to be proved to be consistent with the specification. The mechanisation of these proofs is still not an everyday possibility, and whilst proof checkers can assist, it is still the task of the programmer to develop the proof in the first instance.

The point of this is clear: if we use formal methods such as those described by Gries [Gries 1981], Jones [Jones 1986] or Dijkstra [Dijkstra 1976] to construct our code from our specifications, we give ourselves verification possibilities far stronger than the sampling techniques of traditional testing alone.

Further examples

There are many other examples of this:

*   We can produce specifications and designs that can be executed and hence validated against "normal" operational use, eg using Peter Henderson's **me too** [Henderson 1986, Henderson 1987] and Gerrard Software's *ObjEx* based on the OBJ method [Gerrard 1990].

*   Following McCabe and Schulmeyer [McCabe 1985] we can derive system test cases by analysis of the higher level Data Flow Diagrams for a system.

*   If we use JSP [Jackson 1975] to design a program we start by defining a grammar for the incoming data streams that the program is to process. This allows us to generate representative sets of input test data directly from the grammar.

*   Starting from a Z specification for a program, we can derive test data for that program systematically [Hayes 1986].

V&V potential comes from formalism

You'll have noticed by now that *formal* methods are the ones that have the strongest V&V potential. That strength derives from the fact that if something is formally expressed then its meaning is well defined, typically mathematically. And if something is well defined, we can apply logic to reason about it, and that reasoning will generally be at a general level, rather than a form of sampling. General reasoning – eg "in all cases ..." – is clearly a powerful form of verification that meets our two criteria: that it should be reliable and economical.

Even traditional systematic methods can be improved simply by examining the underlying semantics and strengthening the method by beefing it up where necessary, as we saw in some examples above.

(I think it is worth noting here that I am *not* suggesting that by using formal methods and supporting tools you do away with the need for traditional testing. We have to recognise that any procedure that involves human beings is potentially error-prone and who would want to fly in an aircraft whose fly-by-wire software systems had only been proved correct and had never actually been tested with real data?!)

I have often seen a method defined as a notation and a procedure for using it. I have rarely seen *strong V&V potential* identified as an important characteristic of a method. This is probably because in the past our methods have been so poor in this respect. So when you look for the methods that you are going to use on your project you should be looking at each candidate for a number of properties:

*   A *notation* of course and a syntax defining it, but a notation with well defined semantics too. What does an arrow with a double head *mean*? What does it mean for an arrow to run from one sort of box to another? What are the implied dynamics of the system being drawn? And so on.

- A *procedure* for developing descriptions in the notation. This might be a procedure expressed in terms of heuristics and checklists, since design (eg software development) is a creative and largely non-mechanisable act.

- *Good V&V potential*. We want techniques that help us to check out (test/verify) the descriptions produced, be they specifications, high level design, code, or whatever.

I believe that the V&V potential of a method is at least as important as, for instance, its simplicity in use. It is not enough that we should have an easy-to-understand diagram resulting from the use of a method. That diagram must also be amenable to strong verification. If it isn't then we have trouble ahead. Let me cite one case.

For some years now the world has used activity networks for project planning. An activity network is a network of boxes representing activities, connected by arrows that represent the dependence of activities on each other. Annotation on the chart against an activity box shows the resources required for the activity and the cost of those resources, its planned duration, and perhaps an earliest start date. Figure 7-6 shows a simple PERT chart (or activity network) for a simple project.

The semantics of the chart are well-understood, even if not expressed (as they could be) in mathematical form. Moreover, those semantics are clear enough for us (and, more importantly, a machine) to deduce solely from the information on the chart the resource utilisation over time, the earliest and latest start and finish date of each activity, the total cost of the project, and so on. In particular we can – quite mechanically – determine whether in fact the project we have modelled with a particular chart is indeed feasible. We can in other words test the proposed design of the project against a number of properties that we would wish it to satisfy:

- *feasibility* – can that amount of work be done by those people in the time available with those resources?

- *economy* – is the total cost less than the amount we have to spend?

- *robustness* – is there enough slack in the resource and/or time usage to allow for a certain amount of overrun in key activities? and which are the critical activities, those whose slippage directly affects the end-date?

- *flexibility* – is the degree of inter-dependence such that we could agree to take on additional work on the fly?

- and so on.

With such a tool we can not only test our proposed "designs" for a project, but we can also explore different designs, something that it would be a pleasure to do for software specifications and designs. Computer support for activity network planning is now commonplace. There's clearly a lesson here.

Exploiting V&V potential in tools

This leads us neatly on to another aspect of this business of V&V potential that I think will become increasingly important as the software engineering industry itself becomes increasingly automated. If strong V&V potential comes from increased formality in our methods, and if increased formality implies better defined semantics, then the more important it becomes to increase formality and hence V&V potential so that we can start to get machines to do our V&V for us. One simple example of this fact has been staring us in the face almost since the start of computing: namely the use of compilers.

Suppose you were around in the early days of computing, writing your programs in hex. No doubt you would find yourself writing the logic first in some other, higher-level, language in which thinking about logic was easier than in hex. Once you were satisfied that this high-level description captured the logic you wanted (perhaps in some sort of "PDL"), you would hand translate the logic into hex. After a while you'd probably draw up standard ways of translating your high-level language into hex, making adjustments to the language so that such translations were easier and well defined. In effect you would define the semantics of your language, by defining what it "meant" in hex – the language where the meaning of a program was real. Once you had got your high-level language defined well enough you'd very quickly realise that you could now get a machine to do the translation speedily and reliably for you.

Giving well defined semantics to the programming language meant that the next development step – translating a program into hex – could be done automatically. Verification of the translation became unnecessary in fact: the V&V potential of the high-level language method was *so* high that the machine did it entirely for you! I would guess that these days, if their program does not work, most people would suspect a compiler error last.

So, the lesson is clear: a method with good V&V potential is a method that opens up the opportunity of using tools to automate V&V. What sort of help might we expect from a tool designed for supporting, say, module testing? I suggest we can look for help in three areas:

- automation of the administrative side of the activity, eg looking after printing and the identification of tests, plus perhaps the storage of sessions etc for regression testing, and so on;

- automation of the mechanical side of the activity, eg the running of the software under test (SUT) within some test harness, the application of test data to it, and the comparison of actual results with those expected;

- automation of the generation of test cases.

Which of these is the most important? The last of course. We can have as fine an administrative procedure as we like, and as smooth running a test execution suite as we like. But if the test cases are not good enough (ie reliable and economical) then we are wasting our time. Yet it is in the area of test case generation that we are most poorly served and I would suggest that the reason for this is that the process of test case generation is itself not yet amenable to formalisation. And why? Because, quite simply, our development methods themselves are not sufficiently formal and hence have poor V&V potential.

So strong V&V potential typically opens up the potential for automated checking of some aspects of our work. Let's take an example familiar to many: the use of data flow diagrams (DFDs) during the specification and/or design of a system. With some care, we can define the meaning of the various symbols and arrows on a DFD, and we can devise rules that DFDs must conform to if they are to be meaningful and have certain desirable features. Such rules might be, for instance,

- all data items appearing as the subject of data flows must also appear in the data dictionary

- the decomposition of data flow across levels must be matched by the decomposition of the data which is the subject of those flows

- meaningless data flows (such as from one data store to another without an intervening process) do not appear.

All these checks ("tests") become possible because we have (whether we realise it or not) well defined semantics for data flow diagrams in these respects. Moreover, it is precisely because those semantics are there that we can now design our CASE tool to check our specifications and designs against these rules. To go one step further, if we are using the Ward-Mellor control logic extensions [Ward 1986], we can design our CASE tool to do a degree of simulation of the system's behaviour so that we can validate that behaviour against our intentions.

Elsewhere in this book you will come across examples where a simple tool can we written to automate some form of verification or validation, and that possibility is invariably due to some degree of formality in the methods used. Strong V&V potential means strong potential for *automating* our V&V with all the productivity and quality assurance improvements that brings.

6.4   QUALITY FACTORING AND THE VERIFICATION CHAIN

So far we have only looked at the verification of individual items in isolation. Verification is the determination of whether a deliverable meets its specification. Now, those requirements are simply a set of quality features. As an example let's look at the range of quality features that we might define for a Pascal code module:

- the module satisfies its specification over some predefined set of test cases

- it always runs in less than a certain amount of time

- it occupies no more than a certain amount of memory

- its source is commented to a particular degree

- its source satisfies a certain set of style rules

- it contains no unreachable code

- it contains no variables that are read before being written, or that are written but never read.

And here are some that we might specify for a design in the form of a finite state machine:

- for every event in every state an action and a new state are defined

- every state is reachable by some sequence of events from the initial state $S1$

- the state sequence $S5$, $S7$, $S3$, $S3$ can never occur

- state $S12$ can never be reached without state $S6$ having been reached beforehand.

But where do these quality features come from? The only ones for which we can give a simple answer are those of the final system, because this is the only deliverable for which a full set of quality features is specifically drawn up, namely in the form of the System Specification. That specification will tell us all about the functional and non-functional features required in the final system. But how do we decide what the quality features of the intermediate deliverables are? For instance, what quality features should we define for our design, our code, our test plans, and so on? And what should they be derived from?

The answer to this last question is simple: *from the quality features of the system itself.* There is nothing else from which they might come.

It is here that we need to look in a little more detail at the notion of *quality* and its equivalent description as "fitness for purpose".

I always become worried when people start to use the term *quality* in isolation, especially as an adjective: "this is a quality piece of software", "this is high quality software", "what are you doing about quality?", and so on. There is the suggestion that quality is something absolute, a sort of Platonic ideal that exists somewhere and that we all try to achieve. It is far from this. It is precisely what we define it to be. And, ultimately, *it is what the client wants to pay for.* If system A has more (or more stringent) quality features than system B, then we can expect it to cost more than system B. A car with the property that it is less likely to skid in the wet under braking will cost more than one without that property. To the client therefore, quality is *not* free; there will be a level of quality (or more precisely a set of quality features) that they will be prepared to pay for and that in some way makes economic sense to them. You don't spend £100 (~\$150) on a component that will last 20 years if your need is for a £10 component that will last 5 years.

To illustrate this, let me mention something that has been raised on several occasions at seminars where I have spoken on so-called *Zero Defect Development*. Attendees often assume that "zero defect software" must never fail. In answer to questions I often make the statement that a piece of software could crash and yet be defect free. If the program is for experimental use only or just a prototype that is to be experimented with, we could well specify that it should have a mean time between failures (MTBF) of two hours in continuous use. If we produce a program that only crashes about every four hours we will have satisfied the specification: the program will be defect free in that it possesses all the required quality features. If the program took us two weeks to develop we would perhaps have got value for money. To make it error-free (ie totally correct) would require far, far longer – even if we could ever know we had achieved total correctness.

So the definition of the quality of a system lies with the client. What are they prepared to pay for? How much is economically useful to them? Every client that tells you they don't want a gold plated system understands that – from their perspective – quality is not free.

But as far as you the *developer* are concerned, quality *must be* free, in the sense that to build to a lower quality than that required will lose you money because you will have to rework to achieve the quality wanted ("right first time" is the catchphrase that captures the message here); and to build to a higher quality will cost you more but bring you nothing: spending an extra £100,000 (~$150,000) putting in performance that was not asked for is unlikely to earn you an extra £100,000 in a fixed price contract – that's gold plating and your client will not pay for it.

The lesson is clear: all quality features of all deliverables during development must be derived from the quality features of the system to be delivered. This immediately suggests the notion of what I call *quality factoring*. We take the quality features required of the final system and factor these into quality features in the design, in the code, in the user manuals, in the test specifications, in the project plans – in fact into everything we produce. Let's take an example: performance.

In the specification of some system, let us suppose there is a requirement (quality feature) for a certain level of performance. Let us imagine that it is that the system should be able to process up to twelve transactions per second over a sustained period of ten minutes without any other loading, irrespective of transaction type, each transaction having a transit time of less than 0.5s (with suitable definitions). We can straight away factor this feature into one in our design. Our design must display this level of performance, and we shall want to check that it does. That check might be done with a mathematical model of the proposed design, or perhaps with some prototyping.

Let me give you a real example of this. Earlier in this chapter I described a sonar system I was involved with where our design involved a network of communicating processes that triggered each other depending on the mode in which the system was running (live data, recorded data, or simulated data) and on failure conditions in the surrounding electronics (noisy data, missing clock signals etc). The system was required by the client to support the tracking of a certain number of objects at any one time. Would our design handle this?

The tracking capability was a quality feature of the final system, and could be factored into a quality feature that had to be displayed by our design. How would we check whether our design satisfied it? The answer was to build the basic tasking primitives, to construct a number of dummy tasks of about the right size and duration, to build them into the triggering network we had designed, and to put the whole software mock-up into the target processor and watch what happened with some simple simulated data.

When we tried this we noticed that some processes were getting into memory too late – the design had to be changed so that they went into locked partitions in memory. Others were holding too much memory for too long unnecessarily – they had to be split. After some adjustments to the process network we achieved a structure that gave us confidence that the actual system of processes would achieve the required tracking performance. So far so good.

Now we came to the next level of design where we were designing in detail each individual process down to the module level. We could not forget the performance issue. Our mock-up had assumed a certain size and approximate running time for each process. If these estimates were significantly missed in reality then we could be in trouble. So the performance quality features on the design had to be factored further down into individual modules. If we had been very stringent (and we weren't) we could have set size and execution time limits for each and every module, thereby continuing the factoring right down to the code. In fact we only did it for a selected few that were seen as critical – the others had only broad requirements.

Standing back from this we can see that we developed a chain of quality factoring and that this chain was carried through the specifications: some factor of performance was required in system, subsystem, and module specifications, and the quality factoring passed down the specification chain.

Now this business of performance is a simple one with which to demonstrate the principle of quality factoring, but let's take a slightly less obvious case: "usability". If we have done a good job on the specification of the system, we will have defined the usability of the system in terms that will allow us to check it out in the delivered software. Let's suppose that the definition we came up with is as follows (it's not perfect but it will do for illustrative purposes):

> The system shall be usable with confidence by a new operator without previous experience of computer-based systems within one day of full-time use after up to one day of training. "With confidence" means "without having more than one transaction attempt in ten rejected by the system because of operator error, without referring to the paper manual more than once per twenty transactions, and achieving thirty successful transactions per hour".

How shall we factor this quality feature over intermediate deliverables? Clearly, we shall have to factor features into the specifications for the design, for the help facilities on the system, for the user interface, for the user manuals, and for the training courses and their materials. For example:

- we might require certain ease-of-use features to appear in the user interface, such as a maximum number of key strokes required, or a limit on the possibility of user error through the use of pull down menus and point-and-click working, or the use of visual cues to indicate the stage that has been reached in a transaction

- we might require a minimum level of direct hands-on working in the one-day training course, plus a specified emphasis on the most common transactions that the operator is likely to see

- we might require certain functions in the design of the screen handling software that permit good "undo" facilities

- and so on.

The factoring here is obviously more complex, and two questions arise:

- how do we decide how to factor a feature in one deliverable into a number of features defined on quite different deliverables?

- how do we decide that the factored features in some sense "sum" to the original one?

There is no answer to first question! The question is the same as "how do you design software?". It is a matter for experience, imagination, creativity. And it is the subject of other books.

As for the second, one of the few people to tackle this directly is Tom Gilb in his *Design by Objectives* [Gilb 1987]. Briefly, his method requires you to decompose the various non-functional features until at some point you have testable sub-features at the lowest level. You then identify actions you will take, or features of your system design, or whatever, that (will) contribute in some fashion to those sub-features, ascribing a figure to the "size" of that contribution, expressed as a crude percentage. If the total of the contributions to a given sub-feature is large enough – for instance, over 150% – you judge that you have done enough. This might make a mathematician blanch but, as Gilb put it at a workshop when criticised for his cavalier approach to mathematics, "if you can tell me a better way of doing this, I'll sell it!".

6.5 DEVELOPING A VERIFICATION STRATEGY

This chapter has so far been a rather philosophical one, and I think you, the reader, deserve an explanation of why this has been necessary. I believe the position and nature of V&V in software engineering has generally been poorly understood and poorly treated by the industry. We have simply not looked at the topic carefully enough, in particular at its position within the whole development framework and in the context of our development methods. As a result, we have made a poor job of applying the same degree of Quality Control expertise in the entire process that other manufacturing industries have. They are very much more at home with the idea of looking at the development process when they look at Quality Control. When they want to improve quality they improve the development process, not just the checks on the output.

I hope the preceding philosophy has helped you to see more clearly just what V&V is all about and how it is completely bound up with an understanding of the development process model and with the methods that you use.

So, now that you have a better idea of the background to this verification game, you are in a position to draw up sound procedures for developing the verification strategy for your project. Back to the practicalities of planning software development!

Defining verification activities

In chapter 3 we looked at how a consideration of the risks and uncertainties in your project lead you to a choice of process model for the development. That process model was characterised by an overall WBS such as the one for incremental delivery:

1000   Plan overall development

2000   Produce User Model

3000   Produce Architectural Model

4000   Develop kernel

      4100   Produce Implementation Model for kernel

      4200   Produce Build Model for kernel

      4300   ...

5000   Develop increment 1

      5100   Produce Implementation Model for increment 1

      5200   Produce Build Model for increment 1

      5300   ...

6000   Develop increment 2

      6100   Produce Implementation Model for increment 2

      6200   Produce Build Model for increment 2

      6300   ...

In chapter 4 we looked at how the nature of the system to be built would determine what methods you should use to develop those system models. This analysis allowed us to be more specific about production activities:

3000   Produce Architectural Model

      3100   Produce Logical Data Flow Diagrams

      3200   Produce Data Dictionary

      3300   Produce State Machine for AS Interface

      etc

In chapter 5 we looked at the different forms that verification activities could take: those that are method-specific and those that are not. The discussion earlier in this chapter should have made clear the fact that not only are method-specific the most desirable sort of verification activity, but they are also the most powerful and our choice of methods should be influenced by the method's V&V potential.

We can now bring all this together and elaborate activities like *3300 Produce State Machine for AS Interface* with detail about the verification that will be used to check the deliverable. In some cases, the verification activity might be significantly large: module testing is such a case, where we need a whole test planning and test specification activity itself. In other cases, the verification process might be quite small: checking the properties of the state machine for instance might be only a few hours' work and require no special planning or software.

In the first case, we would want to add new work packages for those verification activities to the WBS. In the second case there would not be the need – we could assume that the verification takes place at the end of the production activity, though in fact we will not rely on our memories: below we will look at how this sort of decision is recorded in a Quality Plan.

> The key point is that in our elaborated WBS we identify a verification activity for every deliverable, either explicitly or implicitly.

We have also seen how the yardsticks against which we can test a deliverable – the basis for the verification activity in other words – can take four forms:

1   a definition of quality features to be achieved for this deliverable for this project, deduced by quality factoring from the quality features of the final system

2   a definition of features that are to be achieved by all such deliverables produced on this project

3   a definition of features that are to be achieved by all such deliverables produced in this organisation

4   a definition of features that are to be achieved by all such deliverables produced for use in this application domain.

Features of type 1 will be defined in a deliverable-specific specification of some sort. Features of type 2 will be specified in a project-wide standard. Features of type 3 will be specified in organisation-wide standards. In some cases it might be that *application domain* or *industry-wide* standards must be applied, as happens for instance in the avionics arena. If you are calling up standards to define the quality features of some deliverable, you can either simply reference those standards if they exist, or, if they have still to be prepared (ie they are project specific) then you should make sure you have an activity in your WBS for their preparation. If you want to define the quality features (or some of them) in a specification to be produced at some time during development then you should ensure that your WBS contains an activity to prepare that specification.

Clearly standards can play a key part here so a section on their role is appropriate right here.

The role of standards

In chapter 5 we touched on the various quality standards covering different aspects of the software development process. Such standards come from bodies at the international, national, and industry arenas, as well as from within individual companies. And I have one reservation about them all (though I must make it clear that I support standardisation activities and serve on the UK national standards committee responsible for standards in software development!).

This chapter has analysed in some detail the fact that (a) quality is fitness for purpose and hence will vary from system to system, and (b) that primary quality features are factored into quality features for intermediate deliverables. The implication of this is that one cannot write a standard for, say, module specifications that applies sensibly to all systems. As an example suppose we were to write a standard that defined what checks were to be applied during code reviews. Such a standard would list items like:

- there shall be no unreachable code
- no variable shall be read before being written to
- the module shall contain a change history record detailing all changes made subsequent to successful completion of module testing
- pointer arrays shall not be used.

But we can easily imagine situations where these quality features would be too stringent: a prototype piece of software intended only to explore some facet of design and then to be discarded, for instance. And we can just as easily imagine a situation where they would not be stringent enough: for safety critical software we might well wish to add a number of additional features (such as amenability to semantic analysis). To have one standard for all situations is clearly an impossibility and so it is vitally important when using standards (whether local to your organisation or international) to be sure that wherever necessary you adjust them to the requirements of the job in hand: fitness for purpose.

The lesson is that we should be careful not to call up standards without thinking about their applicability.

Of course there are some situations where you might not have the luxury of questioning whether a standard is or is not applicable: your client might demand it, or you might be required to use it by legislation. Clearly these are special cases that require special handling. Nick Birrell and I once met the first of these cases and felt it proper to convince our client that our standard was best. We were developing a complex call billing system for telephone exchanges. The client wanted us to prepare the design in the form of flowcharts, but we felt that this was inappropriate to a multi-process, real-time system. Nick had decided to use the SARA design technique, as its fit with the problem was excellent (see [Birrell 1988] for a summary). Flowcharts simply didn't come into the running, but the client's Quality Assurance staff expected them as part of their normal quality standards. It needed some careful argument of our case to get them to agree to a design expressed in the diagrams and text of SARA.

So let me finish this section by voicing a word of caution against the blind use of standards – whatever their source. Quality features will vary from project to project. It is important not to set them too high or too low by simply calling up a standard "off the shelf".

Having got that warning out of the way, let me remind you of the very useful list of software engineering standards to be found in [Hall 1988].

6.6   DEVELOPING YOUR QUALITY PLAN

We are now at the point where we are able to pull all the quality analysis together and make our decisions available to everyone in the form of a Quality Plan. This is a plan that says what you are going to do on your project in the way of Quality Control. (Remember that quality attainment – getting it right first time – is addressed when you consider what process or methods you will use, a decision that is part of technical planning and that is recorded in your Technical Plan.)

Your Quality Plan will therefore

- list all the deliverables you will produce, final and intermediate

- define how their quality features will be defined (specification, local standard, organisation standard, or industry standard)

- and define how those features will be checked for (ie define how the Quality Control will be done).

The list of deliverables will be steered for the most part by the choice of methods.

How the features will be defined will be defined by the four means listed above with the priority order being

1   standards for such deliverables produced for use in this application domain

2   standards for such deliverables produced in this organisation

3   standards for such deliverables produced on this project

4   a definition of quality features to be achieved for this deliverable for this project,

bearing in mind the need to choose appropriate standards for things and not to end up with something that is inappropriate but conveniently grabbed.

How the quality features will be checked for – the verification activities – will have been deduced from your earlier analysis, particularly from the V&V potential of the methods you've chosen to use. If your methods don't offer any way of checking the results or you aren't using any method to speak of then you will need to fall back on the non-method-specific verification techniques, namely inspections, reviews and so on. But they should be your last resort as they are relatively weak and ill-focused.

In some cases you will be able to specify a tool that exists or that you can build to assist in the verification. A static analysis tool can find unreachable code or anomalous data usage for you. You might choose to write a tool that allows you to look for desired or undesirable state sequences in a finite state machine, you might decide to write or buy a tool that allows you to carry out performance predictions for your chosen hardware configuration, and so on. The Quality Plan is the place to record these decisions. If a tool has to be built or bought and installed then you will need to plan activities to do this. Add those activities to your blossoming WBS.

Once you have finished you should, in particular, have definitions of all the arrows in figure 6-6 relevant to your process model; and you should have elaborated your WBS with considerable detail about Quality Control activities.

The contents list for a Quality Plan will depend on local requirements of course, but you will probably have something along the following lines:

1   a definition of where the system is or will be specified

2   a definition of where the acceptance criteria for the system are or will be specified

3   a list of the deliverables – final and intermediate – that will be produced during development

4   for each deliverable a definition of where its quality features are or will be defined; this will be by reference to a specification (existing or to come) and to project, organisation or industry standards

5   for each deliverable a definition of how those quality features will be verified and what records will be kept of the verification

6   indications in all cases of the levels of authorisation that will be required for approval of specifications, approval of verification, and approval of outcome.

Depending again on your local requirements, your Quality Plan might also be an appropriate place to describe

• change control procedures

• fault management procedures

• configuration management procedures

• purchasing procedures

• project reporting and debriefing procedures

• training requirements

• security considerations.

The first three of these are important on all but the smallest project and deserve a book of their own. We saw in chapter 3 how, in some process models, especially those that use iteration or overlapping phases, these disciplines are essential to the successful control of the process. There are extensive systems described in the literature; see for instance [Bersoff 1981] and [Babich 1986].

6.7   CHAPTER RECAP

Whilst we would like to think that by choosing the right methods for software development we will attain the necessary quality, human fallibility means that we have to provide the safety net of *Quality Control*. The earlier a defect is found the cheaper it is to remove it, and to be certain of delivering the desired quality features in the final system we need to check the quality features in every intermediate deliverable. Those quality features of intermediate deliverables

need to be derived principally from the quality features of the final product - a
process of *quality factoring*.

Checking for quality features is *verification*. Good verification is verification
that is reliable and economical. Reliability can be achieved by using
development methods with high *V&V potential*, ie methods that offer good
possibilities for directed verification. The problem of economy is less easily
addressed. The more formal the method the stronger the V&V potential, so
formal methods have greater attractions where there are more stringent quality
requirements. A tool supporting a formal method is also more likely to be able to
assist in verification in a strong way than a tool supporting an informal method.

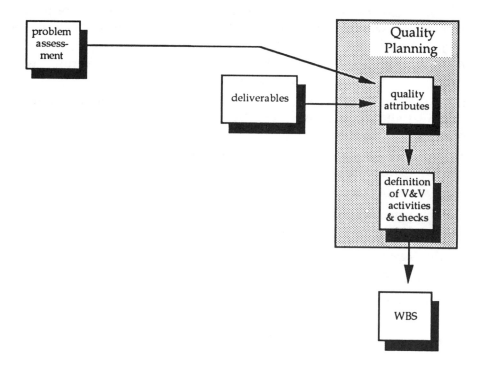

Figure 6-10. The story so far

Quality features can come from four sources: quality factoring from the quality
features of the final system, and from project-, organisation- and industry-specific
standards. All standards must be intelligently applied since, whilst being
generally applicable, they might be specifically inapplicable.

Given the methods you will use and the quality features to be checked you can
draw up a Quality Plan that

• lists all the deliverables you will produce

• defines how you will define their quality features

- and defines how you will check for those features.

Chapter 10 gives the skeleton of a sample Quality Plan.

From this Quality Plan you can elaborate your WBS with specific Quality Control (or verification) activities for each of the deliverables where a separate activity is warranted.

Figure 6-10 shows an expansion of one more box from figure 1-1 – the Big Picture – and shows how the results of technical planning feed into quality planning.

7

PLANNING RESOURCES

7.1   THE CULMINATION OF A JOURNEY

We have covered a lot of ground in the past six chapters. The bulk of this has been about getting information about your project and the system it will build. It has been about making decisions about how the project will achieve its aim: namely to build the system to the right quality, on time and on budget. In this chapter we look at how you use the information you have gathered and the decisions you have made to prepare your *Resource Plan*, and at the factors that affect productivity on your project.

In essence, what has come out of the technical and quality planning work has been a list of the activities and iterations that you need on your project in order

- to handle the risks and uncertainties
- to carry through the methods you have chosen
- to do the V&V that is necessary to ensure quality has been achieved.

This list of activities and iterations will form the major part of your Work Breakdown Structure (WBS). Figure 7-1 gives a detailed view of the original "big picture" that I summarised in figure 1-1. Notice how every decision you have made so far has led to the WBS, and remember my statement right at the outset that from technical considerations we would deduce managerial and commercial decisions. We have now reached that point.

Your next move is to complete some of the gaps in the WBS, to cost it, to deduce the timing and resourcing of the activities in it, and then to write all that up in your Resource Plan.

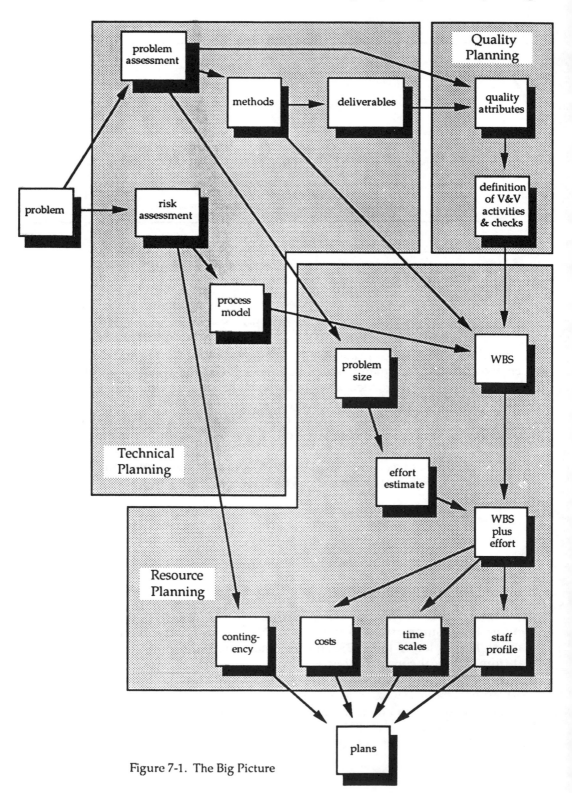

Figure 7-1. The Big Picture

As with your Technical Plan, you need to write all these decisions down for a number of reasons:

- because you will want to communicate them to others, in particular your project team who will use the plan as a work instruction
- because you will want to prove to others, typically line management or your client, that you have a feasible strategy for the project that stands some reasonable chance of success and that is well thought through
- because you have a bad memory.

It is important to remember that these are the only reasons you are writing a Resource Plan. All the thinking and decision-making should now be complete, and recording things is just a straightforward matter of putting pen to paper. The "only" remaining creative skills to be exercised will be to construct your project network and to estimate the duration of activities.

We start with the mechanics of project planning and project re-forecasting. Subsequent sections then deal with other factors affecting productivity (tools, training, and so forth) and with project metrics.

7.2   PREPARING THE RESOURCE PLAN

This section is the culmination of the processes I have presented in earlier chapters: it shows how all the decisions you have now made yield most of the input you require to draw up a full and realistic Resource Plan.

The Work Breakdown Structure

There is a strong tradition of hierarchical structures in our industry and so we take to a hierarchical decomposition of our projects into activities quite readily. If you have not come across a *Work Breakdown Structure* (WBS) before, read this section; otherwise skip to the next.

A WBS is best explained through an example. Imagine the following is a WBS for a project to build a house.

    1000   Negotiation and Planning
            1100   Agree target price with buyer
            1200   Negotiate materials prices with suppliers
            1300   Draw up ground plans
            1400   Get plans agreed by local planning department
            1500   ...

```
2000    Construction
        2100    Clear ground to correct levels
        2200    Prepare footings
        2300    Fabricate roof structures
        2400    ...
3000    Fitting out
        3100    Install electrical circuits
        3200    Install plumbing
        3300    Install air conditioning
        3400    Decorate interior
                3410    Plaster where necessary
                3420    Wallpaper as specified
                3430    Paint as specified
                3440    Carpet as specified
                ...
        3500    Carry out final inspection and cleaning
```

The main groupings of activities are *1000 Negotiation and Planning, 2000 Construction*, and *3000 Fitting Out*. Anything needed to get from the initial agreement to handing over the keys to the new owner must appear within one of these three main groupings. Each grouping is then decomposed into a number of smaller activities. The sum of the subordinate activities is exactly equal to the main activity, no more and no less. This decomposition can be taken down any number of levels, though I have never worked on a project that could not be adequately handled with five levels. I have shown some of the decomposition of house building above. Every activity required to get the house built must appear at some level in the WBS.

(As an aside, I would recommend that you use imperative verbs for the lowest level WBS activities: *Complete System Specification* rather than just *System Specification*. You are after all defining activities! You should also suggest in the verb the required outcome: *Get price agreed* rather than *Discuss price*.)

Note that I have drawn up the WBS for the house building in more or less the order that things would happen in time. Clearly there is some parallelism around: roof structures can be constructed whilst foundations are going in, for instance. But overall there is a flow of time through the WBS. However, you might choose to structure your WBS around the structure of what you are building. For instance, your system might consist of three relatively independent subsystems: Account Transaction Processing, Mail Shot Processing, and Credit Worthiness Assessment. You could structure your WBS thus:

```
1000    Complete overall design
2000    Design individual subsystems
        2100    Design Account Transaction Processing
        2200    Design Mail Shot Processing
        2300    Design Credit Worthiness Assessment
```

```
3000    Implement individual subsystems
        3100    Implement Account Transaction Processing
        3200    Implement Mail Shot Processing
        3300    Implement Credit Worthiness Assessment
4000    Integrate separate subsystems

...
```

or thus

```
1000    Complete overall design
2000    Construct Account Transaction Processing
        2100    Design Account Transaction Processing
        2200    Implement Account Transaction Processing
3000    Construct Mail Shot Processing
        3100    Design Mail Shot Processing
        3200    Implement Mail Shot Processing
4000    Construct Credit Worthiness Assessment
        4100    Design Credit Worthiness Assessment
        4200    Implement Credit Worthiness Assessment
5000    Integrate separate subsystems

...
```

I would favour the second approach because it is easier for the separate teams that you will probably have working on the different subsystems once the overall design has been done to see their own work separated, rather than mixed up with everyone else's. Also, the potential parallelism is expressed at the correct (ie high) level.

Inputs to the WBS

Because you are going to use the WBS as a basis for your costed Resource Plan, there is a major point to be remembered:

If an activity is not in your WBS you will have to do it in zero time and for free.

Completeness is therefore the key attribute of a good WBS, and in this section we shall look at how the results of technical and quality planning provide the major part of your WBS.

I shall refer to an item at any level in the WBS as a *work package*.

Input from technical planning

First, let's look again that the form that these various inputs can take. As we predicted in chapter 2, our analysis of risk and quality leads to the identification of

- an overall shape for your project, eg a three phase project with two intervening review points, or an evolutionary development

- single activities, eg *prepare a system specification using Yourdon,* or *validate specification by animation,* or *verify usability of User Manual*

- decision points at which one of a number of alternative paths is chosen, eg *if a relational database will suffice use one, otherwise develop a purpose-built file-handler*

- dependencies between activities, ie *logic* for your plan, eg *agree interface definition before specification work,* or *validate system against simulator before integration with real hardware.*

The first question we must answer is: how do each of these find their way into our plan?

- A process model obviously has a major effect on the structure of the project because that is exactly what it is about – we saw this in chapter 3. We can expect the structure of the process model to be mirrored in the structure of the WBS. A three phase project with two review points will be best mirrored by a WBS with three major work packages: *1000 Phase 1, 2000 Phase 2,* and *3000 Phase 3.* Within 1000 we could expect to find the first review activity, and within 2000 we could expect to find the second review activity.

  When we come to construct the network we shall reflect the overall logic of the chosen process model in the overall logic of the network.

- Clearly, a single activity appears simply as itself somewhere in our WBS, eg *3145 Verify usability of User Manual.*

- A decision point will generally involve an activity to make the decision, eg *4522 Evaluate the available relational databases,* followed by two or more alternative paths (sets of activities with their logic). The question here is: how should these alternatives be shown?

  Firstly we should note that we should at least have a good idea of the possible outcomes of the decision. If we don't then we shouldn't be planning the project beyond such a critical decision – we should have limited our (commercial) commitment to what we can reasonably predict. So the sort of decision in *4522 Evaluate the available relational databases* is fine: subsequent activities will either be independent of the outcome (do the design with database *A* or with database *B* as the target), or, at worst, might depend slightly on the outcome. For instance, if database *B* is chosen we might need to add further activities for training if we only have experience of database *A*.

  When it comes to constructing the WBS it should therefore be possible to put in *all* activities that might result from *all* the possible outcomes. And when we choose durations we can pick the longest from the alternatives.

This might not sound entirely satisfactory, but our starting point should be to cover against the "worst" case, ie the most expensive outcome of the decision. Later on we might assess the relative likelihoods of the different outcomes given whatever prior understanding we might have, and then adjust the durations on the basis of that. Resource planning is never an exact science!

- A dependency between activities will go straight into a dependency in your activity network which is intended precisely to show such dependencies (see *Drawing the network* below).

In chapter 4 we looked at how your choice of methods is determined by the sort of system you are building. In particular we looked at how generic activities such as

- Prepare User Model
- Prepare Architectural Model
- Prepare Implementation Model
- Prepare Build Model

are defined by the methods you use. So when we draw up the WBS at this stage of the planning process we can be quite specific about what activities we will have, given those methods. Thus, if we are using SSADM, the generic activity *Prepare User Model* can be replaced by a whole set of activities to do with the preparation of Entity Life Histories, Data Flow Diagrams, Technical Options and the like. A good WBS will name these activities and their deliverables explicitly, eg *Prepare and agree Entity Life Histories*.

Input from quality planning

In chapter 6 we looked at how verification and validation were activities that not only appeared throughout the development path, but also were directly related to the methods you chose, the extent to which those methods gave you opportunities for strong verification (V&V potential), and the nature of the deliverables resulting from those methods.

Since verification takes place throughout development you could expect to see verification activities throughout your WBS. Moreover, because of the analysis you have done of the methods and V&V you can do, your WBS can be very specific about the precise verification activities. *2300 Verify design* would be a weak specification of an activity: you should be able to break this down into, for instance, *2310 Verify performance through simulation, 2320 Verify data base integrity preservation, 2330 Validate functionality through prototype screens*, and so on.

Filling in the gaps

Technical and quality planning are designed to help you generate all the crucial activities of your project – those about which you have least knowledge at the outset. But there are of course a host of activities that are almost standard from one project to the next and that, in general, do not represent a major risk. Precisely what they are will depend on your particular environment, but the sort of things I am thinking about include

- preparing documentation plans
- preparing test plans at all levels (unit, subsystem, system, acceptance)
- preparing maintenance documentation
- preparing support material
- handling any change-over from existing systems (data conversion, parallel running etc)
- preparing user documentation
- training users (including preparing material)
- project debriefing
- the collection and analysis of metrics.

I would advise that you construct your own checklist of such activities and make sure you scan it whenever you are drawing up your project plans. If you miss one out and it's non-trivial *you will have to do it for nothing*.

Costing the Work Breakdown Structure

Finally, we come to the one bit of black magic in this book. Under an innocuous sounding heading, we have to tackle the great unsolved problem of software engineering: estimating. How long will it take? How many staff will I need?

It's an advantage if you don't expect there to be some magic formula that will help you here. The only real guide is straight experience. In the software houses where I have worked, when the moment comes for the estimates to be made for a competitive bid, it's the old hands who are wheeled out in their wheelchairs to do the estimate. Experience, experience, and more experience. There are of course various "estimating models" that you can use (and more of these in a moment), but they are only as good as the experience that is crystalised in the constants in their formulae. Any estimating model worthy of the name will give you a way to calibrate it against *your* experience in *your* organisation with *your* sort of staff on the sort of projects *you* normally tackle. In other words – against *your* experience.

It is therefore quite obvious that if you never record your own experiences you will never learn to estimate. Later on I recommend the simple statistics you should keep to help you develop a "feel" for how long things take.

There are two ways to cost your WBS: the *holistic* approach and the *analytic* approach. Let's take them in turn.

The holistic estimating approach

In the holistic approach you start with an estimate of the "size" of the problem you are going to solve, and you derive from it an estimate of the total amount of effort an enterprise like that would take. You then take that total figure and break it down over the various activities using further experience about what proportion of the total project effort each activity takes.

This is not the place for a long exposition or analysis of estimating models – you should refer to the source material – but a glimpse of the processes is all that we need here to show how they fit into the overall resource planning business.

The holistic approach is adopted by, for instance, the COCOMO estimating model [Boehm 1981]. This model has many ramifications so I shall restrict myself to the general scheme and leave the detail to Boehm's classic text.

For the COCOMO model the estimate of the problem size is expressed as the number of lines of code that will be developed for the system. The unit generally used is the KLOC (thousand lines of code). (Suitable definitions of things like a line of code are of course necessary but they are peripheral.) The model then requires an estimate of 15 so-called *cost drivers*:

- required software reliability
- data base size
- product complexity
- execution time constraint
- main storage constraint
- virtual machine volatility
- computer turnaround time
- analyst capability
- applications experience
- programmer capability
- virtual machine experience
- programming language experience
- use of modern programming practices
- use of software tools
- required development schedule.

Scales are defined for these drivers and it should be clear that much of the technical planning analysis described earlier in this book will help you to make estimates of these costs drivers against the scales. The model will then, if suitably calibrated, give you an estimate of the total amount of effort required for the development, plus estimates of how that should be divided over the various phases of development. This would be a starting point for putting figures against the individual activities in your WBS.

Clearly, as you divide the effort down over smaller and smaller activities so you will need to exercise your judgement about what proportions to use. That judgement will come from experience – ie from records you have kept of past actual results. I have figures from a number of projects carried out in the late 1970s. The proportion of effort consumed by each of the major phases is shown approximately in figure 7-2. Figure 7-3 shows the figures for a project I ran in the early 1980s. Figure 7-4 shows the figures for a number of projects in the late 1980s.

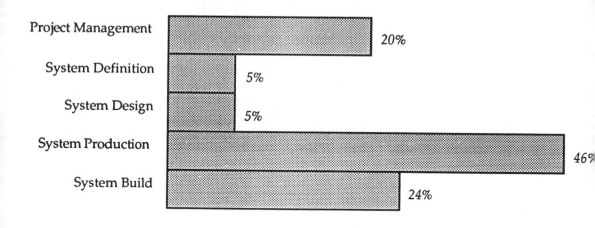

Figure 7-2. Effort profile from a mid-70s project

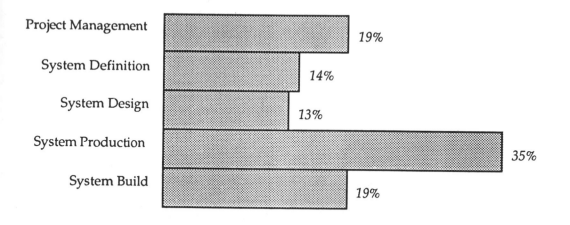

Figure 7-3: Effort profile from an early 80s project

The trend has clearly been towards a greater concentration on the definition and design phases and the effort profile has changed. There are of course no magic numbers that apply universally – projects can vary enormously and the projects in the figures are a tiny sample, but you should establish a profile for projects in your organisation, both so that you can use them as a basis for costing your WBS when estimating holistically, and also so that you can take steps to change the proportions if you feel they are not right – for instance, continuing the emphasis on early activities.

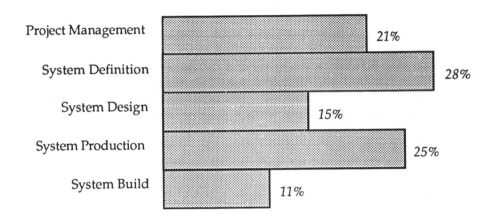

Figure 7-4. Effort profile from a late 80s project

The result of your work will be a costed WBS, with an estimate of the duration of each of the activities in some appropriate unit such as weeks.

The analytic estimating approach

In the analytic approach you start from the detailed WBS and ascribe a duration to each activity. By totalling the estimates for the individual activities you get a figure for the total effort for the entire project. You still need in some sense to estimate the size of the system because when you estimate how long the activity *2534 Code Transmission Algorithms* you will need to have some idea of the "size" of the Transmission Algorithms.

There is little advice that anyone can give you here – you really are on your own! You will need to establish from your own experience and that of others just how long things take. Experience, experience, and more experience.

One tip worth following is to choose an appropriate unit for estimating durations. How do you decide what is "appropriate"? Here are some points to remember when deciding.

If you choose a small unit such as days and have a small number of large activities you will tend to underestimate. If you choose a large unit such as months and have a large number of small activities (down in the one and two month area) then you will overestimate. Never estimate in anything smaller than a day. I once managed a project where estimates were required in hours. This could easily have led to hopeless underestimates, simply because you end up with very large numbers, and very large numbers always look *too* large, and so you tend to scale them down ... The only way I could handle it was to do my estimates in days and weeks and then convert to hours for presentation purposes!

At bid time I would be surprised if anyone could estimate in anything finer than weeks. The acid test is whether I can discriminate between N units and $N+1$ units. For instance, will *2534 Code Transmission Algorithms* take 35 days or 36 days? If this is a meaningless, unanswerable question – I couldn't say which is more likely – then I am using too fine a scale. I move to weeks. Will *2534 Code Transmission Algorithms* take seven weeks or eight weeks? Yes, I can make a judgement on that. So I use weeks as my unit. If I couldn't I would move to months. Will *2534 Code Transmission Algorithms* take two months or three months? No, that feels too coarse. I had a manager once who reckoned "it takes a week for a sh*t or a p*ss". The smallest thing takes a week so there's no sense in estimating in any smaller units!

When doing a holistic estimate we made critical use of proportions for dividing estimates down over the activities in the WBS. These proportions have their place when you are using the analytic approach too. Once you have costed the entire WBS activity by activity you should add up the numbers so that you get totals for the major phases. Then check the proportions they have between them against the "norms" that you have established from experience. This is a typical sort of sanity check that helps you spot anomalies. Where the proportions differ considerably, eg by more than a difference of 5%, I would suggest a careful look at the costings and either the production of a good reason for that difference or a change to the figures.

It is worth mentioning here a major difference between an estimate done for overall planning and an estimate done for actual project control. In the first case, it is only necessary to come up with an estimate of a feasible WBS – it does not have to be *the* WBS. This means that you might decompose your WBS to levels that give you a "feeling" for the work rather than an accurate prediction of the activities that will be done. For instance, you might estimate the duration of the activities in a prototyping exercise at a much finer level than you could be totally confident about. It won't be until you get nearer the prototyping work that you will be in a position to do a breakdown and costing that you would be confident enough about to give a team member to act upon. This is fine. By all means estimate to a level of detail greater than that at which you are really confident *for costing purposes*, eg at bid time. But when you draw up the project plan you should leave your WBS at the higher level, and not refine it further until you have information on which to do it reliably – this will generally be closer to the time.

Making the estimate

Since you now don't expect there to be a magic formula, you will definitely want to use as many methods of estimating as you can in any given situation. In my opinion the analytic method is the one to start with, though I would always expect it to generate an overestimate rather than an underestimate, especially if you have gone to considerable detail in your WBS. This is because you will tend to round up on each figure, and a lot of small roundings up can become a very large rounding up when added together. On the plus side, the more detail you can go into in your WBS the more confidence you can have in being able to achieve your estimate – clearly a lot of WBS detail *should* mean a lot of understanding about how you are going to get the system developed.

Also, by costing the WBS directly, you will find it easier to inject your own experiences of how long things take in your situation – this is clearly not so easy with the holistic methods that require a good calibration to be effective *as well as* experience about the proportions for various activities.

However, if I can I then use holistic methods, no matter how coarse they are, to give a sanity check or two on the figures I get analytically. This is the whole point about estimating: you need as many ways of getting the estimate as you can find. When the results differ substantially you need to ask yourself why that is is, and by answering the question – and it should not take long – you will get more information about either the problem or your uncertainties. Either way, that's good value. It's for this reason that a number of independent estimates by different people will also help. Some people have a better feel about estimating some areas than others. So, by comparing their estimates and finding out why they are different you will know which ones are based on more reliable experience than others and you will start to get an overall feel for the "real" answer.

This is a good moment to remind you that an estimate is not a *prediction*. I have often heard people talking about estimates as if they were referring to the project as some sort of scientific phenomenon about which they were making a prediction and which they were then going to observe to see if their predictions were right. An estimate is a *management goal*. It will only turn out "right" if you as project manager manage the project to *make* it turn out right!

A popular sport for those coming across an estimating model like COCOMO for the first time (and I've done this) is to take an old project, "run it through COCOMO", see what the model says the project should take, and then compare that with what it *did* take. The answers are invariably different. But we should not be surprised – the difference between a future project and an old project is that you can manage a future one, but the old one is history. On the future project you are going to use the estimate as a management *tool* to get things done in a certain time. No doubt on the old project that was run through COCOMO the project manager was using some estimates as a management goal, and hence the comparison is not a valid one.

This is why the apparent poor "accuracy" of estimating models like COCOMO is only apparent. When he calibrated COCOMO against his original 69 projects Barry Boehm found that, in rough terms, the calibration was within ±25% of the actual figure for two thirds of the projects. This sounds appalling. But he goes on to point out that a manager can handle a 25% "error" either way, either by turning up the heat or turning it down (if allowed that luxury!). So an "error" of that size is no big deal. It's important therefore for you to have an idea of just how much ±% you think you could handle when you make your estimate.

Once you have finished you will have a costed "Work Package Analysis" similar to the fragment in figure 7-5. You will later update this on a monthly basis, as I describe below.

plan days	work package		
	1000	Project Management	
		1100	Initiate project
5			1110 Draft and agree Project Schedule
2			1120 Set up project file
15			1130 Prepare Technical Plan
10			1140 Prepare Quality Plan
15			1150 Prepare Resource Plan
			1160 Prepare CM Plan
			...
		1200	Monitor and report on project progress
			1210 ...
120		1300	Administer project
			1310 ...
		1400	Liaise with client
...			1410 ...
15		1500	Close and debrief project
	2000	Prepare User Model	
		2100	Specify requirements
55			2110 Analyse functional requirements
25			2120 Analyse performance requirements
30			2130 Produce outline design
20			2140 Define user interface through prototyping
		2200	Specify system
...			2210 ...
		2300	Specify acceptance criteria
...			2310 ...
	3000	Prepare Architectural Model	
...		3100	...
	4000	Prepare Implementation Model	
...		4100	...
	5000	Prepare Build Model	
...		5100	...

Figure 7-5. A Work Package Analysis

Drawing the network

You now have a WBS with an effort estimate against each activity. The next step is to draw all those activities onto an activity network, adding the inter-dependencies between them.

Missing out a dependency reduces your plan to fiction.

There is no real way to spot all dependencies except to sit and stare at the network trying to decide, for each activity, what you will need to be able to start it. For instance, before you can start coding a module you must have completed its design, of course. But you will probably also need to have the host machine and its development environment available to your programmers. You will need to have written a standard that defines the house style and programming rules. You might need to have the individual programmer trained in the facilities of the operating system they are to use. These are all dependencies to go on the network.

Amongst the activities and dependencies that you will put into your aplan are of course the plan fragments that arose from a consideration of the minor risks and uncertainties that you identified during technical planning. Check that they are all in the activity network and that their associated logic (*before* this and *after* that) is shown as dependencies.

Having got the logic right, you now allocate staff to the activities. You might be working with the names of real people, or simply "programmer 1", "programmer 2" etc. It makes little difference. What you should realise however is that as you allocate staff you are in effect adding new dependencies to the plan: unless the activities are only part-time activities, no team member can work on more than one at a time.

I have often been amazed – and alarmed – by seeing a project manager attempting to manage a significant project simply with a barchart. A barchart contains *no* indications of the dependencies from one activity to another; and in software development, as in any engineering activity, there are many dependencies. If you ignore them, you are working in the realms of fiction.

I first learnt how to plan a project from Peter D whom I worked for on a project on which I started out as Technical Authority and (initially reluctantly!) ended up as Project Manager. We were working on-site at the offices of our client, an electronics company. Naturally, this company had a drawing office and all the accompanying repro facilities (this is in the days before CAD/CAM had come to engineering of any sort). All their engineering drawings were done on large A0 sheets of plastic drawing film that had the wonderful property of taking any amount of pencilling and erasing. Just the medium for a project network. Until I had discovered this, my project plans were constructed with coloured strips of paper for the different activities, coloured according to the person I thought should do them. By placing these on a large sheet with time running from left to right and taking into account dependencies between the strips, I could fashion a plan – until the door was opened and my plan was blown on to the floor.

I moved to the drawing film. And since then I have moved to the personal computer planning tools that provide so much flexibility. There is no substitute for working with an activity network, and any tool that does not allow me to interact *directly* with my network gets a poor rating from me.

Having got the dependencies and the staff allocations onto your network, you now start to play with it. Your aim is clearly to devise a project that takes into account the estimates and the dependencies, *and* that brings the system in on time. This is where the trouble really starts. Almost without fail, the first network will show an end date that is too late – you have come up with "the wrong answer". There are other books on the tricks of project planning so I shall restrict myself to mentioning some of the basic ploys available to you. They all rest on the notion of the *critical path*.

The critical path of a network (and there might be more than one) is the path formed by the longest sequence of dependent activities. In other words if the critical path is shortened the end date comes in. So shortening the critical path is the key to bringing in the end date. Any project planning tool worth its salt gives good visibility to the critical path. Here are some ways of shortening the critical path:

- Long activities on the critical path can sometimes be split into two or more shorter and overlapping activities. There is a danger here if new dependencies are introduced between the subactivities. The whole thing can become quite complex and hard to actually manage when the time comes. Moreover, by making the parts parallel – and hence done by different people – you might need to increase the total amount of effort in order to cope with the increased need for coordination between the staff.

  In other cases a long activity can be split into two parts, the first of which can be started earlier because it is not subject to the dependencies of the whole activity.

  Of course, some activities really cannot be split sensibly – a module design activity for instance. Putting two people on the job really makes no sense. (If it takes one woman nine months to have one baby, how long does it take nine?)

- Better staff can be put on critical path activities. In principle they will do the job more quickly.

- Sometimes activities appear on the critical path simply because of the way you have staffed them. Their dependencies with other activities have not made them critical, but the staff allocated to them are in some fully or over-loaded. For instance, it would be unusual if the activity *Train Users on System* were to prove critical, but it could be that it has become so because the staff you have allocated to it are also planned to do other *truly* critical work.

- In some instances, you can adjust the logic of the network and the activities to reduce the constraints and hence change the critical path's composition. Provided the new logic does not omit important dependencies this is fine.

One tenet that I believe in very strongly is that you should start with the most highly constrained plan you can devise and that you should then and only then be prepared to relax constraints. Not the other way round. In other words, make sure that every possible dependency, however remote, goes into the first version of your network. Every dependency removed or ignored is a risk introduced, and it is only by explicitly removing them that you can know what risks you are introducing and then decide whether you want to take them. Taking risks is a commercial matter and not a technical matter. You should therefore start with a network that is "correct" (ie adequate) on technical grounds and then use your commercial judgment to decide how much risk you are prepared to introduce in the cause of bringing the end date in.

Figure 7-6 shows an imaginary highest level activity breakdown for the first phase of a project to be run as an incremental delivery. Round-cornered boxes are milestones; square-cornered boxes are activities, showing the person who will do the work at their top left-hand corner, and, at their bottom left-hand corner, the number of days effort estimated for the work and the calculated earliest start date. Activities in bold squares are on the critical path. You can see that the delivery of the interface specifications is currently a critical dependency too, and some experimentation with the database to determine its performance is also on the critical path. A moment's thought will suggest that there is no need for it to be so, if it were possible for it to start the moment that planning was complete, rather than waiting for the User Model to have been finalised. There is clearly room for some manoeuvre here.

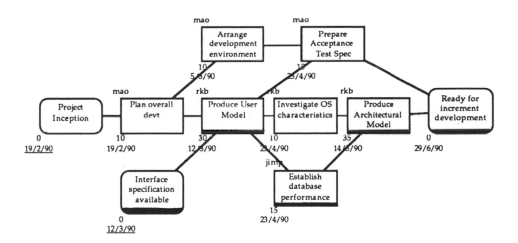

Figure 7-6. A simple activity network

This is not a book on planning with activity networks so I shan't go into a lot of detail here about the use of slack, and hammocks, and lags, and the like, but I have some specific pieces of advice for anyone working with a network:

- Concentrate on where the critical path turns up.

- If a particularly risky activity turns up on the critical path, find a way to get it off: only have safe, predictable activities on the critical path.

- Keep yourself off the critical path: if the project goes critical you should be managing it, not doing the most critical work.

- Give yourself something unimportant to do, such as writing the Acceptance Tests, something that can take the whole of the project without causing trouble. Don't be Technical Authority as well as Project Manager ("I like to keep a close eye on the technical side when I am managing") – that's pure selfishness as well as dangerous. There will be other people who will want to take on the role of Technical Authority – you should not expect to collect jobs like this.

- Don't let inexperienced staff work on critical activities if you can help it: they are already a risk in themselves.

- Don't let individuals work on two things at once unless it really makes sense.

- Don't leave large gaps in people's timeline – time when they would be "resting". There's no need at this stage to ensure that everyone is gainfully occupied every single day. You should leave a little slack in the plan for future use. (More subversion? Sure, but when the time comes to squeeze the project it's like any negotiation, it's nice to have a little you can give away without too much pain.)

Finally, spend as much time as you can just playing with your plan: see what the effect of likely delays would be (try slipping that hardware delivery by two weeks, or doubling the time that weak team member takes to get that code delivered), juggle with staff over the activities, and so on. Your aim should be to see where your plan is delicate, where the sensitivities are – in summary, what its *dynamics* are. Once you know those dynamics you will be able to respond more quickly and more appropriately when something *does* go wrong during the project. You'll know the likely effect almost without having to refer to your network.

This need to play with the network is one good reason for having a computer tool that allows you to interact directly with your network.

Are plans programs?

This is a good moment to re-raise a notion I first raised in section 3.1, namely that our plans traditionally only capture sequence and sequential logic: "this activity follows that activity", or "this activity follows those activities". When we looked at process models in detail in chapter 3 and at the different ways we could manage risk in a project we discovered we wanted to be able to make decisions during our projects ("if this proves to be so, then do this, else do that"), and to have iterations ("do this until something is true"). In other words we would ideally like all the traditional *programming* constructs of sequence, selection, and iteration.

But a "normal" plan, of the sort that has always been drawn since PERT and related techniques were invented decades ago, shows only sequence, as if no decisions were going to be made downstream, and everything need only be done once to be right. What are we to do? It seems that a true plan must be closer to a program; it must be able to "unroll" in a number of different ways, *each of which we have planned in advance.* Having alternative plans is nothing more than contingency planning – but how often do we show this in software development plans? And how often do we show explicitly the possibility of iteration?

Unfortunately we are not helped here by our project management tools. I have not come across any that do anything other than handle straight dependency networks. Until the time comes that I can express my project – as I would like to – as a program that can unwind in different ways (in the same way that the Spiral Model can unwind in different ways for instance), I shall have to resort to half-truths in my networks.

Deducing the effort profile

Once you have juggled staff, activities, and dependencies until you get a project that looks feasible, you can read an effort profile from your network. In fact, a good project planning tool will generate one automatically for you. But, for those of you without access to such things, it will be no problem. Ignore those few days mid-project when someone is between activities. You'll end up with a simple barchart such as that in figure 7-7. Imagine how pointless it would have been to have started trying to draw up such a barchart right at the beginning.

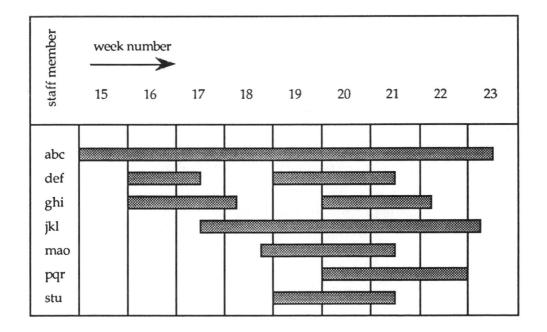

Figure 7-7.   A sample project bar chart by person

Deducing costs and milestones

Now comes the moment of truth – the moment when you have all the information at hand to determine when you can deliver the system and what the total cost will be.

By using the appropriate day cost for each of your staff, you can determine from your effort profile what the total effort cost will be. Again, a decent planning tool will do this for you. To get the full project cost you will need to add a whole host of other costs – often referred to as *materials and expenses (M&E)* – some of which will have been thrown up by your technical planning, and others of which you will need to remember, from checklists, company procedures, or whatever. Here is a selection of some of the things you will need to consider:

- fees for training courses (in methods, in use of support or embedded software, in languages, etc)

- software licence fees for the host development environment (compilers, operating systems, databases, planning tools, CASE systems, comms packages, ...)

- software licence fees for the target environment

- software licence fees for the maintenance environment

- travel and accommodation costs (during training, visiting suppliers, visiting your client, etc)

- hire of equipment for the duration of the project.

If you are bidding for work in a competitive situation, there will be a whole host of other considerations to be taken into account when coming up with the final *price* – for a price is never the development cost alone. When deriving your price you will consider items such as

- inflation over the life of the project

- financing of cash flow (depending on the payment schedule you can negotiate with your client)

- any currency fluctuations

- contingency – an insurance premium to cover residual risk

- profit.

I shall leave the detail of this to you and your commercial judgement – the essentials probably remain the same but the detail will differ from one company to another.

Iterating to the "right" answer

It seems to be a law of nature that when you have done your network, deduced your effort profile and deduced the delivery date and the cost of the project, they always seem out of line with the date and money you have been given. I personally take what is sometimes regarded by colleagues as a rather subversive view of this. It is that when the project manager is drawing up the plan for the first time they should do so *without* regard to the *external* constraints such as required delivery date or budget. This is the one exception to my earlier advice to start with a network with every conceivable constraint in it. They should aim to produce the ideal plan for the job in hand. This doesn't mean they are at liberty to produce a plan that takes as long as they like in delivering the system. I believe they should simply use their best instincts to decide how long it should take and how many staff should ideally be on the project team. And the plan should not assume that overtime will be worked from day one.

Once a feasible and workable plan has been produced, *then* is the time to start squeezing budget and timescale to meet the commercial requirements. The reason for doing it this way is simple: when you squeeze a project you introduce risk, by definition. And you, as project manager, have a responsibility to know precisely what risks you are taking. Indeed, this book has been largely about identifying risks and planning to manage your way through them. Just chucking risk back into the plan now, without knowing you're doing it, would be madness!

The need to squeeze a project arises for commercial reasons, and for perfectly good commercial reasons very often. But commercial decisions are very much about risk analysis: how much risk to take and at what potential cost and at what potential pay-off. So new risk should only be put in a project *knowingly*. And that means squeezing the ideal project to fit the commercial necessities, and *not* starting off with a compressed project with no knowledge of the risks that have been introduced.

I think that this is a lot to do with people wanting to give the right answer – being keen to say they can do things, whilst keeping quiet about the risks that are causing them to curl their toes under the table and to bite their lips in horror.

The aim should be to separate technical decisions about feasibility from commercial decisions about risk taking.

7.3   PREPARING THE MONTHLY REPORT

In this section I suggest a straightforward and reliable way of regularly checking progress and reforecasting outcome. There is nothing special about it, but it falls out naturally from the planning method I have given in the previous section. If you have a project of small to medium size (say up to 50 person-years of effort) you will find it will work quite adequately without major effort on your part. This is because it has been successfully used in the software houses that I have worked in – environments where accurate forecasts of future costs are vital to profitability. If you are running major projects of hundreds of person-years of effort ... I wish you luck. Perhaps you can scale this simple scheme up – I have never tried!

Recording history is of course interesting but the real point of preparing your monthly report is to forecast the future, not to report on the past. So your first step must be to find out where your project stands against the plan in as much detail as you can. Knowing where your project is, you can forecast where it is going – or, rather, where you intend to *manage* it to go!

Recording the past

Your first move must to be to find out exactly where you are on your plan. I assume that you have been doing this regularly anyway and that you don't wait for the end of every month to find out what's going on. But at month-end you do it in detail.

For each work package that has been worked on during the last month find out the number of days that have been used on it. There are many ways you could collect this. A common one is to use some form of contract between the manager or team leader and the engineer. Such a contract would

- identify the piece of work to be done (eg *3462 Prepare Acceptance Test Plan*)
- identify the inputs to be used (eg issue 2.1 of *System Specification* and issue 1.4 of *Project Overall Test Plan*)
- identify the outputs to be generated (eg a definitive issue of a document to be entitled *System Acceptance Test Plan* agreed with the client)
- define the quality level to be achieved, probably by reference to the project's quality plan (the term *exit criteria* is sometimes used here)
- define the amount of effort allowed (eg three weeks) and the required date.

This contract would be agreed with the engineer who would then start on the work. When the work package is finished it is checked by the person who handed out the contract and the actual amount of effort used is recorded on the contract. This should be a basic metric recorded on all projects.

Forecasting the future

Now that you have collected your input data, you can take last month's report/forecast (or the original plan if you are at the end of your first month) and forecast again.

The process is simple:

1 For each work package that has been worked on during the last month but not finished, find out the number of days of effort that the staff member concerned reckons are required to finish it. It is not enough for them to subtract the number they have spent from the number you gave them at the start of the work package! You need a realistic estimate of what there is to go.

   There is of course a great deal of psychology about getting these to-go figures. Suggestions that I have read include asking for *three* figures: the shortest imaginable time it would take, a "reasonable" estimate, and a safe estimate. Which you choose is up to you – you might want to put the pressure on, or you might believe the person is so over-optimistic that you need to advise them otherwise! This is not a book on psychology, so I leave such trickery up to you.

used days	to-go days	plan days	work	package
			1000	*Project Management*
			1100	*Initiate project*
6	0	5	1110	Draft and agree Project Schedule
1	0	2	1120	Set up project file
18	0	15	1130	Prepare Technical Plan
8	0	10	1140	Prepare Quality Plan
13	0	15	1150	Prepare Resource Plan
12	0	10	1160	Prepare CM Plan
...			...	
			1200	*Monitor and report on project progress*
...			1210	...
			1300	*Administer project*
26	85	120	1310	...
			1400	*Liaise with client*
...		...	1410	...
0	15	15	1500	Close and debrief project
			2000	*Prepare User Model*
			2100	*Specify requirements*
62	0	55	2110	Analyse functional requirements
21	0	25	2120	Analyse performance requirements
24	0	30	2130	Produce outline design
32	0	20	2140	Define user interface through prototyping
			2200	*Specify system*
...		...	2210	...
etc etc				

Figure 7-8. A Work Package Analysis updated with effort figures during a project

2   Update your Work Package Analysis (figure 7-5) with the to-go figures you have collected. You'll get something like figure 7-8, which also shows the effort used figure updated ("leaf" activities are in roman type). A little arithmetic will tell you what the forecast total of effort is now, as of today. You will use this as a cross-check in a minute.

3   And now for the most important step: updating your network. (Precise details for doing this clearly depend on the tool you are using.) Delete each completed activity. If an activity has started but not finished, update its duration to the estimated effort to go. If an activity has not yet started you should still give a moment's thought to whether the original estimate is still sensible. Your experience to date on the project might lead you to revise some of the original estimates.

For instance, you might have got some way into coding work and discovered that your original estimates seem to be consistently about 15% under what is actually being achieved. You can turn the heat up under your programmers of course, but you might also take a pragmatic view and adjust your forecasts on the network for the remaining coding activities.

4   You can read off new dates from your updated network, both for intermediate milestones and for the final delivery.

5   Finally, you can determine the total cost to date, total to go, and the overall total and compare the last of these with your project budget ...

As with the original planning work that you did, you will no doubt occasionally find that the cost and date you come up with at the month end is not the "right" answer. If you are forecasting an overrun or overspend, your options are same as ever: reduce the scope of the work, turn up the heat under your staff, or get an extension or more money. But this is getting into territory I don't plan to deal with in this book.

I have known many project managers feel very reluctant to update their network every month. They feel it is an unnecessary burden. But it's clear to me that, if you don't, you are once again ignoring dependencies and the effect they will have on the end date. I cannot understand how anyone can predict a new end date *without* redoing the network. Ignore dependencies and you are in the realms of fiction.

If the above process sounds a lot, I can assure you it isn't. Before the days of spreadsheets on personal computers I used to do the whole thing on pencil and paper. I would reckon on spending about two days at the end of the month preparing a full report including technical, timescale and financial status for my line management and the client in about two days at the expense of a set of calculator batteries. With spreadsheets the effort is reduced to just that required to rework the network – and this is time well spent as you are getting to know the new dynamics of your project, exploring the effect of future events and the sensitivity of your project to different risks. As newer tools become available much of this arithmetic will disappear but waiting for them to arrive is no excuse for not doing the work in the meantime!

7.4   FACTORS AFFECTING PRODUCTIVITY

For a given amount of software to be developed, what factors will affect how long your team will take to develop it? Development productivity is a major topic in itself and I will only touch on it as far as to show the extent to which your technical planning will have generated much of the information you need. Let's return to the relevant cost drivers of Boehm's COCOMO.

Required software reliability

Systems that don't have to be very reliable can be afforded lower degrees of verification activity throughout the development process. The methods used for specification and design do not have to be very stringent. On the other hand, a life-critical system will demand considerably greater expenditure in time and effort at every stage as all deliverables are subjected to considerable stringency in their construction and extensive verification.

Database size

Large databases bring problems of scale, in particular performance. In some cases they will be distributed – a well known technical problem that has no ready made solutions with today's databases.

Product complexity

The more complex it is the greater the risks in development and the greater the likelihood that a complex solution will be required. Complexity = effort.

Execution time constraint

Despite the annual increases in processor power, software engineers never have enough – quite simply they are always trying to do more the more facilities they are given. If you are running your available processor close to its limit, you will need extra effort in producing and checking out an optimised design and an optimised implementation. Such optimisation is both time-consuming and error-prone.

Main storage constraint

The same argument seems to apply to main memory, though perhaps less so than it used to be in the days when the overlaying and process swapping strategy was often a major preoccupation of the system designer. But even today it is possible to find oneself up against the memory limitations of the target machine. Shoe-horning is another consumer of effort. The functionality doesn't increase but the time to get it into memory does.

Virtual machine volatility

One of the uncertainties of a development project that we noted earlier on is the degree to which the underlying virtual machine or infrastructure (OS, DBMS, etc) on which you are building the system remains constant. If your DBMS is constantly being upgraded and you are trying to move with it, you are in severe danger of finding yourself with a design that works under version 3.3 but not under

3.4 for some strange reason. Finding out *why* it doesn't work and then correcting your work eats up yet more unnecessary effort – effort that is not directed towards delivering functionality.

Computer turnaround time

This is a factor that has become a great deal less important since the·late 1970s when Boehm's model was originally calibrated. On-line access for the entire development is generally the order of the day.

Analyst capability

Just how good are your analysts? If they are good, they will not only be productive themselves but they will produce a specification that can be efficiently developed. If they are new to the job, they can be slow and they can generate poor specifications. On Boehm's calibration, the difference between the two ends of the scale can mean a factor of two difference in the productivity of your team.

Applications experience

A team that knows the area that it is working in – radar, payroll, telephones, whatever – is more likely to build a system whose structure reflects the domain structure and hence has that conceptual integrity one looks for in a good design. That makes for greater productivity in a host of ways.

Programmer capability

Little needs to be said about this. Again, in Boehm's calibration, there's a factor of two between the productivity of 15th percentile programmers and that of 90th percentile programmers. I know many people who would say that this is a gross underestimate and that a very experienced programmer can be up to five times as productive as a newcomer.

Virtual machine experience

This has also been raised earlier as one of the factors to be taken into account in technical planning, particularly with respect to the need to experiment with things like your operating system, comms packages and so on, if your team is not familiar with them. Unfamiliarity with the very foundations of your system represents a very great risk – one that needs to be explicitly handled if it is not to have an unpredictable effect on productivity.

Programming language experience

A similar comment applies here.

Use of modern programming practices

The whole of chapter 4 hinged around the choice of good development methods (to extend Boehm's cost driver). In chapter 4 they were looked at as part of the quality achievement strategy, but we have seen that getting things right first time is what quality achievement is about, and this transfers directly into productivity improvement: more right first time means less rework means higher productivity.

Use of software tools

Tools are principally productivity improvers – or should be! Tools typically take over the clerical, mechanical and administrative tasks that we should not be paying our software engineers to do. Well-chosen tools can increase productivity. Poorly chosen tools can damage productivity.

Required development schedule

Finally, Boehm points out that if you have a tight schedule then you will have to (up to a limit) put more people on the job. But more people means more communications, which in turn means lower productivity. In the limit, as Brooks pointed out [Brooks 1979], *adding manpower to a late software project makes it later*.

7.5   METRICS AND INDICATORS

A few years ago Nick Birrell and I worked on the development of a medium size system. We decided at the outset that we should gather some figures about the development to see if we could learn any lessons. The data we collected included the following:

- The amount of delivered source code measured in KLOC (thousand lines of code – we wrote a "line" counting program so we stopped all that argument about what a line of code is).
- The terminal connect time for each subsystem as measured by the operating system.
- The CPU time consumed for each subsystem as measured by the operating system.
- The McCabe cyclomatic number of each module in a subsystem (again we wrote some software to measure this for us).
- The number of errors detected in each module subsequent to the first typing of the source code onto the machine. This required the software engineer, when editing the source of a module to correct an error, to add one to an element in a

matrix in the module header according to the error type and the stage at which it was discovered; we wrote some software that then processed all the headers and reported totals etc.

* The number of test cases applied to each module during unit testing, the figure being derived from the unit test specifications.

We gave careful definitions of terms like *line of code* and *error*. Both during and at the end of the project we got together the numbers and tried to see what we could deduce.

Our little experiment was carried out on a typically sized project for a software house and hence was the sort of project one would like to be able to make predictions about. The project lasted for about two years and included the development of some complex digital video hardware which was microprocessor-controlled. The software development team peaked at six (with around four more building the bespoke hardware). We broke the system into a number subsystems, A through R. Subsystems N through R were for software to run in the micro. The other subsystems were for software running in an attached VAX. But for a tiny amount of assembly language code, all 10KLOC of the software was written in C.

My impression (as a non-statistician) was that there was actually quite a lot of "regularity" in the figures – enough for me to believe that I could use the figures in some way. You'll find them in figure 7-9.

We were starting, like the botanists of the 18th and 19th centuries, from the basis that if we could collect some data we might then be able to deduce some theories which we could use to go on to generate hypotheses. We certainly didn't start out with a theory – though there was some folklore that we thought it would be interesting to check out with real data. For instance, the rumour that the better the up-front design work, the faster the production goes; the more complex a module, the more likely it is to contain defects; and so on.

Certainly there have been experiments and certainly there have been theories, and they are to be found in the literature. But we all know the easy objections: "the sample was too small", "our projects aren't like the one in the experiment", "our environment is different", "the theoretical basis is too shaky", "there are too many variables in the problem", and so on.

One of the objections is that the simple act of measurement changes the experiment (ie the project) – Heisenberg proved this for quantum-sized objects and we know it's true of projects too! (We have already seen a corollary of this, namely that if you set a project a target for some metric then it is likely to achieve it; in other words projects are self-fulfilling prophecies. Indeed, we actually task our project managers to aim for those targets, especially cost and effort targets.) And it is this objection that gives us the clue to how we can use metrics – even the very small sample of slightly consistent figures Nick and I collected. *We can use them in real-time to control projects.* OK, we still aren't able to make *predictions*, but we are able to set targets, monitor progress against those targets and take corresponding action, in other words to manage the project.

sub system	person	connect hours	connect mins/LOC	CPU mins	CPU secs/LOC	McCabe value	test cases	lines per day	edits /KLOC	100*edits /McCabe
A	1	98	10.5	450	48	103	71	27	45	24
B	1	268	12.5	1138	53	236	142	14	27	15
E	2	74	5.0	273	18	158	107	30	101	56
F	3	226	6.1	809	22	260	946	29	106	91
G	3	275	9.6	631	22	249	274	26	157	110
H	4	67	5.5	206	17	-	-	32	139	-
J	5	248	10.9	887	39	208	398	25	97	70
N	4	3	6.9	2	5	3	5	13	77	33
P	4	123	7.1	419	24	92	213	27	86	97
Q	2	50	5.1	181	18	74	72	18	109	83
R	4	27	6.7	55	14	25	394	17	112	110
							averages	24	100	100

Notes

1 Unfortunately person 1 generally forgot to log off at the end of the day and thereby distorted their connect time figures. Their much better "accuracy" suggested by the bug rate (last column) is therefore very likely due to greater skill and care.

2 N was a tiny subsystem and hence not representative.

3 Figures are added together where they are collected at module level.

4 "Lines per day" is a crude measure of programmer productivity. It is the number of lines (by our definition) of delivered source produced from the module specification, design, code and module test activities.

5 An "edit" was defined as any change to the source of a module. Such a change could result from coding errors, design errors, specification errors, syntax errors, changes necessary to overcome hardware errors, slight on-the-fly enhancements to the design, and so on. And of course one design error could lead to changes to several modules and hence multiple counting. However, the edit figure gives an indication of the amount of reworking required from the moment a module was first coded.

6 The system had a handful of residual errors detected after delivery.

Figure 7-9. Some metrics from a project

Here are some examples to illustrate how you can use metrics as *indicators*.. Suppose we set a particular productivity rate that we are going to expect of programmers for a particular task. During the course of the project we can monitor that metric and compare out-turn with target. If we spot places where there is wide divergence, we can investigate more closely. We might find we have a problem, in which case we have detected it quickly and can act. It might turn out to be perfectly acceptable. Even then we have learnt something: how that figure can be affected by certain environmental features. We might not be able to provide an algebraic expression for that effect but it is added to our store of experience. Yes, it's open to abuse but we should in most cases be able to detect it and, if we can't, then we have a problem whichever way you look at it!

Suppose we define a particular threshold for the ratio of errors detected to the complexity of a module. Again, we can monitor achieved values and follow up discrepancies. But we can also let the team set itself the target of coming in under the threshold. We might have set the threshold too "easy" – so we tighten it on the fly. We might have set it too "hard" – why does it appear too hard? can it reasonably be softened? On the next project, we would start with a value which takes into account our new experience.

And when the project is all over we can go back and review the values that we set for the different metrics and get a better feel for what the "right" figure in our environment should be and how different factors can affect it. We are collecting wisdom. Even if we are not producing formulae.

What of staff reaction to this managerial finger on the pulse? On the above project, the figures were discussed regularly and we were perfectly open. We detected no problems from the team. The overheads of collecting the data were small – most of the work was done automatically by a couple of programs. The benefit to the project was that we had real-time indicators of progress and quality which we could use to help us manage the project, and staff were probably kept on their toes in a constructive way. The benefit to the staff was that everyone learnt something about the dynamics of software development by watching their own activity in detail.

So, until the statisticians and behavioural scientists come up with empirically or theoretically derived models I propose that we all get in there and use our metrics in real-time, on our projects.

It was to this end that Nick and I introduced the notion of *indicators* in our book *A Practical Handbook for Software Development* [Birrell 1988]. For each traditional phase of development we list a number of the sorts of things that you could measure and monitor in order to watch some of the inner workings of your project. Most of them can be automated without great effort and hence the running costs can be minimal. Try it!

One of the most crucial indicators I believe is how much software you think you will write. During the project that Nick and I metered we made frequent re-estimates of the size of the system (it wasn't that big as you can see but the principle stands). We estimated blind each time, that is, without looking at the last figures for a component. As the estimates came in we expectantly plotted them to see what was happening.

Figure 7-10 shows our estimates at various stages in development:

- at the start of the project
- twice during system specification
- on completion of overall system design
- on completion of subsystem design
- on completion of module specification
- at the end of coding
- at the completion of module testing , about a year after subsystem design
- at the end of build testing (ie ready for acceptance testing)
- after acceptance testing (ie at the entry to operational use).

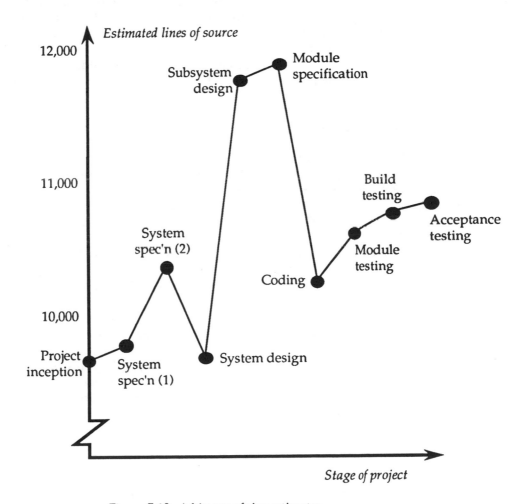

Figure 7-10. A history of size estimates

We estimated in "pages of annotated C", where a page of annotated code was reckoned on average to be 50% all-comment or white space lines and 50% containing language source code of some form (figures borne out on other projects I have observed).

Much of what happened was predictable. Until we really got into subsystem design our estimates were fairly constant – then they went bang! This was I suspect due to a combination of finally understanding in detail all the ramifications of what we were constructing, and of the fact that we were starting to estimate smaller chunks with the consequent increase in rounding up. As we actually got into writing the code, the volume dropped back a bit. Overall we were 20% too low in our original estimates. The relative constancy of the estimates suggests to me that estimating KLOC, even from a system specification, is possible and reasonably accurate for estimating purposes. At the point that we saw a large rise in volume of code we decided to take action to contain the problem. Having that early indication meant we good take early action. There really are very few other indicators that can give you as project manager early warning of possible overrun.

The estimates for some subsystems fluctuated wildly but the overall fluctuation never exceeded 25%. I find it hard to believe after our experience that this sort of data isn't invaluable to the project manager.

7.6   Chapter Recap

Your technical and resource planning work has yielded data in three areas: a process model and plan fragments to handle risks and uncertainties, methods and their deliverables, and a set of V&V activities. You now combine these in a single, hierarchical *Work Breakdown Structure* (WBS) together with other supporting activities. The completeness of this WBS is crucial to the realism of your plan.

You then cost your WBS by ascribing an amount of effort to each activity. You can derive your effort estimates in a variety of ways. If possible, you should use top-down (holistic) *and* bottom-up (analytic) methods, together with any sanity checks that you have.

Once you have a costed WBS, you can construct an activity network that contains all the activities and their interdependencies – the logic of your plan. By ascribing individual staff to the activities, you can derive an end-date and an overall cost. If (when) these prove not to be acceptable you can apply various tricks to shorten timescales. However, all such tricks generally introduce some new risk and so such compromises need to be taken knowingly – they might be acceptable on commercial grounds, and it is important to separate technical idealism from commercial realism.

Assuming you are going to report on progress and assess the future on a monthly basis, you should rework your activity network monthly, updating it to take into account work done and changes in the work to do, especially any reassessments of the team's productivity in the light of its performance so far. Above all, your plan *and* your report are only the hard copy output of a *process* by which you come to understand your project and its dynamics, and by which you make sure that at all times

- you know what you know
- you know what you don't know
- you know how you will find out what you don't know
- and you know what you (and your team) will do next.

8

THE FOURTEEN DILEMMAS OF SOFTWARE ENGINEERING

8.1   CHANGING IS HARD

Over the years I have done a lot of work introducing and encouraging new software engineering techniques into organisations. The response – as one would expect – has been mixed. Some of the blocks that people have to taking on new techniques and tools start to sound familiar after a year or two. They have a similar pattern. Here are some variations on what we will quickly see is a common theme.

1   We can't use a new and unfamiliar method on a fixed price contract because we increase the risk of exceeding our budget and/or timescales. We can't use a new method on a time and materials contract because the client won't stand for the bill for training and learning time, or for the increased timescales necessary to cover our training and familiarisation, or for the risk it represents.

2   We can't use a new method on a real job because there is a risk that we will fail on it as a result. There's no point in trying out a new method on an artificial job created for the purpose because there aren't the pressures of a real job.

3   The first project on which we use a new method must be one on which the method will succeed or the method will lose credibility right from the start. If we use a new method on a difficult project where it could fail then the outcome will not prove anything about the method. If we use a new method on an easy project and it succeeds then we shall have proved nothing.

4   It's not possible to decide on methods at the start of a project because we don't know much about the system and hence what methods would be appropriate. It's not worth deciding on methods after a project has started because it's too late to do anything about training, tooling, planning and so on.

But breaking these dilemmas is clearly something that is necessary if new improved practices are to be taken on. The answer varies considerably and I have adopted a number of different approaches in different situations.

(For a book devoted to the topic of introducing new software engineering techniques into an organisation see [Pressman 1988].)

8.2   BREAKING THE BLOCKS

Let me start by dividing the dilemmas into a number of basic problems faced by those wanting to introduce new methods. I then want to show how technical planning in particular can give you a framework in which to attack them. Here they are:

1   Changing how we do things *before* a new project is started is wasted effort; changing how we doing things *after* a new project is started is effort that is too late.

2   All new things must have proved their worth before I try them.

3   Trying new things on fake projects is unrealistic; trying new things on real projects is foolhardy.

Given that there are so many excellent reasons for not changing, it's a wonder that things do change. Here are some of the reasons that things change despite everything. It's useful to know what they are as you can use them as levers to break the blocks.

* Have a champion. Having someone on the team – ideally the technical authority – who really wants the new technique or tool to work can be 50% of the battle. It means you have someone who is committed to finding ways of making it successful, someone who won't give up at the first hurdle and go back to the old ad hoc methods. When Nick Birrell and I were involved in the telephone call billing system described earlier the choice of design method really was a difficult one: a network of microprocessors operating independently had to be coordinated in the real-time environment of a (non-digital) telephone exchange. Nick had read about Estrin's SARA technique and felt it had a good match – the computational models were a good fit.

    Although neither he nor the team had experience using it, Nick was sure it was the right answer and started by training the team in the techniques at the beginning of the project. He drove the use of that method, adding project-specific detail and removing things that didn't work. Without his champion-ship of the technique it might not have been successful.

* Get your customer to demand new practices. (But please let those practices be good ones and appropriate ones.) It is increasingly common for large procurers of software – typically Government departments or major computer users – to require particular techniques or tools to be used in developments done for them.

As major examples we can cite the US DoD's requirement for the use of Ada, whose development it paid for; or the UK Government's SSADM (Structured System Analysis and Design Methodology) whose design it commissioned through the the CCTA (a government agency) and which is now required for the development of administrative system for government; or the UK MoD's MASCOT method for the construction of real-time systems, and (once) the CORAL programming language intended for use in embedded (typically real-time) systems.

If you want the contract, you use the method required. This concentrates minds wonderfully in the supply side of the industry and the suppliers start to get their staff trained and to buy the tools. This clearly isn't the ideal way of going about things, since blanket rules such as this can be counter-productive unless sensitively handled – as most agencies know. But I suspect that – in the UK at least – the interest in methods has been beneficially increased by such pressures.

- Find new things that really do let people do things better. Most software engineers are really very keen to do a good job. After all, getting software that works is most of the fun. A poor engineer must surely be an unhappy one. Methods can be of interest particularly to staff new to the industry. Old hands, who never learnt a method (perhaps because there weren't any when they started in the industry) are generally more reluctant to learn a method – simply because they have devised their own over years of experience. Throwing that experience away in favour of some "alien" method is not an idea likely to attract anyone, particularly skilled staff. But young minds do not have this barrier to overcome; they accept methods because they are there.

Provided that the methods really do work, and are applied in the right places, and do not conflict with previously held views developed over years of experience, then such methods can be taken on quite smoothly.

The situation with tools is little different. Tools are not a million miles from toys and they can have an attraction for that reason. But from my observations I deduce that the same blocks occur as occur with methods. One of the major reasons that I have found people unwilling to use a new tool is not that it doesn't do X or Y, but that it doesn't automate *precisely* what they currently do by hand. A tool can have as many extra benefits and features, but if it doesn't work the way people work *now* then people won't want to use it: CASE tools that draw different shaped boxes from those used now, or that capture data in a slightly different fashion, languages that don't permit certain control or data structures, and so on. This must make life very difficult for the tool developer.

8.3   HANDLING THE RISKS OF INNOVATION

If a new method or technique is truly seen as a risk and yet you feel it is the correct choice, then you should simply apply the technical planning process recursively:

treat the use of, say, the new method as a risk and decide what process model (or changes to the process model) and what plan fragments you could use to reduce that risk downstream. Then work this back into your plan.

Possible process model changes might include a pilot phase on part of the system before the main development begins, and a parallel development with conventional techniques on any area considered particularly dangerous. Additional plan fragments might be included for increased training, increased familiarisation activities, the use of external consultants in the method at critical points, and reviews of success at critical points (giving you the option of cutting your losses if the worst comes to the worst).

These additional activities will of course initially increase costs and possibly extend timescales. You must decide if those increases are acceptable and this will depend on the perspective you are taking. If your horizon does not extend beyond the current development project, it might be very hard to justify. This can be the case where one department is responsible for initial development and another for subsequent enhancement. It is not in the interests of the first department to invest more than it needs in doing its job.

If your decision horizon extends over the whole life of the project – ie beyond development, through enhancement, to final replacement – then the advantages of the new approach may outweigh increases in the development. This can be the case with a system that is likely to be subject to a lot of change – a little extra spent now to get a firm basis for the future can pay considerable dividends in the longer term. Calculating "life-cycle costs" is hard but can reveal the advantages of early investment.

If your horizon takes in all the projects in a department or company, it becomes easier to take on training, familiarisation, and tooling costs for the benefits that it can bring to you as a software engineering group. An investment (ie increased costs) on one project can lead to savings in subsequent projects, and such savings can be invested in part in further developments, thereby snowballing the benefits.

8.4   Getting the Basic Experience

Ultimately there is no substitute for using new methods on real projects with real pressures. But you might want to get the basic experience in a less risky way. Here are some simple suggestions.

• Use the new methods or tools in parallel with your traditional methods and tools. This could be done on just a part of the system if necessary. It has the advantage of giving you something real to work on without being totally reliant on the results.

For instance, you might be interested in getting familiar with formal methods of specification, let's say Z. Find a part of the system that is amenable to specification in this way and specify that part of the system in your normal way and with Z. Have an activity to compare the results and the costs at the end. Squeeze as many lessons as you can out of the experience. Try Z on a bigger slice on the next system, or do just a part of the specification in Z alone, and the rest with your normal method.

- Less effective is to rework all or part of a completed development using the new method or tool. This is less satisfactory for all the obvious reasons, but it can be effective for simply getting to grips with the method and acquiring a deep understanding of its strengths and weaknesses. The engineers have time to explore and find out how it should be used, rather than unwittingly misusing it but getting by under pressures of time. It is rather like an extended real-life exercise at the end of the training course, with the opportunity to take a harder look at what is going on.

- The lowest risk approach is of course to watch someone else using the method, preferably a team that is expert in its use. This might be possible somewhere in your own organisation or even in another. Watching an expert use a technique can reveal many insights that might take you years to discover by chance.

- Finally, in all cases it is well known that having an expert at hand – ideally on full-time secondment to the project – is essential. It is all too easy for a team starting with a new method to misunderstand basic principles or to use it in an inappropriate and ineffective way, without knowing. As a result they can quickly become disenchanted with the method and write it off as of no use. An expert can guide the team to an understanding of the principles and effective use at the point where they go wrong.

9

RÉSUMÉ

9.1 CLOUDS TO CONCRETE

Whilst I was writing this book, Channel 4 TV in the UK had a four-part documentary on the construction of the Worldwide Plaza building in the West Side of New York. The building – a 770 foot edifice built on the site of the old Madison Square Gardens – was budgeted at $550M to build and was completed in around three years from conception to handover.

I have an interest in the idea of tall buildings for some reason, so I was drawn to watch the series. As the story of its design and construction unfolded, I was fascinated by the similarity between this massive and complex venture and the development of a software system. There are superficial, obvious similarities of course: both are about the development of something usable starting from an idea and some money, and perhaps those similarities are common to any engineering venture with a buyer and a developer. But the similarities went deep enough to make the comparison instructive. Fortunately, the maker of the documentary – Karl Sabbagh – wrote a book [Sabbagh 1989] which goes into the story in much greater detail and it gave me the chance to look more closely at the parallels. I strongly recommend that you read it if you can, because the story illustrates in tangible (concrete?) form all the problems that beset the developer who grapples with that great intangible: computer software.

Before summarising the techniques described in the earlier chapters, I would like therefore to finish by drawing points from Sabbagh's book to illustrate the aims and importance of the techniques.

The story involves the developers (ZCWK), the architects (Skidmore, Owings and Merrill (SOM)), and the construction managers, HRH, plus some sixty subcontractors including the steel fabricators, the site clearers, one of the tenants (Ogilvy and Mather), suppliers of bricks, and so on.

Within the architects, two partners held joint responsibility for the skyscraper: a *design partner* and a *management partner* – much as a software development team could be expected to have a project manager and a technical authority. Within the team they built around them, one architect was designated *technical co-ordinator*, who, amongst his tasks, had to coordinate the designers, structural engineers, and mechanical engineers to make sure they all built the same building. Had the specification always been the same this would have been a straightforward matter. But, of course, it didn't, any more than the specification of a software system remains constant over the development. A small change in design could lead to a major change in engineering. The technical coordinator's task was to make sure that all these interdependencies, and all the impacts that flowed from changes, were spotted and communicated to those that needed to know.

His job also included ensuring that the building complied with the many codes and regulations that surround the construction of buildings. This external standard setting and imposition is not as frequent in software development but is becoming more so, especially in the safety-related area.

At design time, many of the building's performance characteristics had to be tested – from the design alone. Wind tunnel tests on scale models showed how the building would behave in the sort of winds that it was expected to survive. Mathematical calculations gave general answers about the stability and stiffness of the building. Feedback from this modelling led to changes in the design and in particular in the underlying skeleton of the building, what we would call the *architecture* of a software system. Doing this sort of design-time verification is all too rare in software development.

The developers were the procurement body, the tenants the users. The procurement body wants to keep costs down but to increase the take-up of the "system", ie to rent space to the tenants. But users have their own views of how things should be, and they have some leverage to make that happen – no-one can make a user use a system if they don't like it.

Most interesting is the notion of "fast track" building in which people get on with building the building even though decisions have not been finalised on how the building should look. The result is what one might expect: things have to be undone when the details are finally decided, plans have to be altered, costs increase, ... All very familiar to the software developer. The pressures on both sides are well brought out in the book and the lessons transcribe well into the software arena.

Returning to the software theme, before you read on to chapter 10 and its worked example (and perhaps even to chapter 11 with its exercises!), here is a summary of the planning process that I have presented in this book. The terminology should now be familiar and so I have simply brought together the relevant parts of the recaps of the chapters and edited them into one story. Here it is.

9.2   GETTING THERE

The route summarised

Planning a project is a three stage process:

- *technical planning* in which technical considerations lead to inputs to quality and resource planning
- *quality planning* in which quality considerations lead to inputs to resource planning
- *resource planning* where all the inputs from technical and quality planning are used to produce a resource plan that should be achievable, realistic, and low risk.

As a reminder, figure 9-1 repeats the overall route map we started with in chapter 1.

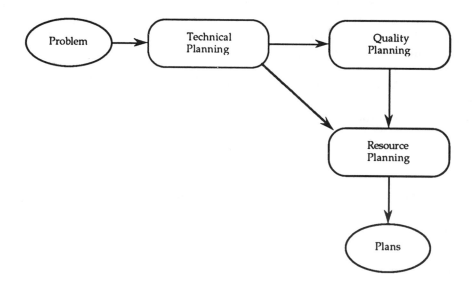

Figure 9-1. The basic route map

Stage 1 – understanding the problem and deriving the process

Step 1.1 – list the risks and uncertainties

All projects have risks and uncertainties and it is these that cause projects to go wrong, ie to overrun in time and/or budget. A central part of your planning process must therefore be the analysis of risks and uncertainties. Step 1 of the first stage is therefore to list all the technical risks and uncertainties.

Step 1.2 – choose a process model for the big risks and uncertainties

Some risks and uncertainties are so major that the overall shape of your project itself can be completely determined by them. Such project shapes – *process models* – are designed to ensure that (commercial) commitment can be limited to what you can reasonably predict. Typically this means some sort of phasing, with each phase being determined or steered by the outcome of the previous one. Different process models can be seen as different unwindings of Boehm's *Spiral Model*. Major risks and uncertainties will therefore lead you to choose a process model. This is step 2 of the first stage.

Step 1.3 – devise plan fragments for the small risks and uncertainties

Other risks and uncertainties are less extensive in their effect on your project's shape, and in particular do not need you to limit your commitment. For these you need only devise activities that will remove or sidestep a risk or that will resolve some uncertainty. You must fit these activities into the overall project in such a way that they happen early enough to reduce or remove exposure to risk. This results in some plan logic saying when in the project they should take place: eg *after* this *and before* that. An activity together with such a piece of logic forms a *plan fragment*. Devising plan fragments for the lesser risks and uncertainties forms step 3 of the first stage.

You will use your chosen process model and your chosen plan fragments later on in the construction of your Resource Plan.

Step 1.4 – choosing methods to match the problem

The next steps are about putting process into the process model: choosing methods. The right choice of methods – ie the methods that lead efficiently to a correct system – requires you to match the strengths of your methods to the key characteristics of the problem you are trying to solve. This is step 4 in technical planning, after the analysis of risks and uncertainties.

Every method is about *modelling*. Most methods model in terms of data and/or control, and model their static and/or dynamic aspects; the dynamics of data and control relate to how things change over time (the temporal aspect) or in space (the local aspect). Every method assumes some form of *computational model* in terms of these aspects. Choosing the right method then becomes a question of matching the modelling "language" and the computational model of the method against the characteristics of the problem you are trying to solve. The method with the best fit is the method most likely to give you an efficient solution to your problem.

During development, whatever the process model you adopt, you will generally produce four different models of a system: a *User Model* which concerns the system in terms of what the users see; an *Architectural Model* which concerns the overall architecture of the solution system in terms of some abstract computational model; an *Implementation Model* which concerns the system in concrete terms related to the target environment; and a *Build Model* which concerns how the system is built from its constituent parts. Different methods produce different (parts of) these models. Your development path should therefore have methods addressing *all* models in some measure if the system is to be developed according to any sort of plan.

Your choice of methods will determine the deliverables that you will produce and the activities that you will need to produce them. Knowing the methods you will use, you can elaborate the process model to include specific activities that will produce specific deliverables.

Stage 2 – putting the quality control and quality assurance in

We can view Quality Control in the general case as a five step process:

1   define the quality feature(s) and level(s)

2   define the feature test procedure

3   carry out the test procedure

4   record the result

5   take and record any corrective action taken.

Step 2.1 – decide what deliverables you will produce

From the methods that you have chosen, draw up a list of the deliverables that you will produce. Be specific about them: *Entity Life Histories* and *Data Flow Diagrams with Data Dictionary*, rather than just *System Specification*.

Step 2.2 – decide on the quality features for each deliverable

For each deliverable decide how its quality features will be defined. Your options are:

•   a specification for that deliverable

•   a project standard for such deliverables

•   an organisational standard for such deliverables

•   an industry standard for such deliverables.

You might choose some combination of these. If you are referring to standards then you should be able to decide which ones at planning time; if you are going to specify features in a specification – such as a module specification – then you need only say so and check that there is an activity to produce such specifications already in your WBS. The quality features of intermediate deliverables need to be derived principally from the quality features of the final product - the process of *quality factoring*.

Step 2.3 – decide how quality features will be tested

Given the features, decide how you will test whether those features have been achieved. For each test either include a new activity in your WBS to do the test, or note that at the end of the production activity the deliverable must be tested in the way you have specified.

Development methods that specifically support Quality Control (V&V) are generally those that are more formal in nature since that formality means that the semantics of the product are well defined and hence properties of the product can be more easily checked for. Many Quality Control checks can be automated if the meaning, ie semantics, of the representation we are using is well defined. In other situations we have to fall back on more general, less formal and hence less powerful Quality Control actions, such as Structured Walkthroughs and Fagan Inspections.

Step 2.4 – draw up your Quality Plan

Each development project should have its own Quality Plan identifying how each of the (final and intermediate) products of the project will be checked for quality. At corporate, project and activity levels the rule is : say what you will do, do it, record it, take any corrective actions. Your Quality Plan says how you will do this for all your deliverables.

Whilst we would like to think that by choosing the right methods for software development we will attain the necessary quality, human fallibility means that we have to provide the safety net of *Quality Control*. The earlier a defect is found the cheaper it is to remove it, and to be certain of delivering the desired quality features in the final system we need to check the quality features in every intermediate deliverable. The quality features of intermediate deliverables need to be derived principally from the quality features of the final product - the process of *quality factoring*.

Given the methods you will use and the quality features to be checked you can draw up a Quality Plan that

* lists all the deliverables you will produce
* defines how you will define their quality features
* and defines how you will check for those features.

From this Quality Plan you can elaborate your WBS with specific quality control (or verification) activities for each of the deliverables where a separate activity is warranted.

Stage 3 – putting the Resource Plan together

Step 3.1 – collect the process model and all activities into a WBS

Your technical and resource planning work has yielded data in three areas: a process model and plan fragments to handle risks and uncertainties, methods and their deliverables, and a set of V&V activities. In the final stage you now combine these in a single, hierarchical *Work Breakdown Structure* (WBS) together with other supporting activities. The completeness of this WBS is crucial to the realism of your plan.

Step 3.2 – cost the WBS

You then cost your WBS by ascribing an amount of effort to each activity. You derive your effort estimates in a variety of ways. If possible, you use top-down (holistic) *and* bottom-up (analytic) methods, together with any sanity checks that you have.

Step 3.3 – construct an activity network

Once you have a costed WBS, you construct an activity network that contains all the activities and their interdependencies – the logic of your plan. By ascribing individual staff to the activities, you derive an end-date and an overall cost. If (when) these prove not to be acceptable you apply various tricks to shorten timescales. However, all such tricks generally introduce some new risk and so such compromises need to be taken knowingly – they might be acceptable on commercial grounds, but it is important to separate technical idealism from commercial realism.

Assuming you are going to report on progress and assess the future on a monthly basis, you rework your activity network monthly, updating it to take into account work done and changes in the work to do, especially any reassessments of the team's productivity in the light of its performance so far. Above all, your plan *and* your report are only the hard copy output of a *process* by which you come to understand your project and its dynamics, and by which you make sure that at all times

- you know what you know
- you know what you don't know
- you know how you will find out what you don't know
- and you know what you (and your team) will do next.

That's it!

10

A WORKED EXAMPLE

10.1   INTRODUCTION

In this chapter I have put together a worked example, developed as an amalgam of many projects I have seen or taken part in, and which we use in our own training courses in Praxis. It starts with an *Invitation To Tender* (ITT) from a company called Snoozo which is in the satellite TV advertising business and which wants a system to handle the scheduling of advert transmission. As you would expect, their ITT is full of problems awaiting the developer. (It's their right to set these problems – that's what they're paying us to solve.) The ITT appears in section 10.2. Quite a bit of detail has been omitted where it is truly irrelevant to the subject matter of this book.

In section 10.3 you'll find the Technical Plan prepared at the time of bidding for the work. It illustrates the maxim "write down what you don't know, as well as what you do know". In section 10.4, there's a draft Quality Plan, again from the bid stage, and in section 10.5, you'll find the starting point of a Resource Plan for the project to do the work. The main point to note from the WBS of the Resource Plan is how its overall structure and many of the key details derive firstly from the Technical Plan and secondly from the Quality Plan. The precise form in which these three plans will appear will depend of course on your own organisation's conventions – I have simply shown the main contents.

You might need to suspend your disbelief over some points, not least that some detail is absent. Remember though that the aim is to illustrate the major lessons of the preceding chapters.

10.2   THE INVITATION TO TENDER

Introduction

This section describes the requirements of a system to support the Snoozo Satellite Advertising System. It is to be used by bidders to prepare a proposal to carry out the work identified below.

Snoozo plc have acquired the rights to transmission channels 6 and 7 of the Boresat European television satellite outside day-time broadcasting from mid-1991 to mid-1996. It is Snoozo's current intention to sell time to advertisers during the so-called "night-time" period. Advertisements will consist of pre-recorded video features of varying length that will be transmitted at the appropriate time to Boresat for broadcasting. In the longer term all-day advertising channels may be leased and this should be borne in mind by bidders.

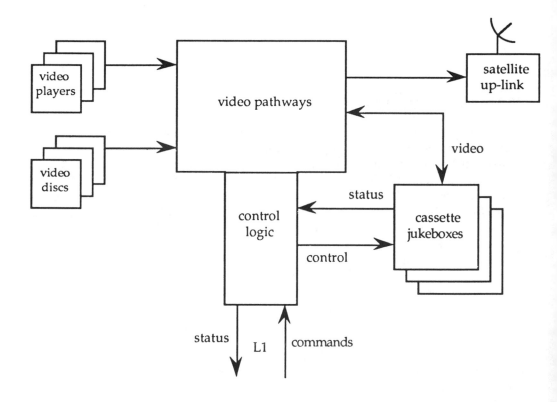

Figure 10-1. Expected structure of SUCS

Snoozo have already contracted with Horsefall Ltd of Auchtermuchty for the development of the video storage equipment, satellite up-link, and associated control system (SUCS).

The SUCS System

SUCS stores, transmits and deletes video adverts on a videotape jukebox under commands arriving on a serial link, *L1*. The structure of SUCS is currently expected to take the form shown in the block diagram in figure 10-1. Briefly, videotapes from advertisers are mounted on videoplayers. On receipt of a command over the link *L1*, the advert is transferred from the videotape to one of the 128 video cassettes in the jukebox. SUCS can also, on command via *L1*, ready up to three jukebox cassettes prior to transmission, and, on a further command, transmit the advert on one of those cassettes to the satellite via the up-link transmitter. SUCS can also carry out some housekeeping activities such as the erasure of cassettes and the ejection of defective cassettes, again on command from *L1*.

The contract to be placed

Snoozo now wish to place a contract for the development of the Advert Storage, Programming and Information Computer (ASPIC) which will

- maintain records on stored adverts
- maintain transmission schedules
- control the Horsefall equipment during transmission of adverts at the predetermined times
- prepare invoices for advertisers on the basis of transmission time used.

The ASPIC system will need to be connected to SUCS for these functions.

Functional specification

ASPIC is required to carry out the following functions:

1 *maintenance of a database of stored adverts*

When a new advert is to be stored on the SUCS jukebox, this will be invoked by an operator on the ASPIC system. ASPIC will keep a database of what adverts are recorded on which jukebox cassettes and will update this database when a new advert is filed. ASPIC will send commands to SUCS (on interface *L1*) to capture the advert waiting on a given videoplayer on a specified cassette. ASPIC will also instruct SUCS to delete adverts when they are no longer required for future transmission and are not marked for future but unspecified use.

2   *maintenance of a database of advertisers, and billing of advertisers*

ASPIC will maintain a database of advertisers who place contracts with Snoozo. This database will also be used to accumulate details of the successful transmission of their adverts so that monthly invoices can be prepared.

3   *storage of newly received adverts*

New advertising videos will be received on a regular basis (typically on a Friday) and they must be stored on SUCS ready for transmission within six hours. This storage must be controlled by the video engineer from ASPIC. ASPIC must instruct the operator in the mounting of the videotape and then send commands to SUCS to transfer the advert(s) to a free jukebox cassette. ASPIC must get from the operator details on the advert(s) including requirements for its transmission, and must update the advert database accordingly.

4   *transmission of adverts*

Although SUCS carries out the transfer of video from cassette to up-link equipment, it must do this under command from ASPIC. ASPIC must therefore take timely action to instruct SUCS to ready the appropriate cassettes and to begin transmissions at the specified times. Timing information will be available from Horsefall. ASPIC must take appropriate action in the event of failure of SUCS. Successful transmission must be noted in the database for subsequent billing. It is a requirement that a blank screen should never be transmitted. In some cases one cassette might contain more than one advert, but no more than 100.

5   *connection with accounting system*

Snoozo is currently updating its company accounting system and there could be a requirement to connect ASPIC to a remote HAL PS/2 personal computer in order to transfer invoice information periodically.

6   *transmission planning*

In some situations it may be necessary for ASPIC to be able to assign transmission slots for adverts according to a number of criteria (tbd) if no explicit time is required. ASPIC must in such situations advise the operator of acceptable and available transmission times.

7   *future expansion*

Snoozo require future enhancements in two areas. Firstly, in some installations videoplayers will be replaced or augmented by videodisc as the input medium. Secondly, the existing jukebox will, in some installations, be increased in capacity to 512 cassettes. Ideally these should be available for the start of broadcasting.

Figure 10-2 shows our understanding of the structure of the combined SUCS-ASPIC system.

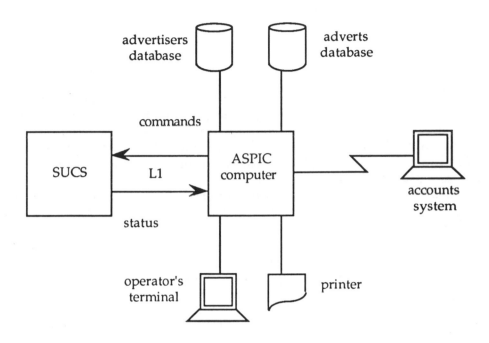

Figure 10-2. The SUCS/ASPIC architecture

The Supply

Bidders are required to present a proposal and plan of work to

- prepare a specification of the entire ASPIC system to Snoozo's satisfaction
- propose for Snoozo's approval a hardware and software configuration for ASPIC
- design and implement the ASPIC system to the agreed specifications
- demonstrate the correct working of ASPIC in conjunction with a single 256-cassette SUCS.

Bidders can propose either to use an existing microHAL II available from Snoozo or to use new equipment. In the latter case the cost-effectiveness of the use of new equipment must be proved.

As from 3rd March 1991 one channel on Boresat will be available to the contractor for testing. Two channels are expected to be available from 12th April 1991. The system must go live on both channels on 15th May 1991.

10.3   THE TECHNICAL PLAN

Introduction

This section presents the Technical Plan for a project to develop the system whose requirements are defined in 10.2.

Snoozo plc have acquired the rights to transmission channels 6 and 7 of the Boresat European television satellite outside day-time broadcasting from mid-1991 to mid-1996. It is Snoozo's current intention to sell time to advertisers during the so-called "night-time" period. Advertisements will consist of pre-recorded video features of varying length that will be transmitted at the appropriate time to Boresat for broadcasting.

Snoozo have already contracted with Horsefall Ltd of Auchtermuchty for the development of the video storage equipment, satellite up-link, and associated control system (SUCS).

The system to be developed is the Advert Storage, Programming and Information Computer (ASPIC) which will

- maintain records on advertisers and stored adverts
- control the transfer of adverts onto SUCS
- control the Horsefall equipment (SUCS) during transmission of adverts at the predetermined times
- prepare invoice data for advertisers on the basis of transmission time used.

Constraints

Risks and uncertainties affecting the software engineering process

1   The specification as it stands is too iffy to give a reliable fixed price for the whole development.

2   An external contractor is already working on the kit that will have to be controlled by ours, and they are geographically distant. The interface that they are presumably working on at this very minute is crucial. Getting it sorted out is an early priority.

3   At some point we will need to get access to the SUCS system but it doesn't look as though it will be available until later. This could delay our verification work.

4   The SUCS will no doubt behave differently when operating with videodisc inputs rather than videotape. Presumably the interface between SUCS and ASPIC will change.

5   The SUCS system will be replicated at some point in the future – how will ASPIC handle more than one SUCS and what implications will there be for performance etc?

6   Will the existing machine handle the load? Is it doing other work at the same time?

7   Who will use this system and what sort of interface would they accept at the single terminal? By all accounts the users will principally be video engineers, so we should plan on a normal forms interface which should be prototyped with sample users.

8   Also, note that real-time activity – the transmission of adverts – in principle causes update of the database; can we afford to leave these updates until during the day-time? What happens if the system fails between transmission and database update? Could the lost revenue be guessed at or what? These are issues for the design and do not lead to process model considerations.

9   There could be problems with the arrival and loading of videos onto the jukebox. What sort of volumes are likely to arrive? Could they all be loaded into the jukebox in time for transmission start-up? Indeed, should the system be able to load new adverts during transmission time? If it can't there could be problems if the option to go to all-day advertising is taken up.

10 The timing information on video transmission is going to be critical and will affect the design of the ASPIC real-time software. It is coming from Horsefall.

11 [etc, etc]

Characterisation of the system to be developed

The system has two parts: a database-based part which is essentially user-driven, probably from menus and operating on a simple database, and a time-critical real-time part that is essentially event- (eg clock-) driven. Some coupling exists. The communications with SUCS take place over a simple state-driven interface.

There is no element of criticality in the system that requires special software engineering considerations.

Client expectations regarding the software engineering process

The client expects to be able to maintain the delivered system on their own microHAL equipment so delivered tools etc must be microHAL-based. They have said they would to buy any licences necessary for their kit.

Choices

Chosen process model

Analysis of the risks and uncertainties suggests that the following features will be required in the project. (Numbering corresponds to risks numbering.) Two risks are sufficiently major to warrant significant process model structuring:

1   Because of the overall patchiness of the specification of the system and those it is connected to, we should split the project into a fixed price definition phase (phase 1) followed by an implementation phase (phase 2). For now the client will accept a budgetary estimate for the implementation phase. By the end of the definition phase we must have determined a fixed price for that latter phase and – if necessary – reduced functionality to bring it to within the budgetary estimate. This means we also do not want to be too optimistic with the budgetary estimate.

The first phase will result in a system definition agreed with Snoozo, a SUCS/ASPIC interface definition agreed with Horsefall, and a budgetary estimate for the second phase. The first phase will include a prototyping activity to establish the detail of the user interface and an outline design activity to aid the pricing work.

4,5 The two subsequent enhancements that are required are even less clear currently. The first two phases should concentrate on the basic system required for the first transmissions, using a 256 cassette jukebox. Activities in phase 2 (see below) should determine the enhancement requirements in sufficient detail for us to ensure that the architecture prepared in phase 2 will support them. Further phases can then be agreed to provide those enhancements once the initial system has been installed and has been proved in operation. If the scoping of the second phase requires it, we could also delay some of the less vital functionality to these later phases.

The overall process model is therefore to be as shown in figure 10-3.

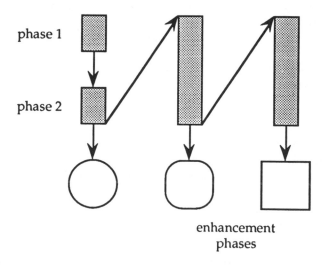

phase 1

phase 2

enhancement
phases

Figure 10-3. Overall process model for the Snoozo project

During phase 1 there must be the following plan fragments (activities and dependencies):

1   *Prepare and agree* a system specification.

   Prepare phase 2 Technical, Quality and Resource Plans at end once system specification has been agreed.

2   *Agree* formal SUCS/ASPIC interface specification in the form of a state transition diagram/matrix, including timings, as part of the system specification activity and before phase 2 planning starts.

9   We need to do some calculations about peak loading times and, if necessary, to agree some constraints on the overall capacity of the system in the system specification.

   Determine worst case video loading timings and resultant loads and check feasibility as part of the system specification activity and before phase 2 planning starts.

5   *Establish* performance characteristics of the system with one and more than one SUCS. Do this during an outline design activity.

6   We need an early activity to find out what spare capacity (of all sorts) there is on the existing machine and another activity to establish approximate loading profiles for the proposed system.

   Establish the level of spare capacity of the target machine and check its sufficiency before phase 2 planning starts and after the outline design is complete.

During phase 2 there must be the following plan fragments:

1   Integration in the second phase should proceed in an order that makes the time-critical parts of the system available first for testing.

3   Since we don't expect to get early enough access to the SUCS system we will have to build some form of simulator to mimic the interface so that we can integrate well before we attach to the Horsefall kit.

   Define, design and build a SUCS simulator, so that it is ready before the start of integration. (Is there some way this can be generated without writing too much code? In particular, can we generalise it for different protocols?)

3   *Integrate* with the SUCS simulator at earliest moment that this makes sense.

4   *Investigate* the effect of using videodiscs during the design so that the architecture can cope with this and as input to the scoping of the implementation phase (phase 2).

5   Since in future the SUCS system will be replicated our architecture must make
    the ASPIC able to handle multiple SUCSs – a consideration for phase 2.
    Performance will also be an issue and we should do some coarse calculations
    early in the architectural design phase to check that, whilst the kit might be
    up to handling one system, it is also up to handling more than one (and
    perhaps finding out how many). We should also do an actual loading
    measurement with the simulator when everything has been put together to
    see just what spare there might be.

    Carry out performance calculations during architectural design phase.

    Carry out performance measurements using simulator towards end of
    integration.

4,5 *Prepare and agree* details of the subsequent phases for the enhancements once
    the system has entered trials.

7   *Prototype* forms interface for users at start of phase 2.

10 We need as a minimum a review activity with them on those timings, as well
    as some dependencies on them in the·plan.

    Review SUCS timing characteristics with Horsefall before starting design.

Chosen development methods

The target infrastructure of the system is a combination of HALos and its
scheduling mechanisms (for the real-time components and overall system
scheduling) and HALdb (for the database-oriented aspects of the system).

    The decomposition criteria will also divide along the line between the real-
time components (controlling for example the link with SUCS) and the user-
driven database-oriented components. For the former, the decomposition will be
into HALos processes communicating through the supplied HALos inter-process
communication mechanisms. For the latter, the decomposition will derive
principally from the screens presented to the user; a secondary decomposition will
cover processes spawned from screens (such as those performing off-line functions,
eg printing or taking back-ups).

    Therefore, for the specification of the database-based aspects of the system
we shall do Chen data modelling to produce an ERA model, prepare screen and
form layouts, and define screen logic and process descriptions in English. For the
definition of the SUCS/ASPIC interface we shall use a state transition model.
For the design of the overall system we shall use a simple decomposition into
concurrent processes and thence a functional decomposition of each process into
modules. The code will be written using HALdb tools wherever possible, with any
remainder being written in C.

Chosen tool support

Since the entity/relationship content of the system is simple, we shall use HALcase on HAL PS/2s for preparing diagrams and data dictionary. Development will be carried out using HALdb tools and C.

Chosen target environment

This has already been specified by the client: [HAL machines running HALos, HALdb, ...].

Implementation

Planned training

Two programming staff will require training in the use of the HALdb tools: this will mean a two week course for each.

Planned development environment

The system will be developed on a microHAL on our premises.

Planned maintenance environment

The development materials will finally be transferred to the client's system where there will be the necessary HALdb, HALcase and C licences (being arranged by the client). Maintenance will then be done there.

Implications

Timescale implications

The two weeks' training for each of the two programmers should be followed by a further two weeks' hands-on familiarisation with the tools.

Financial implications

Training costs of £4,000 (~$6,000) should be allocated. Comms costs of £1,000 (~$1,500) should be allocated to cover charges to the end of phase 2.

Computing Facilities implications

Access to one of our in-house HAL systems will be needed, including access to HALdb and its tools for a team of four, and two HALcase seats. Normal in-house support will be used for back-up and communications within Praxis. At some point during phase 2 a comms connection will be required to the client's microHAL in London. This must be arranged and dates agreed with the in-house support team at the start of phase 2.

10.4   THE QUALITY PLAN

Where the system is or will be specified

The system will be specified in a sequence of System Specifications that expand and clarify the ITT. The first System Specification will cover the functionality to be provided for the initial period in which the Boresat system will be live. Subsequent System Specifications will cover extensions such as the ability to handle more than one SUCS system at the same time.

Where the acceptance criteria for the system are or will be specified

A sequence of Acceptance Test Plans will be produced, based on the sequence of System Specifications.

Deliverables

The following deliverables – final and intermediate – will be produced during Phase 1 and Phase 2 development. Deliverables relating to Phase 3 and beyond are not shown here.

User Model

- Screen and form layouts and logic.
- An ERA model (prepared using HALcase) covering the entities, their relationships and attributes.
- An overall functional description in English.
- A specification of the SUCS/ASPIC link in the form of a state transition diagram.
- An Acceptance Test Specification.
- A Phase 2 system installed and ready for operation.
- A User Manual suitable for video engineers.
- A short training course in the use of the system suitable for video engineers.

Architectural Model

- An outline design from Phase 1 consisting of an overall process interaction diagram, sufficient to do timing and performance calculations.
- A full design in Phase 2 consisting of a DFD in Ward-Mellor form showing data flows between processes and process activation logic, plus process logic for each process, and an ERA physical model (prepared using HALcase) covering the entities, their relationships and attributes as they will be implemented.

- A specification and design for a SUCS Simulator.
- A Build Test Specification for each process and for any intermediate system builds.
- Tested processes.

Implementation Model

- A module calling hierarchy for each process.
- Code in HALdb or C for each module.
- Screens and forms implemented using the HALdb toolset.
- A Module Test Specification for each module.
- A SUCS Simulator.

Build Model

- Build files for each process.
- HALdb scripts for installation of the database, screens and forms.
- HALos JCL scripts for system start-up, process initialisation, and system control.

Other items

- Technical, Quality and Resource Plans for Phase 2 (generally updates of those prepared now).
- Change Control Log.
- Various project-specific standards.
- [...]

Definition of quality features

For each deliverable we require a definition of where its quality features are or will be defined; this is generally by reference to a specification (existing or to come) and/or to project, company or industry standards.

User Model

- Screen and form layouts and logic: de facto standards from use of the HALdb toolsets; layout consistency rules in company standard Q03.3.2 to be used; layouts and logic to be signed off as agreeable by users.

- An ERA logical model covering the entities, their relationships and attributes: de facto standards from use of the HALcase toolset regarding layout; all entities identified by users to be incorporated; the implications of future enhancements are to be incorporated.

- An overall functional description in English: see company standard Q05.2.3.

- A specification of the SUCS/ASPIC link in the form of a state transition diagram: see company standard Q05.2.12; actions must be defined for all events arriving in all states; an interface reset state must be defined that is accessible from all states.

- An Acceptance Test Specification: see company standard Q05.6.7; the tests must take no longer than 20 hours; all screens to be fully exercised.

- A Phase 2 system installed and ready for operation: must satisfy the agreed Acceptance Test Specification.

- A User Manual suitable for video engineers: HCI guidelines as described in company standard Q07.5.1 must be followed; usability and other features to be defined in the System Specification.

- A short training course in the use of the system suitable for video engineers: learning objectives of this course to be defined in the System Specification.

Architectural Model

- An outline design from Phase 1 consisting of an overall process interaction diagram: timing and performance calculations show no more than 30% of available power required for first system and known enhancements.

- A full design in Phase 2 consisting of a DFD in Ward-Mellor form showing data flows between processes and process activation logic, plus process logic for each process, and an ERA physical model (prepared using HALcase) covering the entities, their relationships and attributes as they will be implemented in HALdb: functional features in the System Specification can all be traced to design; timing and performance calculations show no more than 30% of available power required for first system and known enhancements; physical and logical ERA models shown to be equivalent; process activation logic for non-database side meshes with L1 interface specification.

- A specification and design for a SUCS Simulator: normal and erroneous behaviour of SUCS must be simulatable, as well as its timing properties.

- A Build Test Specification for each process and for each intermediate system build: see company standard Q03.4.4.

- Tested processes: processes successfully built and tested against Build Test Specifications:

Implementation Model

- A module calling hierarchy for each process: see company standard Q05.1.3.
- Code in HALdb or C for each module: see company standard Q05.2.2; additionally a project-specific standard will be written covering each of HALdb and C, augmenting Q05.2.2.
- Screens and forms implemented using the HALdb toolset.
- A Module Test Specification for each module: level 2 testing (as defined in company standard Q05.1.7) to be applied.
- A SUCS Simulator: level 1 testing (as defined in company standard Q05.1.7) successfully completed against Simulator Specification; timing characteristics sampled and validated against Horsefall statements.

Build Model

- Build files for each process: see company standard Q07.2.3.
- HALdb scripts for installation of the database, screens and forms: see company standard Q07.2.4.
- HALos JCL scripts for system start-up, process initialisation, and system control: see company standard Q07.2.5.

Other items

- Technical, Quality and Resource Plans for Phase 2 (generally updates of those being prepared now): see company standards Q01.4, 5, 6.
- Change Control Log: see company standard Q04.7.8.
- Various project-specific standards: see company standard Q01.2.
- [...]

Verification of quality features

For each deliverable we give a definition of how the quality features defined above will be verified and what records will be kept of the verification. The definitions of the quality features are repeated from above for ease of reading, followed in italics by the verification activity (VA) to be used.

User Model

- Screen and form layouts and logic: de facto standards from use of the HALdb toolsets – *VA: formal review against the standard;* layout consistency rules in company standard Q03.3.2 to be used – *VA: formal review against the standard;* layouts and logic to be signed off as agreeable by users– *VA: user review and agreement.*

- An ERA logical model covering the entities, their relationships and features: de facto standards from use of the HALcase toolset regarding layout – *VA: none necessary;* all entities identified by users to be incorporated– *VA: user review and agreement;* the implications of future enhancements are to be incorporated – *VA: Technical Authority to confirm.*

- An overall functional description in English: see company standard Q05.2.3 – *VA: formal review against the standard with client participating.*

- A specification of the SUCS/ASPIC link in the form of a state transition diagram: see company standard Q05.2.12 – *VA: formal review against the standard;* actions must be defined for all events arriving in all states – *VA: to be checked during formal review;* an interface reset state must be defined that is accessible from all states – *VA: to be checked during formal review.*

- An Acceptance Test Specification: see company standard Q05.6.7 – *VA: formal review against the standard and agree with client;* the tests must take no longer than 20 hours – *VA: estimates of duration to be made before running;* all screens to be fully exercised – *VA: to be checked during formal review.*

- A Phase 2 system installed and ready for operation: must satisfy the agreed Acceptance Test Specification – *VA: formal test against the ATS with no discrepancies.*

- A User Manual suitable for video engineers: HCI guidelines as described in company standard Q07.5.1 must be followed – *VA: formal review against the standard;* usability and other features to be defined in the System Specification – *VA: tests to be carried out as required by the System Specification.*

- A short training course in the use of the system suitable for video engineers: learning objectives of this course to be defined in the System Specification – *VA: tests to be carried out as required by the System Specification.*

Architectural Model

- An outline design from Phase 1 consisting of an overall process interaction diagram: timing and performance calculations show no more than 30% of available power required for first system and known enhancements – *VA: calculations to be carried out.*

- A full design in Phase 2 consisting of a DFD in Ward-Mellor form showing data flows between processes and process activation logic, plus process logic for each process, and an ERA physical model (prepared using HALcase) covering the entities, their relationships and attributes as they will be implemented in HALdb: functional features in the System Specification can all be traced to design – *VA: formal review against the System Specification*; timing and performance calculations show no more than 30% of available power required for first system and known enhancements – *VA: calculations to be carried out*; physical and logical ERA models shown to be equivalent – *VA: full equivalence to be established by inspection*; process activation logic for non-database side meshes with L1 interface specification – *VA: full equivalence to be established by inspection*.

- A specification and design for a SUCS Simulator: normal and erroneous behaviour of SUCS must be simulatable, as well as its timing properties – *VA: model of Simulator actions must be established by inspection to be equivalent to that embodied by the Simulator*.

- A Build Test Specification for each process and for each intermediate system build: see company standard Q03.4.4 – *VA: formal review against the standard*.

- Tested processes: processes successfully built and tested against Build Test Specifications: – *VA: test each process against its Build Test Specification*.

Implementation Model

- A module calling hierarchy for each process: see company standard Q05.1.3 – *VA: formal review against the standard, and hierarchy to be verified against code*.

- Code in HALdb or C for each module: see company standard Q05.2.2 – *VA: formal review against the standard*; additionally a project-specific standard will be written covering each of HALdb and C, augmenting Q05.2.2 – *VA: formal review against the project-specific standard*.

- A Module Test Specification for each module: level 2 testing (as defined in company standard Q05.1.7) to be applied – *VA: level 2 test case selection to be used, supported by coverage testing to establish that coverage targets have been achieved*.

- A SUCS Simulator: level 1 testing (as defined in company standard Q05.1.7) successfully completed against Simulator Specification – *VA: level 1 test case selection to be used, supported by coverage testing to establish that coverage targets have been achieved*; timing characteristics sampled and validated against Horsefall statements – *VA: formal review against the standard*.

Build Model

- Build files for each process: see company standard Q07.2.3 – *VA: formal review against the standard, and build files to be used to generate software for Acceptance Tests.*
- HALdb scripts for installation of the database, screens and forms: see company standard Q07.2.4 – *VA: formal review against the standard, and scripts to be used to generate system for Acceptance Tests.*
- HALos JCL scripts for system start-up, process initialisation, and system control: see company standard Q07.2.5 – *VA: formal review against the standard, and scripts to be used in Acceptance Tests.*

Other items

- Technical, Quality and Resource Plans for Phase 2 (generally updates of those being prepared now): see company standards Q01.4, 5, 6 – *VA: inspection against the standards.*
- Change Control Log: see IEEE Std 828, *IEEE Standard for Software Configuration Management Plans* – *VA: formal review against the IEEE standard at regular intervals during build phase and immediately before release of the first system.*
- Various project-specific standards: see company standard on standards, Q01.2 – *VA: formal review against the standard.*
- [...]

Approval and authorisation

The levels of authorisation that required for approval of specifications, approval of verification, and approval of outcome are as follows [...].

Change control procedures

[...]

Fault management procedures

[...]

Configuration management procedures

[...]

Purchasing procedures

[...]

Project reporting and debriefing procedures

[...]

Training requirements

[...]

Security considerations

[...]

10.5 THE RESOURCE PLAN

Introduction

This section contains an initial WBS derived from the analysis in the Technical Plan in section 10.3, the Quality Plan in section 10.4, and further activities culled from a Praxis standard entitled *Generic Work Breakdown Structure*. Activities marked with a "t" are from the Technical Plan; activities marked with a "q" are from the Quality Plan; and activities marked with an "s" are from the standard. Unmarked activities are derived from their parent's source.

The two important points to note are

- whilst many activities are common to many projects and can therefore be picked from a checklist, Technical and Quality Planning help you to make them more specific and hence more amenable to accurate estimation

- many key activities are revealed by Technical and Quality Planning, and are unlikely to be picked up from general checklists.

The Phase 1 Work Breakdown Structure

1000   Project management (s)

    1100   Initiate Phase 1 of project

          [...]

    1200   Plan Phase 1 of project

          1210   Draft Technical Plan (done)

          1220   Draft Quality Plan (done)

          1230   Draft Resource Plan (being done)

          1240   Review draft plans within Praxis to provisional status

          1250   Submit provisional plans to client for agreement

          1260   Issue first definitive plans

1300   Prepare budgetary estimate for phase 2 (t)

          1310   Prepare draft Technical Plan for phase 2

          1320   Prepare draft Quality Plan for phase 2

          1330   Prepare draft Resource Plan for phase 2

1400   Monitor and report on project progress

          [...]

1500   Administer project

          1510   Maintain project accounts

          1520   Maintain project documentation

          1530   Control project documentation and records

          1540   Prepare Work Package Instructions

          1550   Liaise with hardware suppliers (Horsefall, HAL) (t)

          1560   Liaise with client (Snoozo Technical Department) (t)

          1570   Agree training needs with line manager and project team

          1580   Conduct staff training

                   1581   Train two programmers in use of HALdb tools (t)

                   1582   Familiarise programmers in HALdb tools (t)

1600   Close Phase 1 of project

          1610   [...]

2000   *User Model*

1. 2100   Specify Requirements

          2110   Produce and agree requirements specification

                   2111   Define functional requirements

                   2112   Produce outline design (t)

                   2113   Define performance requirements (t)

                   2114   Check performance requirements met (q)

                          21141   Check video loading timings

                          21142   Investigate use of videodiscs

                          21143   Investigate multi-SUCS config'ns

                          21144   Establish spare capacity on target m/c

2200   Specify System (t)

       2210   Produce draft ASPIC system specification

           2211   Specify *L1* i/f as FSM (t)

           2212   Review *L1* specification against standard and other quality features

           2213   Prepare screen and report layouts and logic (t)

           2214   Review layouts against standards (q)

           2215   Review and agree layouts with users (q)

           2216   Prepare overall English functional spec'n (t)

           2217   Review func'l spec'n with client against stdd (t,q)

           2218   Prepare logical ERA model (t)

           2219   Review and agree ERA model with users (q)

           221A   Validate ERA model against enhancements (q)

       2220   Review draft ASPIC system specification

       2230   Agree ASPIC system specification with client (t)

The Phase 2 Work Breakdown Structure

3000   *Project management (s)*

     3100   Initiate Phase 2 of project

         3110   [...]

     3200   Plan Phase 2 of project

         3210   Revise Technical Plan

         3220   Prepare provisional Quality Plan

              3221   Prepare configuration control procedures

              3222   Prepare change control procedures

              3223   Prepare fault management procedures

              3224   Prepare documentation plan

              3225   Prepare project standards

         3230   Prepare provisional Resource Plan

              3231   Prepare work breakdown structure

              3232   Prepare activity network

              3233   Deduce staffing and costs

              3234   Choose metrics & indicators to be used/collected

         3240   Agree provisional plans with client

         3250   Issue first definitive plans

3260   Maintain plans thereafter

3300   Monitor and report on project progress

3310   [...]

3400   Administer project

3410   [...]

3500   Liaise with client (Snoozo)

3600   Train staff

3610   Agree training needs (eg via Resource Plan)

3620   Conduct staff training

3700   Install and maintain development environment

3800   Close project (including debriefing)

3810   [...]

4000   User Model

4100   Review requirements since Phase 1

4110   Review prototype user interface (t)

42 00   Specify Acceptance Criteria

4210   Produce Acceptance Test Specification (ATS) (q)

4220   Review ATS against standard with client (q)

4230   Check Acceptance Tests require less than 20 hours (q)

4240   Check Acceptance Tests exercise all screens (q)

4250   Agree ATS with client (q)

4300   Carry out Acceptance

4310   Establish test environment

4320   Conduct Acceptance Test of system against ATS (q)

4330   Review results and agree acceptance

4400   Provide supporting material

4410   Prepare User Manual for engineers (q)

4420   Review and agree User Manual doc'n with client (q)

4430   Carry out agreed usability tests on User Manual (q)

4440   Prepare and agree engineer training plan (q)

4450   Provide engineer training (q)

4460   Check training against learning objectives (q)

4500   Release system

4510   Transfer development materials to client's system (t)

[...]

45n0   Prepare and agree subsequent phases

45n1   [...]

5000   *Architectural Model*

5100   Prepare architecture

5110   Identify target infrastructure

5120   Design overall system structure as DFD + control logic (q)

5130   Validate process control logic against *L1* spec'n (q)

5140   Define process logic for each process (q)

5150   Define physical database structure as ERA model (q)

5160   Validate physical ERA model against logical (q)

5170   Define subsystems and interfaces

5180   Check architecture completeness with System Spec'n (q)

5190   Carry out performance calc'ns from architecture (t,q)

51A0   Review SUCS timing characteristics with Horsefall (t)

51B0   Validate Simulator actions against SUCS spec'n (q)

51C0   Review implications of videodiscs on architecture (t)

5200   Define integration strategy

5210   Prepare Build Test Specification for each process (q)

5220   Define development and test tools

5221   Define SUCS simulator (t)

5222   Validate simulator as ready for integ'n use (t,q)

5223   Build or procure other test tools

5300   Integrate system against architecture

5310   Establish test environment (including SUCS simulator) (t)

5320   Build and test processes against Build Test Spec'ns (q)

5330   Carry out performance measurements with simulator (t)

5340   Review test results

6000   *Implementation Model*

6100   Specify components within architecture

6110   Prepare module specifications (for C modules)

6120   Prepare screen specifications

      6130   Prepare report specifications

      6140   Prepare physical database definitions

      6150   Review all specifications (q)

6200   Construct components

      6210   Prepare modules against specifications (for C modules)

      6220   Prepare screens against specifications

      6230   Prepare reports against specifications

      6240   Construct database tables

      6250   Review/inspect components against specifications

      6260   Review/inspect components against standards

6300   Define component tests

      6310   Prepare module test specifications (q)

      6320   Prepare screen test specifications (q)

      6330   Prepare report test specifications (q)

      6340   Review component specifications against standard (q)

6400   Test components

      6410   Test modules against specifications (q)

      6420   Test screens against specifications (q)

      6430   Test reports against specifications (q)

      6440   Review component test results against specifications (q)

7000   Build Model

7100   Prepare scripts to construct system

7200   Review build scripts against company standard (q)

7300   Prepare scripts for installation of database, screens, & forms (t)

7400   Review installation scripts (q)

7500   Prepare scripts for start-up etc (t)

7600   Review start-up scripts (q)

7700   Transfer materials to maintenance environment (t)

7800   Install system on target environment (t)

7900   [...]

8000   [...]

Notes

- No explicit mention is made of the collection of metrics as this is assumed to be going on "silently" in the relevant activities.

- Unless a specific quality control action is noted against a deliverable the production activity is assumed to contain some form of review as a minimum.

- In Praxis, we have three statuses that an item can have: *draft* (cannot be used as the basis for anything else), *provisional* (can be used but still to be agreed with the client), and *definitive* (in force and agreed with the client); hence the progression through these statuses in the above WBS. In some cases the progression is abbreviated: "prepare provisional issue of X" would generally involve the preparation of a sequence of drafts which would be reviewed or inspected until the quality was deemed sufficient for a provisional issue.

- Much fine detail has been omitted where it does not illustrate the themes of this book.

- The WBS has been constructed initially around the four system models: User Model, Architectural Model, Implementation Model, and Build Model. There is nothing sacred about this.

11

EXERCISES

11.1 HOW TO USE THESE EXERCISES

The following exercises are of two types: those that you can use to check your understanding of what you have read and where you can check out your answer by reference to the text; and those that may require you to be assisted by someone who has experience of managing software projects – perhaps your tutor or a manager where you work – or require you to do some background study. Exercises of

the first type are marked with a ⬛ ; those of the second type with a 🕴 or 👥 .

This book is designed to be read from start to finish and the exercises follow the flow of the book, so they are grouped by chapter.

11.2 EXERCISES ON CHAPTER 2

⬛ What is the overall goal of technical planning?

⬛ Describe the overall process of technical planning. Explain the motives that underlie that process.

⬛ What sorts of uncertainty can there be at the start of a software development project? Where do they stem from?

⬛ What sorts of decisions does an analysis of risk and uncertainty lead us to?

You have to develop a set of fast trigonometric routines for a new processor. What risks and uncertainties might there be at the outset?

You have been asked to develop a new compiler. The old version is too slow. What sorts of risks and uncertainties will there be?

Software development is almost entirely a *design* process. How would this change the character of the uncertainties in it? Compare the sort of uncertainties you might find in a software development project with those you might come across when manufacturing ball-bearings.

What four major categories of system affect the choice of how the system is developed? Give an example of each category from real life. Give an example of a system from real life that has parts that are in any three of the four categories.

Describe the overall process of technical planning in the form of a data flow diagram showing the analysis and decision-making activities and how they feed data from one to the next.

How will technical planning at bid time differ from technical planning at the start of a project?

How might the development of a software system, built and installed for one organisation, differ from the development of a software product, such as a compiler or database management system? And how would these differences change the overall approach to the initial development?

How might the development lifecycle of a compiler differ from that of a spreadsheet system, and why?

11.3   EXERCISES ON CHAPTER 3

What is a process model?

How does a process model differ from a method?

Describe Boehm's Spiral Model. What is its underlying principle?

Describe three possible unwindings of Boehm's Spiral Model of software development and explain the situations in which they would be appropriate.

In what ways does a program differ from a process model?

Why is iteration necessary in software development ?

What sorts of major decision can be necessary during software development, and how might they arise?

Under which situations would it be appropriate to use the V process model? Give specific examples.

Why is prototyping a difficult activity to manage? What specific actions can a manager take to manage those difficulties?

Explain how the incremental delivery process model can be viewed as a particular unwinding of the Spiral Model.

What differences between product and bespoke system development will affect the process model most suited to them?

11.4   EXERCISES ON CHAPTER 4

Describe the overall decision-making process of technical planning.

What the main components of the User Model, the Architectural Model, and the Implementation Model?

Why does prototyping not come into the picture when one is considering the system models?

Why is the computational model that is chosen for a system important?

What sort of *structure clashes* do we get when we design systems?

What features of a system are concentrated on by the object-oriented approach? by JSD? by VDM? by Yourdon's Structured Analysis? by Ada?

Compare the computational models underlying JSD (Jackson System Development) and object-oriented programming.

 You have been given the task of building a steer-by-wire system for a car. Movements of the steering wheel will be detected by sensors and relayed to a microprocessor which, in turn, must transmit commands to actuators on the axles according to specified control laws. There is to be no mechanical linkage. You have been given an outline specification of the microprocessor and of the functionality and control laws that the embedded software is to use. Draft a technical plan for the project. If you feel it necessary to make any assumptions in deriving your plan, make these clear.

11.5 EXERCISES ON CHAPTER 5

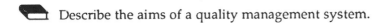 Describe the aims of a quality management system.

Why doesn't having a QMS *guarantee* quality in the result of a software development?

Why is the *recording* of quality control activities important?

Can a piece of software that fails or runs slowly or has a poor user interface still be of the required quality?

Why is the achievement of quality *not* the responsibility of the Quality Assurance function in an organisation?

What happens in Quality Assurance in the software environment?

Are tools more important as an aid to increasing quality or as a means of increasing productivity?

Crosby says that "Quality is free" [Crosby 1979]. Is this true for the purchaser of a system? Is it true for the builder of a system?

What the relationships between ISO 9001, a corporate QMS, a project Quality Plan, and a Work Package Description?

Place ISO 9001's requirements on a QMS in order of importance for the software environment.

What are the five generic steps in Quality Control?

Carry out the five steps of Quality Control for a small module that you have written.

Carry out the five steps of Quality Control for a specification that you have written.

What are the immediate benefits of a review?

What are the long-term benefits of a review?

What social problems might be encountered in a review?

Why are the outcomes of a review recorded?

Are checklists a good thing or a bad thing?

What does a Quality Plan define? What deliverables might it cover?

Is there anything that is produced on a project that might not be subjected to some form of verification or validation?

Are standards a good thing or a bad thing? What the dangers and benefits?

11.6   EXERCISES ON CHAPTER 6

Why does formality in a development method increase the V&V potential of the method?

What potential is there for strong verification of a Data Flow Diagram?

What potential is there for strong verification of a VDM specification?

What is the difference between verification and validation?

The user's requirements are clearly important. But why is the specification of the system equally (or even more important) to the developer?

To what is extent, therefore, is validation of a system against the user's requirements more or less important than the verification of it against the System Specification?

What potential is there for strong verification of code with gotos?

What potential is there for strong verification of code that is Dijkstra-structured?

What is meant by *reliable* Quality Control?

What is meant by *economical* Quality Control?

Study the various testing techniques for module's described in [Myers 1979]; how far can you rate them according to their reliability and economy?

Explain the difference between quality control and quality assurance, illustrating your explanation with one quality control activity and one quality assurance activity in the software development context.

Describe the relationships between international, corporate and project quality standards, in particular how their scopes are related and the extent to which quality control and quality assurance appear in each.

Explain what is meant by *quality factoring*.

Why is the required quality in the final deliverables the determining factor in setting the quality features of intermediate deliverables?

Explain the *verification chain*.

Name some verification activities that should best appear as separate work packages in a Work Breakdown Structure (WBS). Name some verification activities that could be expected to be absorbed within their corresponding construction work packages.

Describe the role of standards in setting quality features for deliverables.

You have been given the task of building a steer-by-wire system for a car. Movements of the steering wheel will be detected by sensors and relayed to a microprocessor which, in turn, must transmit commands to actuators on the axles according to specified control laws. There is to be no mechanical linkage. You have been given an outline specification of the microprocessor and of the functionality and control laws that the embedded software is to use. You have decided that a standard V model development process will be appropriate. Draft a Quality Plan for the project. If you feel it necessary to make any assumptions in deriving your plan, make these clear.

11.7 EXERCISES ON CHAPTER 7

Explain the principles underlying the Work Breakdown Structure and its importance.

Which of COCOMO's cost drivers will be affected by technological change in the next five years?

Why is the calibration of an estimating model difficult?

What are the relative advantages and disadvantages of top-down and bottom-up estimating?

Why is the critical path so important?

Explain the advantage that a network has over a bar chart.

Describe how the results of the technical and quality planning analyses feed input to the construction of the WBS.

Why is it important to record the past during a project?

Look back at projects that you have done or that have been done in your organisation and determine the effort profile over the various phases.

Why can we expect the effort profile to be increasingly front-loaded?

What arguments can be used to justify the costs of tools on a single project? Taking the cost of a symbolic debugger as £30,000 (~$45,000) for a project of five people, what sort of productivity effects must the debugger have to justify its purchase on that project, assuming the project lasts in all one year?

Describe as many ways of shortening a critical path as you can.

Prepare a WBS for writing a book.

Prepare a network for writing a book.

Using the Technical and Quality Plans drawn up in the steer-by-wire system above, construct a WBS for the development and sketch an activity network showing the logic of the plan.

Why are metrics so difficult to use in software engineering?

BIBLIOGRAPHY

[ANSI/IEEE 1983]

IEEE Standard Glossary of Software Engineering Terminology, ANSI/IEEE Std 729-1983. IEEE Inc, New York, 1983

[Babich 1986]

Software configuration management. W A Babich. Addison-Wesley, 1986

[Benington 1956]

Production of large computer programs. H D Benington. In *Proceedings, Symposium on Advanced Programming Methods for Digital Computers*, pp15-27. Office of Naval Research (ONR Report ACR-15), USA, 1956. (Adapted in *Annals of the History of Computing*, 5, 4, pp350-361, 1983)

[Bersoff 1981]

Software configuration management. An investment in product integrity. E H Bersoff, V D Henderson, S G Siegel. Prentice-Hall, Englewood Cliffs, 1981

[Birrell 1984]

Increasing productivity in embedded microprocessor software development. N D Birrell and D H S Blease. In *Australian Computer Conference – Programme and Papers*, pp66-81. Australian Computer Society, Sydney, 1984

[Birrell 1988]

A Practical Handbook for Software Development. N D Birrell and M A Ould. Cambridge University Press, 1988 (paperback)

[Boehm 1978]

The Characteristics of Software Quality. B W Boehm, J T Brown, H Kaspar, M Lipow, G J MacLeod, M J Merritt. North-Holland, 1978

[Boehm 1981]

Software Engineering Economics. B W Boehm. Prentice-Hall, Englewood Cliffs, 1981

[Boehm 1986]

A spiral model of software development and enhancement. B W Boehm. In *ACM SIGSOFT Software Engineering Notes,* **11**, 4, pp14-24. ACM, New York, 1986

[Boehm 1989]

Software risk management. B W Boehm. IEEE Computer Society Press, Washington, 1989

[Brooks 1979]

The mythical man-month – essays on software engineering. F P Brooks. Addison-Wesley, Reading, MA, 1979

[Brooks 1987]

No silver bullet: essence and accidents of software engineering. F P Brooks. Computer, **20**, 4, pp10-20, 1987

[BS 5750]

BS 5750: Part 1: 1987. *Quality systems. Part 1. Specification for design/development, production, installation, and servicing*

[BS 5882]

BS 5882: 1980. *Specification for a total quality assurance programme for nuclear power plants*

[BSI 1979]

QAS 3302/79 Issue 1 *Quality assessment schedule to BS 5750: Part 1 relating to design, replication and distribution of application software for use in electronic computer systems equipment.* BSI, 1979

[Buckle 1982]

Software configuration management. J K Buckle. Macmillan Press, London, 1982

[Budde 1984]

Approaches to prototyping. Edited by R Budde, K Kuhlenkamp, L Mathiassen, H Züllighoven. Springer-Verlag, Berlin, 1984

[Chow 1978]

Testing software design modelled by finite-state machines. T S Chow. In *IEEE Transactions on Software Engineering,* **SE-4**, pp178-187. 1978

[Cox 1986]

Object oriented programming. B J Cox. Addison-Wesley, London, 1986

[Crosby 1979]

Quality is free. P B Crosby. McGraw-Hill, 1979

[Dijkstra 1981]

The Science of Programming. E W Dijkstra. Prentice-Hall, Englewood Cliffs, 1981

[Downs 1988]

Structured systems analysis and design method. E Downs, P Clare, I Coe. Prentice-Hall, New York, 1988

[Fagan 1976]

Design and code inspections to reduce errors in program development. M E Fagan. IBM Systems Journal, **15**, 3, pp182-211. 1976

[Fowler 1931]

The King's English. H W Fowler & F G Fowler. Oxford University Press, Oxford, 1931

[Gerrard 1990]

Formal specification and design time testing. C P Gerrard, D Coleman, R M Gallimore. In *IEEE Transactions on Software Engineering*, **SE-16**, 1, pp1-12. 1990

[Gilb 1987]

Design by Objectives. T Gilb. North-Holland, 1987

[Gilb 1988]

Principles of Software Engineering Management. T Gilb. Addison-Wesley, Reading, 1988

[Graham 1989]

Incremental development: review of nonmonolithic life-cycle development models. D R Graham. In *Information and Software Technology*, **31**, 1, pp7-20. Butterworths, Guildford, 1989

[Gries 1981]

The Science of Programming. D Gries. Springer Verlag, Berlin, 1981

[Hall 1988]

Public Domain Standards Listing. P Hall for BCS/IEE Software Engineering Standards Working Group. IEE, London, 1988

[Hayes 1986]

Specification directed module testing. I J Hayes. In *IEEE Transactions on Software Engineering*, **SE-12**, 1, pp124-133

[Henderson 1986]

Software design using executable formal specifications - a consideration of two approaches. P Henderson, C Minkowitz. Department of Computer Science report, Stirling University, Stirling, 1986

[Henderson 1987]

me too reference manual. P Henderson, C Minkowitz, J S Rowles. Department of Computer Science Report, University of Stirling, Stirling, 1987

[IEEE 1987]

Software engineering standards. IEEE, New York, 1987

[IEEE 729]

IEEE Standard Glossary of Software Engineering Terminology. IEEE Std 729-1983. IEEE, New York, 1983

[IEEE 828]

IEEE Standard for Software Configuration Management Plans, IEEE Std 828-1983. IEEE, New York, 1983

[IEEE 830]

IEEE Guide to Software Requirements Specifications. IEEE Std 830-1984. IEEE, New York, 1984

[IEEE 1042]

IEEE Guide to Software Configuration Management Planning, IEEE Std 1042-1987. IEEE, New York, 1987

[ISO 8402]

ISO 8402: *Quality assurance – Vocabulary*

[ISO 9001]

ISO 9001: *Quality systems – Assurance model for design/development, production, installation, and servicing capability*

[Jackson 1975]

Principles of Program Design. M A Jackson. Academic Press, New York, 1975

[Jackson 1983]

System development. M Jackson. Prentice-Hall, Englewood Cliffs, 1983

[JIMCOM 1987]

The Official Handbook of MASCOT, version 3.1, issue 1. Issued by JIMCOM, available from RSRE, Malvern 1987

[Jones 1986]

Systematic software development using VDM. C B Jones. Prentice-Hall, Englewood Cliffs, 1986

[Livesey 1984]

Experience with prototyping in a multi national organization. P B Livesey. In *Approaches to prototyping,* pp92-104. Springer-Verlag, Berlin, 1984

[McCabe 1985]

System testing aided by structured analysis: a practical experience. T J McCabe & G G Schulmeyer. In *IEEE Transactions on Software Engineering,* **SE-11,** 9, pp917-921

[McDermid 1990]

Software Engineer's Reference Book. Edited by J McDermid. Butterworths Scientific Press, Guildford, due 1990

[McMenamin 1984]

Essential Systems Analysis. S M McMenamin and J F Palmer. Yourdon Inc, New York, 1984

[Macro 1987]

The Craft of Software Engineering. A Macro and J Buxton. Addison-Wesley, Wokingham, UK, 1987

[Mayhew 1989]

Control of software prototyping process: change classification approach. P J Mayhew, C J Worsley, and P A Dearnley. In *Information and Software Technology*, **31**, 2, pp59-66

[Mayhew 1990]

Organization and management of systems prototyping. P J Mayhew, P A Dearnley. *Information and Software Technology*, **32**, 4, pp245-252. May 1990

[Mellor 1986]

Structured development for real-time systems. S J Mellor & P T Ward. Prentice-Hall, Englewood Cliffs. 1986

[Myers 1975]

Reliable Software through Composite Design. G J Myers. Van Nostrand Rheinhold, New York, 1985

[Myers 1979]

The art of software testing. Wiley, London, 1979

[NATO AQAP-1]

AQAP-1 *NATO requirements for an industrial quality system.* Edition 3. NATO, May 1984

[NATO AQAP-2]

AQAP-2 *Guide for the evaluation of a contractor's quality control system for compliance with AQAP-1.* NATO

[NATO AQAP-13]

AQAP-13 *NATO software quality control system requirements.* NATO, August 1981

[NATO AQAP-14]

AQAP-14 *Guide for the evaluation of a contractor's software quality control system for compliance with AQAP-13.* NATO

[NCC 1990]

SSADM Manual (two volumes). G Longworth, D Nicholls. NCC Publications, Manchester, 1990

[Oncken 1984]

Managing management time. W Oncken Jr. Prentice-Hall, Englewood Cliffs, 1984

[Ould 1982]

A workbench for computer simulation of picture coding schemes. M A Ould, N D Birrell, P Radford, N Tucker, D I Crawford. In *Proceedings of the IEE International Conference on Electronic Image Processing*, pp199-203. IEE, London, 1982

[Ould 1987]
Testing in Software Development. Edited by M A Ould and C Unwin. BCS Monographs in Informatics, Cambridge University Press, 1987

[Ould 1988]
Defining formal models of the software development process. Martyn A Ould and Clive Roberts. Published in *Software Engineering Environments*, pp13-26. Ellis Horwood Ltd, Chichester, 1988

[Peterson 1981]
Petri Net Theory and the Modelling of Systems. J L Peterson. Prentice-Hall, Englewood Cliffs, 1981

[Pressman 1988]
Making software engineering happen. R S Pressman. Prentice-Hall, Englewood Cliffs, 1988

[Royce 1970]
Managing the development of large software systems: concepts and techniques. W W Royce. In *Proceedings of WESCON 1970*

[Royce 1990]
TRW's Ada process model for incremental development of large software systems. In *Proceedings of the 12th International Conference on Software Engineering*, pp2-11. IEEE Computer Society Press, Los Alamitos, 1990

[Sabbagh 1989]
Skyscraper. K Sabbagh. Macmillan, London, 1989

[STARTS 1988]
The STARTS Guide. NCC Publications, Manchester. 1987 (2nd edition)

[Tate 1990]
Prototyping: helping to build the right software. G Tate. *Information and Software Technology*, **32**, 4, pp237-244. May 1990

[Ward 1986]
Structured development for real-time systems. S J Mellor and P T Ward. Prentice-Hall, Englewood Cliffs, 1986

[Wolff 1989]
The management of risk in system development: 'Project SP' and the 'New Spiral Model'. J G Wolff. In *Software Engineering Journal*, 4, 3, pp134-142. May 1989

[Yourdon 1979]
Structured Walkthroughs. E Yourdon. Yourdon Press, New York, 1979

ABBREVIATIONS

This section lists the majority of the acronyms and abbreviations that appear in the book and gives their expanded meanings. Further information can be found (where available) by referring to the Index.

BSI	British Standards Institute
CASE	Computer Aided Software Engineering
CCS	Calculus of Communicating Systems
COCOMO	Constructive Cost Model
CSP	Communicating Sequential Processes
DBMS	Data Base Management System
DbO	Design by Objectives
DFD	Data Flow Diagram
ELH	Entity Life History
ER	Entity/Relationship
ERA	Entity/Relationship/Attribute
FSM	Finite State Machine
IEE	Institution of Electrical Engineers
IEEE	Institution of Electrical and Electronic Engineers
IPSE	Integrated Project Support Environment
ISO	International Standards Organisation
ITT	Invitation to Tender
JSD	Jackson System Development
JSP	Jackson Structured Programming
KLOC	Thousand Lines of Code
LCSAJ	Linear Code Sequence and Jump
MASCOT	Modular Approach to System Construction, Operation and Test
M&E	Materials and Expenses

MoD	Ministry of Defence
MTBF	Mean Time Between Failures
OS	Operating System
PERT	Program/Project Evaluation and Review Technique
PDL	Process/Program Design Language
QA	Quality Assurance
QC	Quality Control
QMS	Quality Management System
SADT	System Analysis and Design Technique
SARA	System Architect's Apprentice
SQL	System Query Language
SSADM	Structured System Analysis and Design Methodology
SUT	System/Software Under Test
TP	Transaction Processing
V & V	Verification and Validation
VDM	Vienna Development Method
WBS	Work Breakdown Structure
WP	Work Package

INDEX

A

Acceptance Test Specification 82
accidental difficulties 4
activity network 167, 198
Ada 92
analytic estimating 163
ANSI 118
Architectural Model 74, 82, 124, 195

B

black-box testing 136
blend of process models 67
BS 5750 104, 107, 118
BS 5882 108
BSI 107, 118
Build Model 85
Build Test Specification 84

C

C++ 88
champion 188
change control 58, 105, 149
characterising the required system 18
checklist 160
checklist for reviewing a Technical Plan 27
checklists 112, 113
choice of development methods 18
client's requirements 20
COCOMO 13, 161, 177
completeness 125, 135

compliance analysis 136
computational model 76, 89, 91, 195
conceptual integrity 4, 87
concurrent system 19
configuration management 58, 105, 149
consistency 125
contents list for a Quality Plan 149
contents list for a Technical Plan 24
contract review 104
contractual considerations 36
control-oriented system 19
controlled reworking 88
corrective action 106
cost drivers 161, 177
critical path 168
critical software 20, 147
cross-development 20
cyclomatic number 179

D

data flow diagram 79, 137, 140
data-oriented system 19
decomposition criteria 82
deliverables 36
Design by Objectives 102, 144
developer related quality features 99
development environment 20, 93
development of software products 56
DFD *see* data flow diagram

E

effort profile	162, 171
entity life history	80
entity-relationship model	
	see ER model
entropy of the system	62
ER model	79, 89
error detection	111
essential difficulties	4
estimating	160, 165
Evolutionary Development Process	
Model	18, 35, 54, 68
exit criteria	114
Exploratory Process Model	
	18, 36, 68

F

factoring of quality	129
Fagan Inspections	114, 197
fault management	149
Finite State Machine	
	80, 83, 89, 110, 134
formal methods	
	20, 111, 130, 131, 136, 137
functional equivalence	125
functional quality features	3, 98

H

| holistic estimating | 160 |

I

IEEE standards	118
ikiwisi	45
Implementation Model	
	74, 84, 124, 195
Incremental Delivery Process	
Model	18, 35, 58, 68
indicators	179
inspection and test status	106
inspection guidelines	115
intelligent look-ahead	88
interface risks	62
internal quality audits	106
Invitation to Tender	20
IPSEs	66
ISO	118
ISO 8402	98, 102
ISO 9001	103, 104, 118

J

| JSP | 76, 82, 89, 137 |

K

| kernel | 62 |

L

| life history of a Technical Plan | 26 |
| lifecycle | 11 |

M

maintenance environment	94
management responsibility	104
managing prototyping	54
MASCOT	20, 38, 78, 89
materials and expenses	172
mathematical proof	111
me too	137
meta-models	32
methods	5, 10, 71, 89
Metrics	179
model-view-controller	82
module	73
Monthly Report	173

N

| non-functional features | 3, 98 |

O

OBJ	137
object-oriented design	82, 84, 88, 89
object-oriented development	57
object-oriented programming	76
Objective-C	88

P

performance	49
Petri Net	80, 83, 131
plan fragments	68, 167, 195
planning the client's maintenance	
environment	22
planning the development	
environment	21
planning the training	21
planning tools	167
plans	5
process model	6, 11, 17, 30, 158, 194

product development 62
productivity 176
Prolog 75
prototyping 45, 86
prototyping objectives 52

Q

QMS

  see Quality Management System
QMS accreditation 107
quality 71, 98
quality achievement 71
Quality Assessment Schedules 107
Quality Assurance 71, 102, 103
Quality Control
    71, 103, 108, 114, 116, 123, 128, 196
Quality Control record 117
quality factoring 3, 142, 196
quality feature 98, 99, 146, 196
Quality Management System
    103, 104, 113
Quality Manual 104, 119
Quality Plan 26, 116, 148, 197
quality planning 5, 194
quality policy 103
quality records 106
quality standards 118, 119, 146

R

reducing risk 31
Requirements Expression 81
requirements on a QMS 104
research environment 66
research-oriented projects 18
Resource Plan 24, 153, 197
resource planning 5, 194
reviews 111
risk reduction manoeuvres 68
risk/risk reduction pair 69
risks and uncertainties
    9, 32, 48, 49, 194
risks of innovation 189
rolling hexagons model 124

S

sanity check 165
SARA 147, 188
security 149

semantic analysis 136, 147
silver bullet 4
Simula 88
simulation 45
SmallTalk 88
software acquisition 2
software engineering standards
    see quality' standards
Spiral Model 32, 56, 64, 68, 90, 195
Spiral Model as a meta-model 35
SSADM 20, 38, 80, 89, 92
stagewise model 30
standards *see* quality standards
state transition diagram 80
static analysis 111
strategy 5
structure clash 74, 87
Structured Walkthroughs 111, 197
system model 38, 71, 72, 74
System Specification 81

T

target environment 20, 93
target infrastructure 82
Technical Plan 12, 70, 91, 116
technical planning 5, 11, 194
testing 129
tools 5, 21, 92, 139, 189
training 94, 106, 149

U

User Model 74, 81, 124, 195
user related quality features 99

V

V Process Model
    18, 35, 38, 68, 86, 125
V Process Model with Prototyping
    see VP Process Model
V&V 197
V&V potential 4, 90, 129, 130, 137
validation 123, 124
VDM 38, 78, 80, 89, 130
verification
    109, 123, 124, 128, 145, 148, 159
verification chain 129
virtual machine 83
VP Process Model 18, 35, 45, 68, 88

W

Ward-Mellor	140
waterfall model	31, 39
white-box testing	136
Work Breakdown Structure	
	36, 90, 153, 155, 197
work package	157
work package analysis	166

Y

Yourdon Structured Analysis and Design	38

Z

Z	130, 137
zero defect software	141